MW00368201

# 15 LIES
# WOMEN ARE
# TOLD AT WORK

# 15 LIES WOMEN ARE TOLD AT WORK

. . . . AND **THE TRUTH** WE NEED TO SUCCEED

## Bonnie Hammer

**SIMON ELEMENT**

New York   London   Toronto   Sydney   New Delhi

**SIMON
ELEMENT**

To My First Three Mentors:

My mom, who taught, nurtured, guided, and grounded me

My dad, who taught me there is *no* such word as can't

My brother, who taught me when things get tough, get tougher

# Contents

Introduction                                              1

## STARTING OUT

1: Follow Your Dreams /
   Follow The Opportunities                              9
2: Know Your Worth /
   Work On Your Worth                                   27
3: Have Friends In High Places /
   Find Truth-Tellers In Every Location                 41
4: It's What's On The Inside That Counts /
   What's On Our Outsides Matters, Too                  63
5: You Can Have It All /
   You Will Have Choices                                85

## STANDING OUT

6: Fake It 'Til You Make It /
   Face It 'Til You Make It                            103
7: It's A Man's World /
   Only If You Let It Be                               119
8: Talk Is Cheap /
   Talk Is A Valuable Currency                         137

9:  Good Things Come To Those Who Wait /
        Great Things Come To Those Who Act          163
10: There's Nowhere To Go But Up /
        Success Has Multiple Directions             181

**STEPPING UP**

11: Trust Your Gut /
        Check Your Gut                              201
12: Don't Sweat The Small Stuff /
        Sweat All Stuff                             219
13: The Winner Takes All /
        Winning Isn't Everything                    237
14: Don't Mix Work With Play /
        All Work And No Play Makes Everyone Dull    255
15: If It Ain't Broke, Don't Fix It /
        If It Could Be Better, It Might Be Broken   281
16: The Only Constant In Life Is Change            299

Acknowledgments                                    304
Notes                                              309

# Introduction

I was upside down on a roller coaster when I decided to write this book.

It was March 2022. Along with other top executives at NBCUniversal, the company where I've worked in some capacity for the last three decades, I was in Orlando for the annual top management meeting.

We were all "relaxing" at Universal's Islands of Adventure theme park when the head of business affairs and operations dared me to ride the park's new Jurassic World VelociCoaster. For better or worse, I have a hard time saying no to a dare. The ride went about as smoothly as you might expect, zooming on a seventy-mile-per-hour roller coaster with four loops and a 155-foot drop amid animatronic dinosaurs. The souvenir photo of me says it all: My hair is everywhere, my cheeks look like a skydiver's, and the horrified expression on my face can only be summed up as "What the hell am I doing?"

But while I was hanging upside down, that's *not* what I was thinking. Speeding through prehistoric caves and soaring past screeching dinosaurs, the central thought on my mind was: There are a lot of men on this ride, happily screaming, laughing, and embracing the thrills and chills. Where are all the women?

The more I thought about it, though, the more I realized that there's a glaring misconception about women that says we have to take ourselves very seriously if we want *others* to take us seriously. It's a misconception that says we'll only be effective and respected leaders—or become them—if we stay in our lane, refrain from mixing work with play, and, most of all, avoid embracing the ups and downs of riding the metaphorical roller coaster in our professional lives. My seventy-plus years of life experience have taught me the exact opposite. Taking risks, having fun, letting your hair down, putting yourself out there, and being a genuine part of the team that you lead . . . Those things don't make weak leaders. They make great ones.

As I walked off that ride, I started thinking about all the misconceptions—and lies—that women are told at work. And once I started, I couldn't stop.

At every rung of the professional ladder, whether you are new to the work world, on the cusp of a first promotion, or on the path to a top job, there are too many "rules" rooted in pithy dictums, mantras, and maxims that too many people—and too many women—continue to believe. They sound nice. They roll off the tongue. They seem like an easy enough script to follow, and they feel like a time-tested playbook.

In theory, they might make sense. In practice, though, they're a dangerous (and dangerously clichéd) instruction manual for the modern workplace and world.

That's why I wrote this book: to call bullshit on these clichés. Some of this traditional "advice" is relatively harmless, like the piece that tells you not to have fun at work, to forgo the chance to scream and laugh your way through three minutes on a roller coaster. But most of it isn't. In ways big and small, it's holding women back. Taken together, it helps explain why, for every female leader who exists in any industry, there are a thousand women who didn't make it. (Hint: It's not because they didn't "lean in" far enough.)

Of course, this isn't to discount the sexism—both subtle and flagrant—that still pervades most industries and still undermines women. Trust me, as a woman working in corporate America, I know the problem well. But the idea that it's all sexism? Well, that's bullshit, too.

What's needed in today's work world isn't empty mottos, impossible promises, yet another aphorism, or a set of ten one-size-fits-all corporate commandments that don't actually fit any of us. We just need someone to tell us the truth, even when it hurts, and help us filter out the rest.

In a way, my own work life has made me uniquely qualified to do just that. From the 1970s on, I've been behind the scenes of some of the most pivotal moments and movements in television history, taking us from the beginnings of cable TV to today's watch-anywhere multimedia. Working in entertainment has given me some very colorful stories, but what I have learned in a volatile and evolving industry applies across professional life, whether you are in an established corporation, an indie startup, or anything in between.

From my first "production assistant" job in Boston public television, where I literally had to clean up after a kids' show's shaggy canine star (who also earned a lot more than me), I've survived, occasionally face-planted, and ultimately thrived in one of the most competitive and unforgiving industries—media and entertainment. (At one point, 129 million Americans tuned in every week to watch channels that I ran.)

I was the woman, believe it or not, who helped transform WWE and professional wrestling from a niche sport into a male soap opera. A few years afterward, I posed to Steven Spielberg that he'd cast the wrong child actress for his new show, *Taken*, and suggested we go with a ten-year-old named Dakota Fanning instead. I even helped the

Kardashians make their mark on America. I'm also accountable for hiring a relatively unknown American actress to star in a legal drama that we were about to start filming in Canada. Meghan would go on to become British royalty, while the show, *Suits*, is presently experiencing its own second act as a top ten global hit on Netflix.

My most recent work is playing catch-up in the streaming world for NBCUniversal, overseeing the launch of Peacock, where *Yellowstone*, *Vanderpump Rules*, *The Office*, and *Top Chef* now live. In the 1990s I created the award-winning "Erase the Hate" campaign to combat all forms of discrimination. Today, that effort is needed more than ever.

I've been called the Queen of Cable. And in a victory for irony, I've also been named the most powerful woman in Hollywood—all without ever heeding my multiple bosses' many pleas to move to California. I'm not above selling a good, feel-good story to people, even if it's unrealistic. You could argue I've made a living doing just that. (Even the stuff labeled "reality TV.") I know firsthand that there's tremendous value in telling stories that portray a different world from the one we live in . . . but not when it comes to our careers.

Sometimes, we just need the facts. We just need reality, without the quotation marks. We just need the truth. That's what this book is: the honest and unfiltered truth. Because too much of what women are told at work—*"follow your dreams," "know your worth," "fake it 'til you make it," "trust your gut," "you can have it all," "don't mix work with play,"* and so many more—is a lie.

I see it every day. I've been mentoring women since I first got started in television—from the all-women team of producers I led back at the Boston morning show *Good Day!* in my early thirties to the Women's Leadership Masterclass program that I have run at NBCUniversal. A big part of my job is explaining why the script that women have been spoon-fed into believing we should follow is failing them, and then teaching them how to flip it. Now I hope to inspire working women everywhere—in any industry, at any stage of their careers. Consider this book the pocket-sized, portable mentor you didn't know you needed . . . or maybe the one you've been desperate for.

Chapter by chapter, I'll explore the lies we've been told. I'll explain what the truth really is, using research, real-life anecdotes, and plain common sense. I'll describe the life experiences that led me to my perspective. And then I'll help you "nail it," pun intended, with easily digestible, usable, and shareable advice.

The chapters are loosely organized around three different stages of our work lives, from those who are just starting out, to anyone who wants to stand out in a shifting role or new field, to someone who is stepping up to embrace greater responsibilities. But the advice within them is applicable to anyone in the work world, at any stage—from executive assistant to C-suite executive and every role in between.

A disclaimer before we get started: If you're looking for another magical mantra to follow, one that promises to get you to your dream destination in half the time while barely breaking a sweat, you'll probably be disappointed. After all, every career is a journey—and the journey is almost never straightforward. There's no shortcut or silver bullet. But that's what makes it so rewarding.

My goal is to help you enjoy the hell out of the ride . . . just like I did on the VelociCoaster.

# part one

# STARTING OUT

## HOW TO OWN YOUR FUTURE

- Recognize when dreams hold you back

- Realize your worth is ever-changing

- Know what makes the best mentors

- Use your outside to reflect your inside

- Understand what it means to "have it all"

# 1. Follow Your Dreams /
   Follow The Opportunities

**What We're Told:** *"Follow your dreams."*

It's the first piece of advice most of us are ever given: as kids in the classroom, as students on campus, as graduates preparing to enter the workforce, and as working adults. We are told that jobs are for pursuing passions, not just paychecks. If we do what we love, money and success will follow. If we love what we do, we'll never work a day in our lives. And the corollary to all that dreaminess? If we don't find employment doing whatever we find most fulfilling, we're somehow failures.

**The Truth:** *"Follow the opportunities."*

We don't have to follow our dreams to end up with our dream jobs. In fact, I'd argue the opposite. When it comes to careers, "follow your dreams" can be nightmare advice. That's because most of us enter the working world without knowing what those dreams are.

We might think we do. We might even feel certain of them. After all, Americans are spoon-fed a diet high in dreams. They're the cornerstone of our cultural canon, the basis of fairy tales, superhero stories, and countless Disney and DreamWorks movies. And they aren't just relegated to fiction and fantasy. Phrases like "I'm living the dream," "It's a dream come true," "The man (or woman) of my dreams," and "Beyond my wildest dreams" are part of our lexicon. Athletes say these words in post-game interviews after winning big and making it to the finals. Actors repeat them in acceptance speeches as they clutch a shiny statuette. Even contestants on dating shows utter them after receiving a rose and surviving for another week.

From our youngest years, we are asked about our career dreams: "What do you want to be when you grow up?" Obviously, we have no experience at being anything other than a kid. So why not aspire to be a pro athlete or a pop star?

As we get older and prepare to enter the workplace, some of us still hold on to our childhood or teenage dreams, or we find new ones. Certainly, we are more mature and thoughtful at age twenty-two than we were at age five or fifteen. The sources influencing us are likely to be more logical: our favorite course in college, the recruiter we talked to at an on-campus career fair, or a summer internship that stimulated us intellectually or socially. But like our younger selves, we're still picking from a grab bag of options largely chosen for us by others or offered from limited experiences.

Even if we have a better understanding of what work is, our understanding of who *we* are is still limited. Consequently, most of us don't have a clear idea of what we truly want to be when we grow up—especially not at the start of our careers. And that's a cause for celebration! The point of living is to learn as we go (and grow). That should be the point of working, too: to try new things, to meet different people, to understand ourselves better—what we like and what we can't stand, what excites us and what bores us, what fills us with joy on a Monday morning and what fills us with dread on a Sunday night. We spend a third of our lives on the job. It just makes sense that whatever we fantasized about doing while dozing off in Econ 101 probably isn't what we'll want to be doing thirty years later.

But instead of understanding how lucky this makes us, how much freedom we have, all too often we just feel lost. Because we've been taught to find direction in our dreams—that they should be like a North Star to guide us. We may feel envious of people who seem to have a fixed dream to follow to help them on their way.

Here's the thing: Professional dreams can be incredibly limiting. When we enter the workplace convinced that we already know what we want to do—and are committed to doing it at all costs—what we're saying, in essence, is that there's nothing left for us to learn or be curious about, nothing that could change our minds, nothing else that would make us happier or more fulfilled. We're saying that even though our careers are only just beginning, we already know what we want out of them. With that mindset, we risk sleepwalking through life and hitting snooze on a host of bigger, better opportunities that come our way, opportunities that we never could have dreamed up.

Just like we can't be what we can't see, we can't dream what we don't know. So, at any one time, our wants and wishes for the future have a near-infinite number of blind spots. They include every industry we haven't yet worked in, every company we haven't yet encountered, and every job we haven't tried doing ourselves.

The world of "I don't know" is big and always getting bigger. New industries emerge all the time. New companies launch every day. The newer they are, the less likely we are to know about them. Even if we do, the more entrenched we are in our dreams, the less likely we are to want to step foot on unfamiliar territory. Instead, we live in the comfort of a decision we made years ago. But what feels like a seatbelt keeping us secure can also be a trap confining us.

Those of us who *aren't* committed to a specific dream, on the other hand, have the opportunity to follow new opportunities. Where the dreamers close themselves off, the non-dreamers stay open. Our culture likes to think of them—of us—as lost, but the best way to make one's way has always been to stay alert and be willing to turn left, right, or back to try a new route when necessary. We can't do that when our eyes are closed and we are dreaming about something else.

Does that mean we should discard dreams wholesale? Of course not. There's nothing wrong with having them and holding on to them, even when they seem unlikely, and the odds are stacked against them coming true. Dreams can motivate us, guide us, and serve as reminders of what's most important to us. And achieving them feels great in a way that's hard to top.

But there's a difference between possessing dreams and allowing dreams to possess us. There's a difference between keeping a dream alive while remaining open to other opportunities and closing ourselves off to everything other than our capital-D dream. All of us—and all our careers—would be better off if we did way more of the former and way less of the latter. Life's most exciting and least expected adventures are found when we refuse to be restricted and restrained by what we've previously imagined.

Maybe the random opportunity we say yes to gets us nowhere. Or maybe we're great at it. Maybe it makes us truly happy. Maybe it ends up exceeding our wildest dreams. Maybe it *becomes* our wildest dream. Only now, unlike our childhood fantasies, we'll be equipped with a real understanding of what it entails, what it requires of us, and whether we're up for it—which makes it a whole lot more likely to become our reality and, quite literally, *a dream come true.*

## MY TAKE

At the height of my career, I was called the "Queen of Cable TV." I didn't get there by following my dreams—childhood, adolescent, awake, asleep, or otherwise. I got there by ditching them.

When I was growing up in the fifties and sixties, television was little more to me than a part-time babysitter. Back then, a time before cable (and *long* before streaming), there were just three channels to toggle among. Don't get me wrong—I loved each of them as much as the next kid. I have fond memories of watching shows that defined my childhood, like *My Little Margie* and *Lassie*, starring a telegenic collie I chose to name my family dalmatian after. But I had no grand aspiration or wild dream to someday be the person responsible for bringing those shows to life. If the only way my relationship with TV evolved when I reached adulthood was that it stopped babysitting me and started babysitting my kids, I would have been fine.

TV was a pastime. Photography, on the other hand, was a passion.

I was gifted with my first camera—a Kodak Brownie point-and-shoot that cost one dollar when it originally went on the market in 1900—at age twelve, as I was leaving for Camp Brookwood in Glen Spey, New York. I spent the next seven weeks bringing that Brownie everywhere and documenting my days: the campgrounds, the activities, the food in the mess hall and canteen, my bunkmates, and even the few boys my friends and I deemed cool (but definitely not the many we didn't). After I returned home in August, I took my black-and-white film rolls to be developed; when the photos came back, I mailed the best ones to my best friends across the country and hung the rest on my bedroom wall—a kind of mid-twentieth-century Instagram. I was hooked.

I loved the way the camera let me freeze time and place, and the power it gave me to capture a feeling and tell a story.

Years later, when I was a student at Boston University, my camera was different—I'd upgraded the Brownie to a fancy black Nikkormat with manual controls for light, shutter speed, and lens aperture—but I was still drawn to photography. I declared photojournalism as my major. When I graduated from BU's College of Communications, I walked off campus with a dream of spending my life working behind the lens.

Over the next few years, I pursued my passion with a passion. For my first gig out of college, I worked in the Newbury Street photo studio of Bela Kalman, a legendary Hungarian-born, Boston-based commercial photographer. More precisely, I got a job working in his darkroom, developing and processing his photos. It didn't take long for my hands to reek of chemicals and my fingernails to be perpetually tinted yellow. Isolated from both natural and artificial light *and* human interaction, it took even less time for my sanity to pack its bags and threaten to walk out the door for good. It's not that I hated the job—we just had irreconcilable differences.

I thanked my lucky stars when I was promoted to "front of house" and was tasked with helping Bela take photos on set. I got the chance to step into the literal light, but my metaphorical moment in the sun was short-lived once I realized that I had zero interest in commercial photography. In a way, it was the antithesis of the photojournalism I loved: stilted instead of candid, a distortion (or at least contortion) of reality instead of a reflection, shot inside with artificial everything instead of outside with natural light and backgrounds, rehearsed instead of capturing what the photographer Henri Cartier-Bresson called "the decisive moment"—the spontaneous visual convergence of everything that makes an event significant.

Aware of my essentially entry-level status, I searched for another position in the image industry that felt like a better fit. That led me to the education department at Houghton Mifflin, the textbook company, where I was hired as a photo editor. Having "editor" in my title made me feel important, but the reality was I spent my days flipping through catalogs, trying to find the perfect photo to complement a paragraph about the Gettysburg Address or a math problem in which Sally ended up with two apples and Stanley started out with seven. The work was really a mix-and-match game of sorts, pairing other people's words with other people's images, and I hated playing.

Next, I tried to find something in photojournalism itself. But the only roles open to someone with my limited experience were the photography equivalents of ambulance chasers, rushing to the scene of a crime or an accident and snapping sensationalist shots. That wasn't me either. I believed the camera's role was to reveal and expose, but never to exploit. My interest was in capturing the complexity of human emotion at its most organic and *least* overdramatic.

Today, I'll also confess what I refused to concede back then: I didn't want the broke-artist life—especially if I wasn't doing the type of photojournalism that I was passionate about. But I wasn't ready to give up on photography just yet. Dreams are like drugs; they're hard to quit. Even when they hold us back, trip us up, and make us crazy, we find ways to shift the blame onto ourselves. It can't be that the dream itself—that thing we've been nurturing inside us for years or even decades—is defective or damaging, right? Maybe we're just using it wrong. I told myself that if only I had more time, more exposure, and more opportunities in the field of photography, then the success, happiness, and certainty I was desperately missing were bound to follow.

That thinking led me back to Boston University for a master's program. Unofficially, it was another year to flirt with photography and figure out how to turn my fantasy into reality. But my most formative experience was off campus, at a throwaway internship I only took to satisfy a mandatory degree requirement.

My internship was as a freelance photographer for a new children's show called *Infinity Factory*, airing on WGBH, the local PBS affiliate. By freelance, I mean I was working for free. By photographer, I mean I would chase the show's kids and resident dog around the set to take whatever candids of them that I could, often begging the humans and the canine (almost always unsuccessfully) to slow down for a second.

Nearly all the publicity surrounding the show featured at least one of my photographs—in publications that included *Time* magazine and the *Boston Globe*. That crumb of success tasted great. It even reminded me why I'd had my photography dream in the first place.

In a twist of fate, with graduation just a few days away and my internship all but over, three of the show's production assistants were fired. And I got an offer to transition from freelance, on-set photographer to full-time staff member—to replace one of the production assistants, the lowest level on the television totem pole. At the time, I knew almost nothing about the industry. But I had known from the moment I first stepped on set that there was something in the air I wanted to keep breathing, keep learning, and keep exploring. Plus, I needed a job.

I weighed my options: the dream that hadn't really gotten me anywhere versus the opportunity that might take me God-knows-where. I decided I would rather spend my days calling "Lights, camera, action" than yelling "Cheese!" I said yes to becoming a PA, said goodbye—at least temporarily—to a career in photography, and ultimately said hello to a career in television. The rest, as they say in the industry that I've now worked in for nearly five decades, is history.

What I learned from that experience has stayed with me ever since. There's nothing wrong with loving something so much you want to make a living from it. But if you're addicted to your dreams, you risk sleepwalking past a better opportunity that might change your life. Worst case, you take it and hate it. But if you're lucky? You might end up with another dream, one that lands you in a real dream job (or many).

That's what happened to me. In a way, *not* following my dreams became the impetus for how I plotted my career. Instead, I followed the opportunities. I started in television that way, and I have stayed that way. It wasn't a conscious choice, but I was curious—and without a single dream to race toward blindly, I was able to take my time looking around (and learning about) all the industry's nooks and crannies.

My "accidental" choice turned out to be the smart way to go. With each new opportunity, I learned new skills, forged new connections, and earned newfound respect from people and places I would have never encountered otherwise. I developed new ideas of what my dream might look like.

Even the two sharpest left turns I took when my career was still finding its sea legs, two positions I reluctantly accepted at WGBH that I originally had zero interest in—managing the budget for a documentary series and learning about the mechanics of CDs and three-quarter-inch videocassettes as the network's director of "new media"—were not for naught. These roles equipped me with experience and knowledge in areas that many people working in television lacked, including the economics of getting a show on the air and the evolving technology used to do so. That allowed me to better understand the industry I was working in.

Here's the best part: The old dreams and new ones, the passion projects and more practical professions . . . they aren't mutually exclusive. Mine sure weren't. (My first producing credit was on a TV series called, I kid you not, *The Photo Show*.) Working in TV, I used the traits that made me a good photographer—an eye for lighting and color, a knack for framing a shot, a gift for capturing audiences, an ability to tell a story in a single image and convey emotion without words—to become a strong producer, an even better network executive, and, eventually, the "Queen of Cable TV." You could argue I never even ditched the dream. I simply opened up my lens and widened my exposure, from a single medium—photography—to media at large.

I still love taking photos. But because I was able to zoom out and see the bigger picture, my career and life have had more depth, color, and brightness than I ever could have dreamed. The camera is still my best friend. It's just not my boss.

## NAIL IT

While I didn't end up with a career in photography, the early years I spent behind the camera still changed the course of my work . . . and my life. They equipped me with both hard and soft skills that set me apart on the job. But they also taught me how to look more broadly at what was in front of me and really see what, if anything, was there—how to weigh my preexisting dreams against new ones, how to seize opportunities (and know which ones were worth seizing in the first place), how to make the best of wherever I ended up, and the most of whatever I was doing.

So . . .

## Know Your Subject

Before they even take out their cameras, great photographers seek to understand the subjects in front of them. Given that each of us is the subject of our own lives, we owe ourselves that same understanding. As you begin plotting your career, ask the big and hard questions. First, ask yourself where your dream came from: Is it your own, or was it instilled in you by someone else? If you've "always" wanted to do

### Find the Workplace That Works Best for You

More than anything else, knowing and understanding yourself means being able to distinguish between what you'd ideally want to *be* and what you actually like to *do*. That's important when you have a dream, and even more important when you feel like you have no direction at all. So figure out not just what you bring to the table but what kind of table you want to be sitting at. What would make you feel like you were "living the dream"?

- Are you an introvert or an extrovert?
- Are you a solo operator or a team player?
- Do you like using your brain all day, or would you rather use your hands (and stay on your feet)?
- Would you rather be a big fish in a small pond or a small fish in a big pond?
- Are you creative, a boundary-pusher, or more by-the-book?
- Do you want to travel or stay put?
- Do you prefer structure or autonomy?

something, ask yourself why. Really listen to the answers, even if they weren't what you expected. Figure out when the dream came to you and what's compelled it to stick around.

Know that sometimes, a dream in theory crashes headfirst into the reality of what a career in that industry or field looks like. You might love the Constitution and hate the lifestyle of a lawyer. You might relish writing but want to spend your days interacting with people like the social animal you are. And sometimes, the dream you want desperately might not want you back; the two of you may even be a match made in hell. While giving up on it may seem depressing, there's a bright side: As soon as you push aside a dream that isn't working for you, you can start working toward one that will make you truly happy.

## Survey the Landscape

Survey the professional landscape before settling in. Stay curious. Keep an open mind (and open eye) before you decide exactly what it is you're looking for.

If there's an industry or field you want to enter, do your homework: Talk to everyone you can who operates in the world you're trying to break into. Research the big players—the leading companies, executives, and innovations—and learn what sets them apart from the crowd and each other. Find out what the day-to-day or even year-to-year of a job in that world would look like at each level of the ladder. Understand what people who begin their careers in this industry go on to do, and where the people leading this industry began their own careers. Equip yourself with accurate information about salaries, growth, and work-life balance.

If there's someone you admire and whose career you wish to emulate, reach out to them on LinkedIn with a thoughtful, personalized note, and figure out whether there are opportunities for you to fol-low in their footsteps.

And if there's a specific job you truly dream of having, make sure you know all the positions you'd first need to occupy to get there. If those don't seem appealing to you, and if the path to your dream feels more like a nightmare, it might be time to reconsider the dream.

## Balance Light and Dark

Great photos require the right balance of lightness and darkness—too much of one and not enough of the other obscures or distorts whatever reality the camera was trying to capture. That can happen at work, too. For the 99.9 percent of us who don't start out working in a job or a field of our dreams, the day-to-day can feel downright demoralizing. It's easy to look at all the opportunities we aren't re-ceiving, all the progress we aren't making, all the accomplishments we aren't racking up, all the fun we aren't having, and all the re-spect we aren't earning. But the darkness, we should keep in mind, is normal—and it exists in every job, even those that seem straight out of a fantasy.

At the same time, it's also important to find the light. Are you meeting new people? Gaining new skills? Maybe you're getting cool opportunities to explore a different part of the city, country, or world. Maybe the only thing you're learning is what you *don't* like to do—that's still getting you one step closer to finding and doing something you love.

Be sure to look for the light and dark in any *potential* opportunity, too, especially one that's somewhat out of left field. Our own pessi-mism, preconceptions, and prejudices often prevent us from seeing something for what it is (and also what it can be). So, ask yourself: Best case scenario, where does this opportunity take me? But don't

## Email Etiquette: Dos and Don'ts

Whether your cold email or LinkedIn message gets warmly received or gets you iced out—whether it gets a reply, gets forwarded to an assistant, or gets deleted immediately—depends almost entirely on what you say:

- DO: Personalize your note. Note why you're reaching out to *this* person (and not one of their colleagues), explain how you learned of them (Did you read a profile? Go to the same college?), and talk about how your interests align with their work.
- DON'T: Make someone feel like they are one of ten people on your checklist or copy and paste text from one letter into another. If you reach out to multiple employees at the same organization, expect that they'll talk.
- DO: Explain your interest in their profession/company/industry in a way that sounds genuine.
- DON'T: Ask them to refer you to others in the company before they've met you.
- DO: Ask for a conversation, not a job offer.
- DON'T: Take five paragraphs to make your point. People are busy, and the longer your message, the more likely it ends up in the trash.
- DO: Follow through! If someone offers to have a phone call, always take them up on it—or at least write back to explain—even if you've accepted another job in the time since they responded. Industries are small, and memories are long.
- DON'T: Come across as obsessed. Flattery and interest are great; stalking isn't.
- DO: Be humble. Demonstrate humility, not arrogance.
- DON'T: Act entitled to their time (or a meeting over coffee).
- DO: Say thank you in advance for taking the time to read your note.

be naïve about the answer; don't accept a job because you're relying on the 0.0001 percent chance that you'll become CEO within two years or the equally rare possibility that you'll have no bad days. If you can be realistic with your expectations and remember that no job is entirely amazing (or entirely terrible), you're a lot more likely to find happiness and fulfillment—not just in your dream job but in every job that you work at along the way.

## Zoom In and Out as Necessary

When you're evaluating an opportunity, looking at both the big picture and its smaller details is critical—because the way things seem on the surface isn't always how they are up close. In terms of the big picture, ask yourself whether the job seems like a runway to your next destination or a dead end. Even if the role is in an industry you know little about with a company you've never heard of, there are still many ways it can set you up for success: the mentors you might meet, the management experience you might gain, the leadership you might practice, the way you can differentiate yourself from other people who may have similar backgrounds or ambitions.

Alternatively, what seems like a dream job at the company of your dreams, working under an executive you dream of becoming, can sometimes be nothing more than a first-class ticket to nowhere (or end up moving you one step forward but two steps back).

To avoid the second scenario, zoom into the details and minutiae of a job before you accept it—especially those that may not be advertised. Read up on the corporate culture and envision how you would fit into it—and whether you'd want to. Study up on the people who've held your role, or similar ones at your company, before: Are they happy? Do they stay long? Do they stick to their own areas of expertise, or is cross-team collaboration encouraged? Do people play by the rules or color outside the lines? Do they feel satisfied with their work-life balance? What position did they previously hold? And what do they go on to do? Answering these questions may not lead you to your dream job right away. But looking at the whole picture *will* increase the odds that you know what you're getting into, which will increase the likelihood that you feel fulfilled once you're there. And *that*'s a prerequisite for a job of anyone's dreams.

### It's Okay to Walk Away

Whoever said winners never quit probably isn't a winner. The truth is, they do . . . all the time. If you're no longer learning, growing, or enjoying yourself on the job, and there's nothing else you can get out of it, it's okay to walk away. Just try not to burn any bridges on your way out.

### Lock Your Focus

A photo in progress can have everything working in its favor: a great subject, a mastery of the equipment, just the right background, impeccable lighting, and an intentional and well-thought-out frame. But if a photographer fails to focus their camera (or smartphone), everything leading up to the moment of capture—and the final product itself—might end up being a waste. The same is true when it comes to our careers. We can prepare for an opportunity in all the right ways, but if we get distracted once we get there and start treating where we are as second fiddle to somewhere else that we'd rather be, the opportunity (and everything we did to achieve it) will end up a waste, too.

So give your full focus and attention to every position you accept and challenge you take on, *especially* once you've found something you're passionate about—something that will make you eager to wake up in the morning. Even if the role and its accompanying responsibilities seem irrelevant to your dream—even if they're tedious, boring, and different from what you expected—act as if succeeding at the job is critical to fulfilling your wildest wish. Ask the right questions. Find someone to learn from. Put in the same amount of work and dedication. That's how you will be better prepared when the right opportunity comes your way.

## THE FINAL WORD

When we're head down in our dreams, we limit ourselves. We often miss the opportunities in front of our faces—opportunities with exceptional potential. So instead of committing to a single path early on, stay open, eager, and curious. That's how we figure out not just what makes us happy but what makes us tick. That's how we learn what our real passions and strengths are—and get practice putting them to use. That's how we gain skills and insights and experiences we may not have been looking for. To live our dreams, we have to keep our lens wide open, find the opportunities out there, and explore them.

# 2. Know Your Worth /
# Work On Your Worth

**What We're Told:** *"Know your worth."*

Throughout our lives, people—women especially—are reminded to know our worth. Walk into a gift shop or go on to Etsy, and the mantra is plastered on greeting cards, T-shirts, throw pillows, and coffee mugs. Instagram life coaches proclaim, "When you know your worth, no one can make you feel worthless." And in a world where too many of us too often undervalue, undersell, and underestimate ourselves, "know your worth" can feel like the perfect antidote: an encouragement to never accept less—less pay, less responsibility, less respect—than we deserve. To never settle for anything that unsettles us.

**The Truth:** *"Work on your worth."*

When we're young, most of us are worthless. And we should expect to be treated that way.

Before I get canceled or called out on social media, let me be clear. I'm not telling you to put up with a cheating boyfriend or let your landlord go for months without fixing the broken drain in the shower you share with three roommates and a formerly stray cat.

What I am saying is that our personal worth and our professional worth are entirely different things. Conflating our value on the job with our value off of it is like sticking our hand out the window in New York and thinking it'll tell us the temperature in New Delhi.

Yet too many entry-level and early-career employees seem to miss this memo. As a result, I've watched them trip up on the job, and occasionally fall flat on their faces, when their otherwise enviable self-worth manifests as entitlement—not to being treated with decency and fairness but to rapidly ascend to more money, responsibility, and power.

Some people think it's a generational problem—that today's twenty- and thirty-year-olds have been overly coddled, and this is the result. If there's some truth to that, then many in my generation must shoulder some blame.

As parents, teachers, coaches, and administrators, we spent decades building young people up by artificially inflating their egos. Throughout their childhoods, we doled out participation trophies, gold-star stickers, and As for effort, which essentially made success and failure synonyms. During the college application process, we sent some of them "courtesy deferrals"—rejection letters that let them down easily by postponing the delivery of bad news rather than, well, delivering it. Once they got to campus, we spared them from discomfort (and from having to reckon with a real world that is often offensive) through safe spaces and trigger warnings.

It's no wonder that, by the time they start work, too many young people feel betrayed—or at the very least bored—by tasks that don't inspire or obviously benefit them. They were told they could do anything, and now they're being told to get three iced coffees from Starbucks.

But that is only part of the story. After all, long before there were participation trophies, courtesy deferrals, and safe spaces, there were people who grunted at grunt work. So while this might seem like a new phenomenon, it's not. Who among us *doesn't* want roles and responsibilities that fulfill us physically, emotionally, and even politically?

It's a tale as old as time, largely because it takes time to learn a simple truth: People are born with personal worth, but we have to *earn* professional worth. The experiences, education, and esteem we've accumulated before we start working don't automatically follow us to the office, stick to us like glue, and signal our value to everyone we interact with—our bosses and our peers. Even if we had a great internship or graduated as valedictorian. Even if we had the strongest resume of any applicant, and the recruiter or hiring manager loved us. That's simply not the way work, well, works.

The moment we step into the workplace, we start fresh. When our careers are beginning, often that means doing things—the menial labor, the un-sexy assignments, the mindless tasks—that we might feel are beneath us or that we're too good for. But someone has to do it. Why *wouldn't* it be us?

On the job, people will only know our worth once they know our work. That takes time. It takes effort. It takes consistency. It isn't based on our potential or promise. It's based on our results. Until we've proven ourselves, our value add exists in showing up—and maybe not much more.

So, drop the ego and get to work. If it doesn't feel great, stick to it anyway. As long as you're learning, as long as you're making connections, as long as there's a runway to something else that you can take off from eventually, don't throw in the towel. Trust me, if the only work you're willing to do at the beginning of your career is the big, prestigious, high-paying stuff, you'll probably never end up doing it . . . at any point in your career.

Of course, some jobs are truly worth leaving—the dead ends, the abusive bosses, the all-work-no-life-and-no-end-in-sight balances. But even the jobs that aren't will still test your patience and make you question what the frack you're doing. If Buddha's right and "life is suffering," then guess what? So is work.

There's a reason we don't call it play.

## MY TAKE

I learned my "workplace worth" fresh out of graduate school when I stumbled into my first real job in television as a production assistant for *Infinity Factory*, a children's show that tried to make math fun and easy to learn.

While I chased the entire cast around the set to capture photos for promotional materials, I saw the production assistants in action. Each assistant was assigned to a different cast member, ranging in age from seven to twelve, to help run lines, copy and collate scripts, fetch snacks, and even pick out their outfits.

Underwhelming perhaps, and hardly glamorous—but it seemed like good experience.

So when three production assistants were fired in a single day, and I got a job offer to replace one of them, I said yes. I knew what I would have to do, and I knew I could do it. Even if the position made me the most junior employee on staff, I'd be critical to at least one person on *Infinity Factory*. Then I was assigned my cast member: Winston, an English sheepdog and the show's only non-human talent. My primary responsibility was to follow him around the set, carrying a pooper scooper. My responsibility was shit. Literally.

I won't lie. I was pissed. More days than not, I felt underutilized, undervalued, underappreciated, and way overqualified. (I'm only human, after all . . . a human who was outranked by a slobbery, four-legged sidekick who could pass for a shag carpet.) I had two university degrees. Winston, on the other hand, was a nepotism hire—a proto-"nepo baby"—the precious personal and un-housebroken pet of one of the show's producers. The icing on the cake? I'm pretty sure the dog was paid more than I was.

But even though I may have felt like working for Winston was beneath me, I didn't show it. Instead, I acted like a college student gunning toward an honors degree in pet-sitting—and I treated each doggie bag I filled like an extra credit opportunity. When I was asked to take on the additional responsibility of shopping for the (human) cast members' wardrobes at the Harvard Coop, I acted like I'd won the lottery. And to a certain degree, I had.

Something about the lights, the cameras, the directors, and the production team running around the studio made me want more. I knew I was in the right place—definitely the right industry, at least—and that, at some point, it would be the right time. But not until I put in the time. So I plastered on a smile, picked up the crap, and paid my dues. I also paid attention to everything around me, observing, learning, and growing as much as I could in my current role. Unbeknownst to me, I was also preparing for the next one. When an associate producer position opened up, I was promoted, having already proven I was eager and able to take one (and tackle number two) for the team.

Decades later, I made this point to my son, Jesse, when he was straight out of college. At the time, he was working in the only type of entry-level job that exists at talent agencies—especially when your mom refuses to make calls or use connections on your behalf—the mailroom. "I'm spending my days packing boxes and sorting mail," he would say to me repeatedly. "They're not letting me use my brain."

"What did you expect?" I'd respond. "You took an entry-level job in the mailroom!"

To Jesse's credit, he didn't share his frustration with anyone in the agency. While he couldn't help but bring his ego to work with him each morning, he was wise enough to box up his complaints and take them home with him each night. And boy did he take them home. But on the job, he put on a smile, played the game, and powered through. Eventually, he worked his way up the ladder at the agency.

Now in his thirties, Jesse can clearly see how backward his mindset once was. Before he'd actually done much in the field that he was looking to build a career in, he wasn't worth anything to anyone. His work ethic had never been demonstrated. His ideas had never been put to the test. He might have had a lot of promise, and his bosses might have seen that. But until he had proven himself, his value was only theoretical.

The only way he could prove himself? Swallow his pride and put in the time.

That's what I did—not just at *Infinity Factory* but throughout the early stages of my career. I knew that if I wanted to be considered a valuable asset by my colleagues and bosses, I needed to add some concrete value to their days. Since I didn't yet have a long rap sheet of results or a resume of relevant skills, that value came from showing up and doing what needed to be done.

At the time, I saw it as a survival tactic. But now I know there's a real method to this madness. It's how everyone should *want* to start their careers and chart their way forward. The long hours I put in, the odd tasks I took on, the self-respect I kinda, sorta suppressed at the beginning of my professional journey—all of it prepared me for what came next and truly paid off in the long run.

As I slowly but surely climbed the ranks in the TV industry, I knew how to handle the ugliest, smelliest, un-sexiest parts of the business.

I'd seen and done it all. In fact, I would say that I was *only* able to work my way up to the top *because* I had started at the very, very bottom.

And no, I don't just mean Winston's.

## NAIL IT

If we want to move up at work, we have to *up* our worth—and on the job, that worth is determined by what we do, not how we feel. That's particularly true for entry-level employees; they aren't worth much because they haven't done much, which is why their pay, title, and responsibilities are modest. But it's also true for everyone else. When a CEO has a bad quarter, when an engineer makes a failing product, when a model bombs on the runway, or a writer doesn't make the bestseller list, their worth also goes down. While our pasts count for something, and our potential matters, too, it's what we do in the present that makes us worthy. And being worthy is what sets us on the path to more: more money, more responsibility, and even more gratifying and satisfying work.

So . . .

### Wake Up (And Stay Up)

The more you put into a job, the more you'll get out of it. That includes your time. I'm not directing you to sacrifice your social life or forgo fun, and I'm definitely not recommending that you overexert yourself in the fast lane only to crash with inevitable burnout. But if you feel overlooked, underappreciated, or lost in a sea of similarly skilled and compensated colleagues—or if you're up for a promotion—the easiest way to differentiate yourself and prove your worth is to be the first one at the office each morning and the last one to leave at night. If actions speak louder than words, then getting in early and staying late screams "I'm committed!"

## Show Up

The pandemic unleashed an era of remote work and some unexpected upsides—like shorter commutes and meetings in our pajama pants ("business on top, bedroom on bottom"). But when Zoom became a noun and FaceTime and Teams replaced face time and team meetings, we lost something real: the casual but often consequential encounters that come from working in an office, on-site, with peers and superiors. At the bottom of the corporate ladder, an unplanned conversation in the elevator or unscripted interaction by the water cooler (or the La Croix–stocked fridge) helps you climb. Being seen gives you critical visibility. So if you have the chance to work from an office, take it. I can't predict exactly *how* it'll help your career, but I can promise you that, somehow, it will.

After all, you'll never be worthy of being in the "room where it happens" if you're never *in* the actual room.

## Step Up

If you want to increase your worth at work, literally increase what you're doing at work. You don't have to tattoo "PICK ME" or "I'M IN" to your forehead, but perhaps pretend they're both already inked on there. Become the yes-woman (or -man) in your office. Be the first to volunteer for a task, even when your gut doesn't want to. See no assignment as too menial or too challenging to take a whack at. Especially at the start of your career—before you've acquired a niche, knowledge base, or knack for the industry that makes you irreplaceable—your best shot at standing out is by simply stepping up.

## Look Up

There's an irony in working the lowest job at an organization: You may feel "worthless," but you probably have significant exposure to senior staff and executives—those at the organization who are worth the *most*. It might come from getting them coffee, scheduling their day, or answering their phones. But exposure's exposure. And the time you waste feeling down about yourself is time you could be spending looking up and seeing who's around you. When my son, Jesse, was in the mailroom, he realized he could make the best of his time sorting and delivering letters and packages to agents by learning about their interests, weaving them into a quick bit of small talk, and using that to connect. He turned an underwhelming experience into a networking opportunity, and you can, too.

## Study Up

Generally, your first few jobs should be about learning as much as you can. (At the start of my career, I was making minimum wage . . . and sub-minimum a dog's wage.) So don't bother measuring your success solely by your salary. Instead, be a sponge and absorb the world around you. If there's something you don't know, find a way to learn it. Lots of companies have internal growth programs, subscriptions to LinkedIn Learning, and stipends for employees' "continuing education," and lots of employees never take advantage of them. Don't make that mistake. Seriously—that is free money you're throwing away and a new skill or idea you're opting not to learn.

## Team Up

It's true that "great friendships are forged in fire and born of adversity." No wonder soldiers stay close long after they've been sent home from battle. The same is true for coworkers. It's easier to get through work when you are part of a team. Fight the urge to view your colleagues as competition. Instead, form and foster those collaborative workplace friendships. They aren't just invaluable when you're at the bottom. They often help you rise to the top, too. There are infinite reasons why I consider my first few jobs worth it, and a dozen of those reasons are the friends I made there and still keep in touch with. We all ended up in different places. But none of us would have gotten where we are today without the friendships we made along the way. And each of us is better off because of them.

## Kim Kardashian's Secret Worth? Hard Work

There's a myth that success has come easy to Kim Kardashian, but I can tell you from personal experience, having greenlit multiple Kardashian shows and spinoffs, that Kim works her very photographed butt off to prove her worth. When she was tapped to host *Saturday Night Live*, she made a point of showing up early and staying late. Once the episode's production started, she worked with stylists to get the right look for the audience. She worked with comics and the show's writers to not only learn her lines but perfect her timing and delivery. When *SNL* opened "live from New York," Kim was completely prepared, and she knocked it out of the park. When building worth, there's no workaround or substitute for old-fashioned hard work, something Kim's mom, Kris Jenner, taught her daughters. Kris promoted and supported them and instilled a serious work ethic. Is it any surprise that they have dominated as reality stars and influencers for so many years?

## Chin Up

When I'm hiring for a team or doling out a promotion, the first thing I look at—before talent, experience, or references—is attitude. I don't care if you've won three Emmys or have a photographic memory. If you're a negative person, there's a negative chance you're getting the job. One pessimist, naysayer, or whiner can sour the culture of a workplace, or create such an unpleasant vibe that it de-motivates everyone else around them. Fortunately, the inverse is true as well. A genuine smile and can-do demeanor can make all the difference when you're being assessed for a role. Even when you don't check off every prerequisite or requirement for the job, a positive attitude is like a halo effect. It makes the rest of you seem better—and makes people eager to be around you. I hired my current coordinator, Dana, for this exact reason.

## Dress Up

If all the world's a stage, then the office is no exception. And there's no way to predict our audience. So put in the effort and make your presence a present. That doesn't mean putting your feet in stilettos—it just means putting your best foot forward. If you don't feel great about the job you currently have, start dressing for the one you want. Follow the advice given to every NBC page about how to dress when not in their signature uniforms: Wear whatever you want, but always ask yourself, "If I bumped into the CEO in the elevator, would I be proud to introduce myself?"

## Bottom Up

There's a misconception that starting from the bottom is something to be ashamed of. Nothing could be less true. Unless someone was born on third base or with a well-connected silver spoon in their mouth, everyone starts somewhere. I've learned that starting from the lowest levels of an industry or company actually makes your leadership stronger, more compassionate, more knowledgeable, and more effective by the time you get to the top. You won't just understand every aspect of your organization and field, you'll also have real empathy and appreciation for people currently doing the work you once did. You've literally been there. You know what's worth stressing about and what isn't worth your—or anyone's—time.

So don't be embarrassed about where you start out. Instead, embrace the bottom with humor and humility—and learn everything you can while you're there.

### Account for Your Worth

Once you've shown and know your worth, demonstrate it to the companies you apply for (or the company you're already working for). Don't settle for bread crumbs. In interviews and negotiations, don't only sell yourself, give the company an opportunity to sell itself, too. Be clear about what you're looking for in a job and what your deal-breakers may be. Be honest about where you see yourself in five months (or five years) and ask questions that prompt the company to answer honestly about whether or not your expectations are realistic.

## THE FINAL WORD

Back to Winston one last time. The truth is that by the time I was promoted to producer, I was basically finished with putting up with a dog (and his crap). After all, I'd already put in the time and proven myself—and as a result, I was no longer "worthless." But after all these years, from picking up shit to running shit, there's one thing I know for certain: Putting in the work is how you prove your worth. And it's *always* worth it.

# 3. Have Friends In High Places / Find Truth-Tellers In Every Location

**What We're Told:** *"Have friends in high places."*

For all our talk of meritocracy and hard work, it turns out that pulling ourselves up by the bootstraps is, literally, physically impossible. (Blame gravity.) But if it worked, even metaphorically, that route would make for a slower, bumpier rise to the top . . . at least compared to the alternative: finding someone who is *already* at the top and is willing to pull us up. No wonder people say it's all about who you know. With powerful, well-connected allies to lend a hand and look out for us—with "friends in high places"—who needs a ladder?

**The Truth:** *"Find truth-tellers in every location."*

At work and in life, there's no elevator to success. If we want to get to the top, we have to learn how to climb.

That's where mentors come in. Ask anyone at the pinnacle of their field what the secret to success is, and chances are they'll tell you about a great mentor they had along the way—someone who pushed them to be better. It's no wonder, then, that in today's corporate culture mentorship is all the rage. According to some recent figures, 84 percent of Fortune 500 companies have formal mentoring programs, including *every single one* of the top 50 companies in the United States.[1] While the details vary, the broad contours of these programs look the same.

Largely because of these programs, when we talk about mentors today, we think of the following criteria: Someone more senior than us. Someone working in the same field. Someone with good connections who is available and enthusiastic about introducing us to other well-connected people. Someone to cheer us on when we succeed and cheer us up when we fail. Someone who will make our climb up the corporate (or political, nonprofit, communications, legal, tech, or you-name-it-industry) ladder seamless and swift. And, of course, someone who has officially taken us under their wing and identifies as our mentor.

These are the qualities of what I call "supportive mentors." At work, they're our friends in high places. They're often the first to believe in us, go to bat for us, and build up our confidence. And they're the type of mentors most formalized mentorship programs aspire to provide.

But despite contributing to the development of these programs at my own company, I have to be honest: Most of them are lacking—through no fault of their own—for two main reasons.

The first is that the strongest mentor-mentee relationships are often organic, not organized. They are the result of chemistry between two people, and no amount of scientific study can predict when or with whom that bond will form. Those people at the pinnacle of their fields, the ones who credit mentors for their rise to the top, are rarely talking about someone assigned to answer their inquiring emails or designated to treat them to coffee and advice once a month. Of course, it is possible to find real mentorship through a formalized mentorship program; organic relationships *can* evolve out of organized ones. But relying on these programs to find a genuine mentor isn't a reliable way to get ahead.

The second failure of these formalized, organized programs stems from the first: There's an entire category of mentor they don't even account for—the "challenging mentor." As the name implies, these mentors challenge us. But more than that, they're often really challenging people. They can be difficult to deal with. They refuse to go easy on us. They put the "tough" in tough love. And with them, it *really* is tough. (It also rarely, if ever, feels loving.)

The concept seems almost novel now, but originally, that's what a mentor was meant to be. The word itself comes from the name of a character in Homer's ancient Greek epic *The Odyssey*—Mentor—who served as a counselor to Odysseus and his son, the young Telemachus. Throughout the story, Mentor pushed back and challenged the two warriors when they felt despair or performed below par.

But it's another Ancient Greek, the philosopher Socrates, who truly embodied the ideal of the challenging mentor. As a teacher to Plato, one of history's most famous mentees, Socrates never went easy on him. In fact, Socrates was more of a sparring partner, constantly pushing Plato to further explain what he was saying. Their relationship is the basis of the Socratic method—think college professors asking hapless students follow-up question after follow-up question until their answers are watertight. In the moment, it seems sadistic. Yet the goal is selfless: to sharpen and refine the students' thinking by forcing them to consider (and reconsider) what they believe and why.

If supportive mentors are our professional friends in high places, then challenging mentors are scrappy sparring partners, constantly raising the bar. While supportive mentors tell us we're great, challenging mentors tell us the truth—even when it's hard to hear. They often cause us to double-check both our instincts and our work, and they can double or triple our frustrations.

This type of mentorship is almost impossible to formally facilitate, especially in a structured and human resources–approved work setting. Who among us is so eager to hear the many ways we're messing up or missing the mark that we'd willingly enroll in a program aimed at exactly that? And what HR department wants to be on the hook for facilitating a relationship that is by its very nature difficult, even combative?

There's no getting around the fact that challenging mentorships are more complicated than supportive mentorships. But I'd argue they're also more critical to our growth and success, and that they do more for us in the long run than even the nicest supportive mentors could. History and literature would argue that, too.

And yet something seems to have been lost in translation. Forget about not wanting a challenging mentor. Today, most people can't even see challenging mentors for what they are. Anyone lucky enough to have a challenging mentor in their life—or someone who could potentially fill that role—often doesn't even realize it. Instead, we may view challenging mentors as jerks and bullies who make us uncomfortable by expecting us to do things that feel nearly impossible and holding us to standards that feel almost irrational.

But sometimes, we really do need to be prodded and probed and pressured into doing something we would otherwise never attempt, so we can learn what we're capable of. Maybe we're sent back to the drawing board for yet another round of edits on a script we can't seem to crack—and then we finally write that perfect line of dialogue. Maybe we're assigned the most out-there case of any associate at our law firm in our second week on the job—and then we find a star witness who wins over the jury. Maybe we're given just two hours to make a presentation for the CEO that should take us triple the time—and then we knock it out of the park. Had we never been pushed, we never would have tried. Had we never tried, we would never have known.

There's a reason that so many animals simply push their young into the water when "teaching" them to swim: to show them they already can.

And sometimes we need to be called out, criticized, and brought down to earth once we've done something we shouldn't have—or before we try and fail. The same way that cheering someone as they dive headfirst into a three-foot-deep kiddie pool isn't good encouragement, blind faith and unconditional applause aren't good mentorship.

Trust me: When a leader or executive references a mentor who helped them along the way, they aren't talking about the person who said, "You can do it!" They're talking about the person who *showed* them that they could do it—whatever "it" was—by expecting more of them than they expected of themselves. Or they're talking about the person who sat them down and said, "Actually, you *can't* do it . . . but here's what you could do instead."

None of this means supportive mentors are bad to have. We need different things from different people at different stages in our lives. If someone a little more senior with a few more years of experience takes us under their wing during our first week at our first job, shows us the ropes, and walks us around the office introducing us to colleagues in other departments, that's great. But work isn't a fairy tale. These "friends in high places" aren't the office Rapunzels, able to let down their hair and lift us up to their lofty towers. If we want to get to the top, we need to be surrounded by people who push us to complete the climb—not just those who give us a hand to hold. We need people who challenge us, because that is what prepares us for all the challenging times ahead.

## MY TAKE

I've been mentoring women—and men, too—for almost five decades, since a few years into my first job. Today, I spend my days giving advice to people at every level of the company through every medium, about any topic. The first line of my job description has a mentor-y ring to it: "strategic advisor to the CEO."

But I've also had mentors even longer than I've been one. Before you ask: None of them was ever my official "mentor."

My first mentors were my father and my brother. My father was a supportive mentor—the one who built up my confidence and repeated phrases like *you can do it* and *there's no such word as can't* whenever I needed some extra motivation. He was my biggest champion and cheerleader, and he let me know it. When I was twelve—yes, twelve—he sat me on his lap in the front seat of the car, placed my hands over his on the steering wheel, and taught me how to drive, years before I was eligible for even my permit.

My brother, on the other hand, didn't care about hyping me up or boosting my self-esteem; he had better things to do with his time and energy. A child prodigy who entered college a few months before he turned sixteen, he ended up becoming chief of neurosurgery at one of Stanford University's teaching hospitals. (I've since learned that in the world of medicine, neurosurgeons are stereotyped as perfectionists with God complexes; my brother fit that bill.) Clearly, he liked a challenge—both taking them on *and* doling them out—and he was the ultimate challenging mentor to me, his kid sister.

When my brother was in medical school and I was beginning high school, he invited me to go skiing with his friends. I didn't know how to ski, but he said he'd teach me, and I believed him. He assured me I was fine to skip the bunny slopes ("They're for toddlers, Bonnie"), so we rode the chairlift together to the top of the mountain. Once there, he looked at me, smirked, and said "See you later, sis!" Within a few short seconds, I couldn't even see him. The day was cold, but I was fuming.

Motivated by my need to scream at my sibling and ask him what the hell he was thinking, I eventually made my way down, helped by his friend Don, whose waist I held on to as his skis sandwiched my own.

My brother's response? "I wouldn't have left you at the top if I didn't think you could make it to the bottom. You're here in one piece, aren't you?"

I guess he was technically right. Don had helped me, but I'd also made it down the mountain without first learning on the bunny slopes. In all the times I've gone skiing since, I've never needed a bunny slope.

In their own ways, both my father and brother prepared me for the mentors who followed. (Because I was one of the very few women in my field, most of my mentors were *men*tors.) At USA Network, I had two supportive mentors who helped me to both hone and own my voice.

Dave Kenin was my boss's boss when I was first hired at USA. He ran all of its programming. When I brazenly sent him a suggested schedule for Friday nights—rejiggered so a series I'd worked on would air at a different time and completely different from the schedule he'd already created—he responded with a lengthy note explaining, hour by hour and show by show, why my proposal absolutely wouldn't work. But he ended it in a way that made me feel good rather than silly about reaching out: "All that being said . . . I love your memo. I love that you're playing with scheduling. I love that you're thinking. Keep these memos coming."

Then there was Steve Brenner, who was USA's chief operating officer during my early years and then the network's copresident of operations. When I was negotiating a new deal to keep *The Ray Bradbury Theater*—a science fiction anthology series by the acclaimed author—on our channel, Brenner championed me in my fight to cut unnecessary costs. I'd never negotiated anything before, and I might not have had the best or most refined tactics. I'm sure there was something to critique about my approach. But Brenner's unabashed enthusiasm for what I was doing helped me succeed. From that day on, he was always in my corner, and whenever I've negotiated anything since, his encouraging voice is always in my head.

These men each taught me more lessons than I could fit in a book—much less a chapter. And they both reported to the woman who had founded USA Network, Kay Koplovitz, a trailblazer in the cable television industry and now a trailblazer in venture capital for women entrepreneurs. But it's the challenging mentors, the ones in the mold of my brother, that I'll be spilling the most ink on. Just like we might not know who Muhammad Ali was if not for Sonny Liston, Joe Frazier, and George Foreman—tough opponents who forced Ali to defy expectations and pushed him to greatness—I, Bonnie Hammer, probably wouldn't have written this book (or had the career I've had) without some very tough opponents of my own.

In college, my chop-buster-in-chief was Harris Smith, an ex–US Army sergeant who taught photojournalism. That was my major, and I knew I had a good eye, but Harris—who taught me for two years and four straight semesters—made me realize that wasn't enough. He believed skill alone was insufficient. To succeed in his book meant giving each photo I took my all, even if I could have produced something good with half the effort. (And he could tell the difference.)

These were the pre-digital days; I'd spend hours in the darkroom waiting patiently for my images to emerge. Sometimes, I got the exact shot I wanted. Sometimes, it—and I—let me down. Editing wasn't allowed: no cropping, no blowing up, no adjusting the focal point. Harris believed anyone could submit a great photo, but not everyone could capture one. He saw the purpose of his class to teach us how to *see*, and that's what he was judging (and why we had to submit the negatives of each photo we took).

Once, I submitted a homework assignment that was admittedly subpar, at least compared to what I was capable of: a mundane shot demonstrating little artistry or focus. I'd had a date that weekend, as if that were an excuse for not giving the work enough time, thought, or effort. Harris wasn't having it. In front of all my classmates, he held the photo up in the air, called it "pure junk," kicked me out of class, and told me I was invited back only once I'd captured a new image that was worth his and the class's time.

I was humiliated. But I never gave him less than my best again— and in the process, I discovered my eye was even better than I'd thought.

Another person whom I often felt was too demanding? Barry Diller, a brilliant contrarian and my ultimate boss at USA Network and Sci-Fi Channel (and the owner of both at the time). Barry was legendary in the entertainment industry even back then. As VP of development at ABC in the 1960s, he had pioneered the concept of the made-for-TV-movie *and* the miniseries. He was CEO and chairman of Paramount Pictures during the decade when the studio produced

TV hits like *Laverne & Shirley* and *Cheers* and blockbuster movies like *Grease, Terms of Endearment,* and the first two *Indiana Jones* films. In his eight years running 20th Century Fox, he launched the Fox TV Network and greenlit *The Simpsons.* And that's just the beginning.

I can't think of anyone in the world, especially the entertainment world, from whom I could have learned more. But in my first year with Barry, I did not see it that way. He was often demanding, and sometimes demeaning or straight-up scary. He questioned *everything* I did. He accepted no surprises. In hindsight, he almost made Harris seem sweet—and in reply, I painted "DILLER" in capital letters on the six-foot punching bag I used for my weekend kickboxing classes so I could punch, kick, and grunt out my aggressions before I returned to work for Barry on Monday. Never have I rued the day I met a person so much. Never have I dreaded someone's calls or emails more.

Things began to change on a Friday afternoon. It was a snow day, so while my son was at a playdate, I was sitting home alone, preparing to finally unwind for the weekend, when, at 3:00 p.m., I received an email from Barry with the subject line: "Your Decisions." At the time, I was trying to get the green light for a show on the Sci-Fi Channel called *Crossing Over,* which featured a medium named John Edward. Barry's question seemed simple—but it was supremely frustrating: "If psychics are real, why are they on Sci-Fi? And if they are not, why are we working with this guy at all?"

The email didn't demand an urgent response, at least it didn't say so. But then again, it was Barry Diller, and he was my boss, so I responded. Almost immediately after pressing send, I regretted it. I had a feeling I'd just agreed to a weekend-long conversation—and in the days before email on phones, that meant I was now glued to my desk chair.

I was right. Like clockwork every few hours for the next two days,

I'd get a new email from Barry, written in colorful, capitalized, size-16 font, with another counterpoint. To each, I'd respond not just to the question he asked or point he made but with everything that went *into* my decisions: my thinking, my facts, my counterfactuals, my logic and rationale, my doubts, my backup options and plans B, C, and D.

After one too many back-and-forths on the semantics of the spirit world and the business we were in, I was ready to raise a white flag. But before I did, I made one more point: "Barry, whether you or I believe this guy is the real deal is irrelevant. It's all in the eye of the beholder," I wrote. "Mediums and psychics are neither fact nor fiction but something in the middle. So they belong on a channel that's already home to ghost hunters, extraterrestrial encounters, and paranormal activities—anything outside of what we know to be true."

At 11:00 p.m. on Sunday night, he wrote back and ended the inquisition with four words: "Your argument wins. Go."

Before that grueling weekend, I thought Barry hated me or, at the very least, that he was out to get me. (I've observed this tendency in so many other women; when someone isn't "nice" to us the way we're used to, we assume they don't like us.) But I also realized that what Barry expected of me wasn't unreasonable—even if it often felt that way to me. All he wanted was for me to come armed with clear arguments and fight for my opinions as tenaciously, intelligently, and passionately as he fought for his. When he asked me questions, he wasn't telling me I was wrong—he was hoping to be convinced that *he* might be.

Eventually, I even learned how to spar with Barry. I needed a thick skin, a funny bone, and smarts—which meant doing my homework so I knew what I was talking about, so I was able to push back, so I wouldn't cave under pressure . . . a lot like him.

After working for Barry, I was fearless. No matter what came my way, I was always able to repeat this mantra to myself: "If I survived Barry Diller, there's no one I can't survive and nothing I can't do." Today, I consider Barry not just a former boss and an eternal mentor but also a dear friend.

From both Harris and Barry, I learned something that has stuck with me ever since: Good mentors are like cheerleaders. Great mentors are like coaches. But the best mentors, the ones who change our lives (or at least our career trajectories), are like drill sergeants. The first two can help us win a game. But it's the challenging mentors—the drill sergeants we encounter—who prepare us for battle and help us win a war.

And it's often the mentors we don't account for who end up counting the most.

## NAIL IT

At work, where I've mentored hundreds and helped develop mentorship programs for many more, I frequently hear: Life would be a lot easier if it came with a list of dos and don'ts. Unfortunately, most advice worth following isn't that simple. It has to be occasion-, profession-, and personality-specific. The best mentors know that. But how to find that mentor in the first place—and how to use that mentor once you do—well, those are questions and answers I can tackle a bit more easily, with a list of dos and don'ts you can follow.

So . . .

### Do: Find the Truth-Tellers

While it's great to have friends in high places, it's more effective to have challengers. The former can make us feel good, but it's the latter that will *make us better.* Unfortunately, challengers are hard to spot in the wild. People don't exactly wear badges across their chests identifying themselves as "sadist who is actually acting selflessly" or "bully on the outside, cheerleader on the inside." Fortunately, there's a trick I use to find them: I actively seek out the truth-tellers.

In college, that's what led me to Harris. He had a reputation for brutal honesty, especially when his sky-high standards weren't met. He was known for treating the students in his photojournalism class less like students and more like photojournalists; by the time they walked out of his class, that's exactly what they were. I could have chosen an "easy A" professor, someone with lower (and less militaris-

## Take It Like a Champ

Being able to hear feedback, recognize where it's coming from, and eventually seek it out proactively is the mark of a good mentee—and the sign of a maturing leader. Hoda Kotb checks both boxes. Hoda, now one of the most popular anchors on morning television for the *Today* show, comes from a serious journalistic background. She's a multi-award winner who worked her way up and is as warm and authentic in person as she is on the air. Over the decades that we've both been part of the NBCUniversal universe, she's reached out plenty of times to catch up and pick my brain. She's my favorite kind of person: always looking to grow. I still remember her response to some tough love I once delivered: "Thank you for the wake-up call."

While I don't know every mentor she's had throughout her career, I know one thing for certain: Hoda Kotb made it to the top of morning talk because she doesn't shy away from truth-tellers—she looks to them and learns.

tic) standards who simply wanted to nurture and support my passion for photography. But had I done that, I wouldn't have learned half as much, because they would not have tested my limits and pushed my potential in the same way.

That's what sets challenging mentors apart. They won't lie to protect us from whatever reality we have to face. They tell us the truth—even if it hurts—because they know that hearing it will help us down the line. They make us so uncomfortable because, more often than not, we know they're right.

## Don't: Ask Permission

In corporate America, it's not uncommon to hear the question "Will you mentor me?" But when done right, mentorship is a commitment on both ends; for the mentor, before we know a person and their work, it's hard to want to commit. So don't ask permission to be mentored. Don't propose a relationship that implies an obligation of effort, time, and talent that might scare someone away. Instead, ask to grab coffee and come armed with thoughtful questions.

That's what Meghan Markle did after we hired her for *Suits*. At various points throughout her seven seasons on the show, she would reach out to me with positive, well-thought-out questions about how she could make the most of her time on set, how to become more than a secondary player on the show, how to build the depth of her character and its role, how to more fully engage with the director, recommendations for who could coach her to become a more distinguished actor, and even how to navigate security concerns once they arose during filming for her final season (without inconveniencing everyone else). She had the humility to seek out my opinion—rather than to demand advice or favors—and she was smart enough to never overstep. So, make like Meghan.

## Do: Think Outside the Box

Formalized mentorship programs can be great ways to meet senior people at your workplace and in your field. (If you have the chance to be part of one, take it!) They can also be limiting. After all, when people are told that the conference room on the eleventh floor at 2:00 p.m. on a Wednesday is where they'll find a mentor, some won't bother looking anywhere else.

In my experience though, the best mentor-mentee relationships are made in happenstance and only maintained through hard work. If you're looking for a mentor, think outside the box of your workplace's official mentorship program. Instead, ask yourself who in your life—at your organization, in your industry, or completely outside of both—impresses you, challenges you, makes you think differently, tells you the truth, and, most importantly, seems to be taking an interest in teaching you. Whether it's the hard or soft skills, ask yourself who you can continue to learn from. Then look to them as mentors. Sometimes, they are even right in front of you.

Deenise impressed me with her work ethic when I hired her as my assistant in 2005. But as we worked together, Deenise quietly began looking to me as a mentor. It was so natural and organic that neither of us ever had to talk about it. A single mother from Guiana, Deenise was incredibly organized and thorough. She quickly learned that a key component of my job was attention to detail—whether it be for the brands I oversaw, a gift that needed to be sent, or writing a personalized thank-you note. Deenise didn't just master the role; she shone at every aspect and eventually started organizing events for the entire team. She found the best venues, selected the perfect menus, and even found the ideal color for the flowers. We were two detail-oriented peas in a pod, and I was always relieved to be able to leave the planning in Deenise's hands. When she came to me with questions, they were focused on ways to grow in and eventually beyond her role. She was so good that Amazon noticed her, too, and now she runs the streaming division's event promotions. Her title captures how wide-ranging her talent is: project manager of communications for global media and entertainment. You can bet that I've celebrated her success.

Remember: Mentorship existed long before organized mentorship programs (or office buildings) ever did. There are lots of other ways to find people who will challenge, encourage, and inspire you to succeed.

### Don't: Focus on the Label

While I loudly and proudly attribute my success to the many mentors I've had, according to some standard definitions, I've never actually had one. Neither Harris nor Barry ever identified as a mentor of mine—and I never identified them as such, either—until long after. The same is true for Henry Becton, my boss at WGBH who had an outsized tolerance for my twenty-something self popping into his office and using him as a personal advisor and sounding board. The mentorship I've experienced and benefitted from was never named, has never been formalized, and only ever became apparent in hindsight.

In short: I had mentorship without the label. Today, I'm noticing the opposite phenomenon. In pursuit of a capital M mentor— someone who will figuratively affix the label to their lapel—people are missing out on informal opportunities to learn from, grow under, and work alongside people who have so much to teach. The benefits of mentorship come from what we do, not how we describe the person we're doing it with. Focus on learning from as many people as you can. Once it walks like a mentor and talks like a mentor, you can call it whatever the hell you want.

## Do: Give and Take

Mentorships shouldn't be transactional, but *you* should be practical. And practically speaking, someone is more likely to invest in a relationship with you if you can make that relationship a win-win that's worthwhile for them, too.

When an editor I know was still in college, she turned one coffee with an established reporter for a national newspaper—already the jackpot for an aspiring journalist like her—into a years-long mentorship. How? She connected the mentor to younger sources when they were needed for quotes in articles (and even went on the record herself a few times). She'd update the mentor on interesting trends or the latest stories impacting young women before they became national news. And when the mentor ended up writing a book, she helped with the research.

While it's nice to think of mentors as selfless souls who are solely interested in developing the next generation of talent, the reality is that all of us are human—and all humans are, to some degree, self-interested. So look at mentorship as a two-way street. Take the time to develop genuine connections with the people you admire, figure out what they need, and then offer to assist whenever, wherever, and however you can. Maybe that means taking notes for them during meetings. Maybe it means introducing them to someone you happen to be better acquainted with. Whatever it is, find a way to give and not just take.

## Don't: Take It Personally

The best mentors are challengers. They can occasionally seem almost cruel. I've wanted to strangle a few of mine. But too many women tend to take "tough" and "blunt" personally. We assume that when

## Track the Traits

It's always a *little* subjective. But if you're unsure whether someone difficult will end up teaching you, track the traits (Toxic versus Tough Love) and see which boxes they check:

**Toxic**

- ☐ They actually scare you.
- ☐ They curse you out.
- ☐ They sexualize comments.
- ☐ They blame you for things outside of your control.
- ☐ They take credit for your work.
- ☐ They raise their voice too often.
- ☐ They fire people too frequently or people quit prematurely.
- ☐ They have no respect for your time when you're off the clock.
- ☐ They often pit employees against each other.
- ☐ They make disparaging comments or criticize coworkers behind their backs.

**Tough Love**

- ☐ The people who work for them go on to great things.
- ☐ They expect you to perform when you're on the clock, but respect when you're not.
- ☐ They hold you to high standards, but not higher than the standards they hold themselves to.
- ☐ They make you work hard, but they work just as hard.
- ☐ You're proud to say you work for them.
- ☐ Their tough, even harsh, feedback has been proven correct.
- ☐ They own their decisions, good and bad.

someone is hard on us, it's because they want us to fail—and not because they know we can do better and want us to succeed. We forget that we don't need to like someone to learn from them. In fact, we might learn more if we don't.

If you think a boss is too unfair, challenging, or demanding, or that a supervisor is out to get you—stop thinking about it so much. When appropriate, shift your mindset from "I'm being mistreated" to "I'm being mentored." Yes, shitty people abound in every industry. But if you work for someone, chances are they're on your side—it's their side, too, after all. If they're being difficult, it's probably because success rarely comes easily.

An important additional point: While challenging mentors are often our bosses, not all challenging bosses are mentors. There's a difference between someone who is so demanding they seem insufferable and someone who seems to demand (and even enjoy) your suffering. There's a difference between someone who is trying to grow and stretch you and someone who is trying to break you.

I do believe Jane Fonda was right in her 1980s workout videos, where her catchphrase was "no pain, no gain." But if a job is all pain with none of the gain—if you're constantly being put down without ever being taught how to pull yourself back up—then forget about maintaining a mentorship, feel free to cut the cord, and maybe even quit. You don't have to put up with a toxic workplace, however you define it.

## Do: Look Around You

We tend to view mentorships as relationships with an inherent power imbalance. There's a mentor and there's a mentee, right? Not necessarily. One of the most formative (and enjoyable) mentorships in my career was with someone around the same level as I was: Carole

Black, who had a reputation in the media industry for being exceedingly optimistic, savvy, sincere, and personable. Some might call her my peer mentor. I also call her a mensch.

When USA Network was going through one of its many changes in ownership, I called Carole up out of the blue to ask for some advice. She was the chairman and president at the rival Lifetime Entertainment and a glass-ceiling-smasher as the network's first female president. Back then, I doubt she knew who I was. But she took my call and was gracious, forthcoming, and unbelievably insightful.

Since then, she's been one of my biggest cheerleaders. As two strong women in a male-dominated industry, we've chosen to view each other as compatriots, not competitors. When *Taken*, a Sci-Fi Channel miniseries by Steven Spielberg that I'd championed in the face of long odds, won an Emmy, she stood up in the audience and applauded as loudly as my own team. When I'd give a presentation at some industry event, I knew I could rely on an email from her afterward that said something like: "*CIAO BELLA*, YOU JUST KILLED IT."

Look around for a peer mentor—someone to celebrate victories, commiserate losses, and strategize with as you both make your way in the working world. In short, find yourself a Carole Black.

## Don't: Mistake Mentoring for Networking

As a mentor, my goal is to help people navigate complex situations. But that means I'm here to teach them how to read a map, not to be their chauffeur to a second destination. Many people seem to think that mentorship and networking are the same. They think the purpose of this one relationship is simply to beget other connections. As a result, they take advantage of the barest minimum their mentor has to offer while making their mentor feel taken advantage of. It's a lose-lose situation. If you want to expand your professional network,

## My Accidental Successful Mentorship: Priya and Padma

Sometimes the best mentorships come from introducing two people and then getting out of the way. I met Priya Krishna when she and my son, Jesse, and his now wife, Elizabeth, became friends in college. I quickly learned that Priya had a deep interest in food and cooking; she started writing about food while still an undergraduate. I was able to introduce her to Padma Lakshmi, who among her illustrious career highlights was a host of *Top Chef* on Bravo. I knew Padma from how immensely helpful she had been on our TV campaign "Erase the Hate." Priya started by helping out as Padma's babysitter. But immediately Padma took Priya under her wing and guided Priya toward her dream of releasing a cookbook (*Indian-ish* was a bestseller in 2019) and achieving the coveted position as a food writer for the *New York Times*. Padma and Priya are a wonderful example of generous mentorship—and an accidental perfect mentorship match.

go to a networking event. (Go anywhere, actually. Networking happens organically if you put yourself out there and say yes enough.) But if you want to expand your abilities, responsibilities, and horizons, find a mentor.

## Do: Keep in Touch

While some great mentorships start out at work—including most of mine—the best ones don't end there. I stayed connected to Barry long after we stopped working together, and now I'm on the board of one of his companies, IAC. I'm still learning from him. Every once in a while, I even get to teach him a thing or two.

Keep in touch with everyone who mentors you and anyone you

go on to mentor. When you hit a career milestone—a new job or a promotion—send your mentors and mentees an update. After all, they helped you get there in some way or another; acknowledging that is an easy way to let them share in the moment. Similarly, when you learn of their news—the good, the bad, the ugly—reach out to say how happy, heartbroken, or humored you were to hear about whatever happened. When you see something that makes you think of them—a magazine article, a historical factoid you know they'd appreciate, a celebrity look-alike, an old photograph of the two of you—say something. Take it from someone who's maintained relationships with nearly every mentor and mentee I've ever had: It's a good idea and a great use of time.

## THE FINAL WORD

It's great to have supportive mentors—the "friends in high places" who serve as our advisors, sounding boards, teachers, therapists, cheerleaders, and confidants. But we also need the other kind of mentors. We need challengers, critics, and opponents. If my five decades in corporate America have taught me anything, it's that women don't have enough of the *second* kind of mentorship—even and especially today, as formalized mentorship programs abound but niceness is the name of the game. To succeed when the world feels stacked against us, we need mentors who will tell us when we're wrong and push us to get it right. We need challenging mentors.

# 4. It's What's On The Inside That Counts / What's On Our Outsides Matters, Too

**What We're Told:** *"It's what's on the inside that counts."*

Most of us have heard the adage: It's our insides that matter most. As adults, it's something we often tell ourselves, a comforting rejoinder to insecurities about our wrinkles, our frizzy hair, our blemishes, or our out-of-style and out-of-shape clothes. Our true value is found in our brains and hearts, our personalities and priorities, our skills and stories, our interests and intentions—in the things our eyes can't see. In the end, isn't that what determines our lot in life?

**The Truth:** *"What's on our outsides matters, too."*

Unless you're a radiologist or the operator of a TSA airport body scan machine, you're judging people by what's on their outside. Just like they're judging you by what's on yours.

Everyone does it. We've all heard the saying "You never get a second chance to make a first impression." The data says the same. While the exact amount of time is a matter of debate, experts believe it takes somewhere between seven and twenty-seven seconds to form a solid impression of a person—with a landmark study from two Princeton psychologists suggesting it takes even less time, just a tenth of a second, to start developing opinions about traits like trustworthiness and likability.[1]

Forget about having a conversation to get to know someone, understand their background, or bond over shared interests and hobbies—that crucial tenth of a second is barely enough time to blink. But once these impressions form, they endure, and they can have outsized influence over everything from our romantic prospects to the jobs we're hired (or passed over) for. While it might be nice to think our work speaks for itself, it isn't true. We speak for our work—and we often do so before we even get the chance to open our mouths.

I mean that literally. Dr. Albert Mehrabian, a former professor at UCLA and an expert in communication, has found that *what* we say makes up only 7 percent of people's first impression of us. By contrast, *how* we say it makes up 38 percent. And another 55 percent, the majority, is determined by what people see when they look at us.[2]

Clearly, a lot more than what's on the inside counts, and it counts for a lot more than most people acknowledge or even understand. Disregarding that reality, especially at work, is an exercise in self-sabotage. But I want to be clear: Our "outside" does not mean beauty, athleticism, or even physical attractiveness. Instead, it's everything we present to the outside world—in other words, our presence. Caring about that isn't superficial; it's fundamental.

Our outside is our body language and facial expressions. It's our eye contact, smile, posture, and even our handshake and grip. It's the way we dress, style, and groom ourselves. It's the tone, pitch, and volume of our voice when talking, and the interest (again, eye contact) we express when listening. It's the mood we're in, the emotional state we project, and the confidence we exude. The minute we walk into a room, these external attributes can influence how trustworthy, competent, powerful, credible, personable, energetic, interesting, professional, detail-oriented, and creative we seem. They don't just speak volumes about us. They scream. And when harnessed effectively, they don't just help us stand out in a room. They ensure we resonate in a space long after we leave.

Our external attributes give us the opportunity to shine, but they can also end the race just as we're approaching the starting line. While we can't control whether someone underestimates us because of our gender (or projects other conscious and unconscious biases onto us), we can at the very least try to manage their hasty judgments—for instance, whether someone sees a slob when they look at us and concludes our entire life is a mess. Let's be honest: Sometimes that conclusion is right.

Is it *fair* that people who don't pay attention to how they dress come across as less competent and credible on the job, even in industries and fields that have nothing to do with style or aesthetics? Some say yes, because a person who neglects one aspect of their life might be more inclined to neglect another. But even if it isn't fair, that's the way it is. People want to understand the other people around them and will search for clues in everything. Either we can sit around whining about it, or we can make it work for us and empower us.

Decades of working in television have taught me that what we see isn't always what we get. Of course, the visual and visible parts of ourselves don't tell our whole stories. But how we look and carry ourselves—our vibe, really—is a way of saying what's on our minds before we open our mouths. It's a shortcut to fitting into a role before someone even offers it to us; why do you think so many actors and actresses dress in character when going out for an audition? And it's *not* exclusive to Hollywood or the TV industry. More female politicians than you'd expect have hired image consultants for these exact reasons. Then there's the booming personal coach industry that exists to help women at every level of their careers . . . and men, too. To convince someone we can do a job, we have to put in the work and appear convincing.

But despite how important our external presence is, alone it's not enough. Someone may judge us as powerful or influential based on our perfect posture or our perfectly timed hand gestures. (It's true—these traits can make us seem in charge and in control!) Yet if that impression doesn't resonate beyond the surface, it will dissipate immediately, and we're not going to remain powerful and influential for long.

It's not about the outside counting more than the inside, or the inside counting more than the outside. The better way to look at it is this: Our outer self is a *proxy* for our inner self.

But if who we present to the world isn't consistent with our values, deeds, abilities, instincts, and words, the whole house of cards will eventually crumble. Our outside has to align with who we are on the inside. It absolutely, positively has to be authentic to who we *actually* are.

Does that mean we should all just be ourselves then? Not quite.

Lately, I've watched "be yourself" fall into the trap of too many other feel-good mantras. It's been taken at *total* face value, almost too literally, and seen as an allowance to do the bare minimum so long as it feels "authentic." But if what we're aiming for is greatness—in our lives, in our careers, in our relationships—then greatness is what we have to embody to get there.

So, consider this: Don't just be yourself. Be your *best* self instead.

## MY TAKE

A few years ago, a woman from the TV industry moved into the same coastal Connecticut town where I live.

I'd only met her once in passing at a large corporate gathering. We worked for different divisions of different companies and had different roles and responsibilities. But now that she was essentially my neighbor, I made it a point to welcome her by walking over to her house with my husband and a bottle of champagne. We exchanged pleasantries and played the "Who do we know in common?" game, though I'd be lying if I claimed to remember much else from our first conversation. What I do remember is our *second* conversation, in which this fellow industry insider turned to her husband and said, "Even before we met, I felt like I knew Bonnie. Because I knew the 'Bonnie brand.'"

Initially, I was a little confused. "*I* have a brand?" I was more than familiar with the concept generally, having rebranded multiple cable channels during my tenure leading each network. But I had never thought about having one, or being one, myself. The more I did, though, the more it made sense. Although what my new neighbor didn't know was that my "brand" had also involved some trial and error—it didn't simply appear overnight.

I've never taken the generic route in my life—not in how I dress, talk, behave, think, or carry myself. I've never copied anyone. And given that the opposite of generic is a brand, then in the process, that's exactly what I've cultivated.

Think of it this way: Yes, a great presence requires a memorable exterior, but as with any product, the packaging is only part of the experience. The most successful brands have great slogans, ads, spokespeople, *and* incredible products that tie it all together. Apple, considered the number one brand in the world, is a perfect example. You say the word and a clear image emerges in people's heads: They clearly see the billboards and commercials, they can picture the exteriors and interiors of the stores, and they can even try predicting the design and user interface of future products. Apple's dedicated fans span the globe, and they will buy or download anything Apple, even before knowing what it is, because they trust the brand and know what to expect and what they're going to get in terms of quality, creativity, and utility.

In the same way, an authentic personal brand is what you get when your presence is consistent with and authentic to who you really are—when your inside and outside match. It's what people are referring to when they say your reputation precedes you.

Think of Anna Wintour, *Vogue*'s longtime editor in chief. Over decades in fashion and editorial, her iconic bob haircut (which she started sporting when she was fourteen) and oversized black sunglasses (which are actually corrective lenses) have become her trademark. Her brand, which doesn't bend to fads and trends, works because it's more than skin-deep—and instead is perfectly aligned with what we'd expect from one of the most influential voices in fashion, and the leader of one of the globe's most influential magazines: a bit aloof and almost otherworldly, utterly timeless, and necessarily discerning.

Another great personal brand? MSNBC star Rachel Maddow. Like Wintour, she has a trademark haircut (short) and signature glasses (thick-rimmed). Her visual signature—which also includes a blazer over a T-shirt and jeans—works because of what it hints at deeper down: someone hard at work (and deep in thought) who's too busy to spend time fussing over outfits. As a highly rated presence on cable news, Maddow assumed the role of incredibly approachable wonk.

Politics aside, the stories she'd report on were always thoroughly investigated, often unexpected, and delivered with the zeal of your smartest friend letting you in on something she just learned. There's a reason Maddow has dominated cable news and was, at many points, one of its most-watched hosts: Viewers felt like they knew her, which made them trust her because they knew and trusted her brand.

And occasionally, sometimes, a personal brand actively dismantles existing stereotypes, as well as conveys who you are. Poet Amanda Gorman's exceptionally polished image—impeccable tailoring, classic lines, bright colors, and an elegant presentation—stand in stark contrast to the far more bohemian and even hippie-ish image many of us have of poets. Amanda's commanding style conveys to us that we should take both her and her words seriously. She is telegraphing from the moment she enters a room or steps to a podium that she is a woman of substance, while the colors and occasionally the patterns that she chooses also clearly signal that she is bright and optimistic. She's commanding both our eyes and our ears.

Within my world, I guess I have a visual brand, too. I'll admit that I've always been a bit of a fashionista. I love clothes, shoes, and jewelry, and I'll never be ashamed of my leather pants or the time I spend trying to find the right pair. What I wear is part of who I am, and the trademarks of my personal style are also key tenets of my persona.

For starters, I'm incredibly detail-oriented and even obsessive about every part of my image. My clothes have to be tailored to fit, my nails have to be perfectly filed and clean (yes, I keep an emery board with me at all times and a nail brush in my desk drawer—I have two dogs, and all their dirt and dander ends up under my nails), my hemlines have to be immaculate, even my socks have to fit just right and match the rest of my outfit. I'm the same way with my work. Even relatively inconspicuous inconsistencies and imperfections—on set, in a line of dialogue, the wrong color outfit on a character—can throw off an entire show for me. Everyone who knows me, or knows of me, knows this.

In terms of what I wear—my approach has always been to go a little left or right of whatever was center. When women began dressing for the corporate world in pantsuits and pumps, I went with midi skirts and boots. Now that midi skirts are in vogue, I've switched to pants—leather, patterned, coated. I'm not looking to stand out; in fact, I tend to dress monochromatically, with no loud colors or distracting patterns. But I'm also not trying to blend in. My approach to professional life is the same: Without making too much noise, I've always found a way to be heard.

My style ethos could probably be summed up as "mostly practical with a necessary dollop of play." When I dress, I quite literally mean business. On all the red carpets I've ever walked, I've never worn a floor-length gown; after all, I'm there as an executive and have no interest in being mistaken for something else—and even less interest in tripping over myself. My goal is to be told, "You look great," not "I love your dress." I use clothes to elevate and complement who I am, not to overwhelm or distract. In every outfit I don, I'm never too formal and am always sure to incorporate something fun—a statement necklace, a cool belt, an interesting jacket, a pop of color. The same is true for every team I've ever led: Formal and conventional are overrated; fun and comfort (while still coordinated and put together) are critical.

My shoes follow the same ethos, stylish but always practical, which means no impossibly sky-high heels, even if my five-foot-four frame could use the extra few inches (I only break this rule for black-tie events, which I also pregame with two Advil). I've never been the kind of executive to sit behind a desk all day—I'm always on the move, bopping around from floor to floor, studio to set, restaurant lunch with an agent to meetings with cast and crew—so I can't be slowed down by blisters or swollen toes.

Like Anna Wintour and Rachel Maddow, my "do" is also part of my brand. My hair-story has a history. For the first half of my career, I went to painstaking lengths to maintain my natural, wild curls—until a (male) boss, during the earliest days of video calling, screamed, "Hammer, get your damn hair out of the f*cking camera!" Admittedly, it was a bit out of control.

These days, it's basically verboten to comment on someone's looks, especially something negative, especially at work. Trust me: I wasn't thrilled about the comment back then either. Years later, I'm grateful for it. I wore my hair curly only because I'd always had curls. But the upkeep—the gels, the heat lamps, the styling tools—was tedious and time-consuming. So I made a change. Even though a brand should stay consistent, it also must be receptive to feedback and evolve when necessary. That goes for personal brands, too.

It took a few tries, but eventually, I found a hairstyle that was "less distracting" and ended up suiting me even better. The face-framing layers and eyebrow-skimming bangs I've sported ever since are much easier for me to maintain—requiring fewer products and less time to style. Like a great purse, my hair can easily be dressed up or down, which was perfect for the long days I'd spend on set before rushing off to some fancy industry dinner with no time to shower, change, or even brush my hair in between.

The unexpected cherry on top? The new do has even helped me age gracefully without compromising on my personal decision to thus far avoid having any sort of cosmetic work done. My motto? Bangs, not Botox. (In an over-tweaked industry, my broken-and-never-fixed nose probably sets me apart as well.)

With curly hair, I was just "being myself." With my current hair, I'm able to be my *best* self—which isn't always found in the first hairstyle or wardrobe we try.

Even my drink of choice is part of my brand. I'll almost always order a tequila on the rocks because I believe—as a matter of principle *and* taste—in never diluting something good. That goes for everything from what I drink to a network slogan to a good idea buried in convoluted word salad. If I like it, I want it in its purest form. (I'm also a bit of a control freak and like to know what I'm getting: at the bar, at work.) One establishment's espresso martini might taste radically different from another's. But a bottle of Clase Azul is the same around the block and around the world.

That's my brand. It's not just what set me apart in a tough-as-nails industry. It's what made the people hiring me always feel like they knew what they were getting. It was never a gamble because my reputation and track record preceded me.

It's also what made the people who were working *for* me know what they were getting, along with what was expected of them. They knew the incredibly high standards I held for myself. That set the bar, and perhaps raised it, for the standards my team had to at least strive to meet when they delivered something to me.

Before any big meeting or presentation at USA, the final question was always "Is it Bonnie-ready?" That meant something concrete: Were there typos? Was the formatting correct? Was there a one-sentence distillation of the idea or argument included? Would it bore someone to sleep? Was there a fun element—a cartoon, an anagram, a joke—to mix things up? Had the whole team been consulted and considered?

But it also meant something less tangible: Had every option been thought through and exhausted? Did it look as polished and professional as possible? Did it smartly make its point, or did it feel forced? Would it fit into its intended context, or would it feel distracting and out of place? From the very first page, was it packaged like a project we would greenlight? Would it match our network's brand?

One of the first things I did when I took control of USA was establish a brand filter: Every series we greenlit needed to be character-centric, with lovable but flawed characters; it needed to be a drama with a dollop of humor; and it needed to be shot under literal and metaphorical blue skies. That was the USA brand; it transcended any single show and provided a road map of sorts for our decision-making. It didn't guarantee success, but *did* make it more likely.

In the same way, my team was able to funnel their work and ideas through a "Bonnie Filter." They knew what I looked for, what was important to me, and what I couldn't stand and wouldn't stand for.

When my new neighbor in Connecticut talked about my "brand," I think this is what she meant. But the "Bonnie brand," while authentic, didn't come naturally or effortlessly or even immediately to me. Our best selves take work.

In my early thirties, when I was working at Lifetime as a young director of original programming, I had what's called a "360" performance review—in which I was evaluated anonymously by people I reported to, people I worked alongside, and people who reported to me. Unbeknownst to me, these types of reviews were common in corporate America, and long story short, my results were startling. According to the review, some people thought I was unapproachable and off-putting. They considered me an overconfident know-it-all. I remember feeling shocked, largely because I was actually quite insecure: I had no idea what I was even doing at Lifetime. It was my first position overseeing development as opposed to hands-on producing—and I definitely knew how little I knew.

The bottom line: I was completely lacking in self-awareness.

The review prompted a lot of self-reflection until I realized the issues: Afraid to ask questions about what confused me, I strove to figure things out by myself, which signaled that I believed I knew everything offhand. Afraid of appearing insecure, I projected a false sense of confidence, which came across as haughty. Afraid to appear unprofessional in my first corporate TV job in New York, I was cordial and kept my distance, which others read as unfriendly and unapproachable. My demeanor was the exact opposite of how I felt inside—there was no alignment—and it was getting me into trouble.

The 360 was a wake-up call for me and came at a pivotal point in my career. When I crossed the street, literally, to begin my next job at USA—where I ended up working for over thirty years—I did things differently. Yes, I focused on being friendly and collaborative, which is my nature and how I'd always been before Lifetime. (I never wanted to come across like a know-it-all again.) But more than altering any one thing, my general demeanor changed. From then on, there was never any daylight between how I felt internally and how I acted externally. Rather than try to cover up my insecurities and vulnerabilities, I shared them with others. Self-awareness became my prized possession.

I know firsthand that it's hard to see ourselves the way others do—and even harder to see the light if no one's willing to shine it on us. So now I make it a mission of sorts to give this authentic and generous (even if it doesn't feel like it) feedback, especially about traits that might elude a person and even obscure their underlying talents.

My former head of research had a steely demeanor. In meetings, her refusal to crack even the slightest smile was giving people the wrong—and rude—impression. For the record, she's one of the warmest and most accessible people I know. But as a woman working in numbers and data, she understandably wanted to be taken seriously—at least as seriously as her male counterparts, considering she was better than most if not all of them. She believed she could only do that by delivering the definitive facts she'd gathered with a humorless, unflappable affect. She was aiming for neutral and honest, but instead, she came off as judgmental and intimidating about the projects and programs she was assessing.

When I told her that her delivery and demeanor were interfering with her stated priority—to engage with people and teams and help them frame whatever they were working on—she was incredibly receptive. Like me, she simply needed a wake-up call; the second I gave her one, she started loosening up, smiling more, and even making jokes at her own expense (or the data's). That adjustment to her approach, which had nothing to do with her actual work and everything to do with the perception of it, paid off. As more and more people warmed up to her, she became "the Queen of Research" and everyone's favorite to work with. Eventually, she was promoted from the head of research for USA and SYFY to the head of research for all of cable to the head of research for all NBCUniversal TV platforms.

For the marketing lead of the rebranded SYFY Channel, the issue was how his gelled-back hair and pocket squares helped cultivate a personal brand that worked against him. He was astoundingly good at his job, which I knew firsthand as his boss. He was smart, funny, and an all-around class act. But his perfectly coiffed locks and his overly immaculate (and visibly expensive) suits made him seem almost plastic. The character he approximated most was a collector's edition Ken doll—nice to look at but meant to be displayed on a shelf in his original box. At least that was the perception of the people I reported to, the powers that be who could have promoted him but held off.

He knew other brands like the back of his hand, but he didn't seem to understand his own. He was a marketing whiz, but he seemed to forget he was marketing himself, too. His personal style was completely misaligned with the more casual audience he was meant to win over—both externally with SYFY viewers, and internally at a time when NBCUniversal's CEO was someone whose ideal day would be spent in blue jeans on a Montana ranch.

So, while I advocated for him with leadership, I also advocated for him *to him* by being honest: "People need to believe you're real and relatable," I said. "Instead, you're coming across as overly produced." Fortunately, like my research head, he was receptive to feedback—my intervention, if you can call it that, worked. As soon as he cooled it with the pocket squares and hair gel and started dressing more understatedly, his personality, work, and work ethic shone through. He got the promotion he'd long deserved—and went from marketing at one network to running another . . . where his pocket squares would have found their place and fit in with the audience if he wanted them to.

Change isn't easy. I get it. It's particularly hard when we're told to change our external appearance after a lifetime of being told that what's inside us is all that matters. But after decades of carefully developing my own brand and seeing what has worked—and hasn't— with others, I know that the outside and inside are deeply connected.

If we want to develop a brand that's remembered, respected, and held in high repute, then everything matters. What people see from us *must* be what they get from us.

## NAIL IT

Of course, what's on the inside counts. *Of course it does.* But our outsides count, too, and choosing to ignore that reality isn't a neutral act. When we disregard our image and appearance, we aren't inviting the world to take a closer look at our truest selves. Instead, we're erecting obstacles that obscure who we are and prevent others from seeing it. We're putting ourselves at a disadvantage and setting ourselves up for disappointment. There's so much we can't control in life; why not control what we can? From head to toe, there are simple things we can do to set ourselves up for success; then and only then can we let our insides take care of the rest.

So . . .

### Maintain Your Posture

You may never watch your back—at least not without a mirror—but what you do with it can totally change how someone sees you. Good posture can make you appear not just taller but also more confident, self-assured, poised, attentive, and attractive. Bad posture often communicates boredom and a lack of interest—even if you're deeply engaged. Unless you're trying to send someone a hint that your mind is elsewhere, remember that how you carry yourself sets the tone for how others perceive you.

Save the slouch for the late-night couch. Keeping your spine straight both looks better and improves your presence, while also making you feel more centered and confident. Poor posture interferes with breathing deeply, whereas proper posture—when sitting *and* standing—helps your body maintain and regulate its energy levels better throughout the day and even increases your stamina and focus.

## Make Eye Contact

Looking into another person's eyes is a great way to show interest in getting to know them—and is an equally great way to invite them to get to know you. During a conversation, eye contact is an unparalleled way to demonstrate respect, interest, and understanding, whether you're the one talking or not. It can even foster intimacy and connection between people, as neurons in the brain are activated with eye contact and help us understand another person's emotional state. What's more, our eyes are a tell. Easy eye contact makes us appear honest and confident. Averting our gaze, on the other hand, makes us appear anxious, dishonest, or a little bit of both. And a spaced-out, glazed-over look—or staring deeply into our iPhone screens—sends the impression that we are disinterested, disrespectful, and even confused.

But while you are looking someone in the eye, don't forget to respect the other person's personal space.

## Listen Up

If you want to be seen and appreciated wherever you go, then make sure that everyone in your presence feels acknowledged and appreciated, too. Actively listen to them; this builds rapport, reduces misunderstandings, encourages collaboration, and increases empathy. When someone else is talking, fight the urge to start planning what you're going to say next. Instead, engage your ears. (Then nod along and ask questions to show just how engaged you are.) If you really want to make an impression, perk up whenever you're around people—even when no one is talking yet. In the elevator with coworkers? Take out your AirPods. You'll be surprised by the information you pick up on just from listening in. Plus, the more you look open to conversation, the more likely someone else is to initiate it.

## Put a Smile On

There's no substitute for a smile. You can be as warm and friendly as possible on the inside—but if your outside expression doesn't reflect that, no one knows, and no one cares. A smile, on the other hand, is an active invitation for other people to engage. It makes you seem approachable and relatable, conveys confidence, and even helps you relax in stressful situations. So, say cheese.

## Practice Good Hygiene

I know this sounds ridiculous and shouldn't have to be said, but— especially after years of many of us working from home or doing hybrid work—you probably recognize that some of your colleagues seem to have forgotten that Zoom filters don't extend into real life. If you look like you can't be bothered to give yourself a second thought, people will wonder how much thought you're going to put into your job. So, check your teeth, your breath, your hair, and your outfit. Just say no to anything resembling bedhead or loungewear. Practice good hygiene and take care of yourself—a little extra care goes a long way.

## Watch Your Arms

When it comes to presence, our arms are a key piece of armor. Keeping them loose and relaxed by our sides exudes openness and approachability, while using them to gesticulate purposefully and enthusiastically conveys energy and passion—all of which help us launch a charm offensive on whomever we're engaging. Of course, those aren't the only two options. In the words of the great Kenny Rogers, which should be heeded by everyone who claims to care about body language, "You gotta know when to hold 'em, know when to fold 'em."

If we want to demonstrate warmth, we can use our arms to hug—or hold—someone when it's appropriate. When it isn't, or when in doubt, we should hold *ourselves* back. And unless we're hoping to communicate coldness and create distance from someone (or some situation), we should avoid folding our arms across our chests like an angsty teenager. Whether or not we mean to, we'll come across as defensive and discomfited—as closed off as our arms themselves.

And if you've got sharp elbows, sandpaper them down. In an effort to get ahead, people often—intentionally or not—push others out of the way (or simply away). They act either overly competitive, overly defensive, or uninterested in sharing or collaborating. Spoiler alert: Sharp elbows will only bruise *you* in the long run.

## Keep Your To-Gos Handy

In the case of natural disasters, it's recommended to keep a to-go bag packed and ready by the door. And given that work in the twenty-first century often requires a midday outfit change, save yourself the stress and pack an office to-go bag. I always keep on hand a blazer (in case I came in casual and have to dress up for an unexpected meeting), comfortable shoes I can walk in (in case I have to rush somewhere), a nicer pair of shoes (in case I have to go out somewhere), and a neutral pair of pantyhose and black tights (in case mine rip, which they often do). As your status increases, the to-gos you need probably will, too.

## Ask the Mirror

Appearance is a tricky topic. So often, hair or other personal features are used against women—and especially women of color—to deem us unprofessional. While changing my hairstyle was the right decision for me, it certainly isn't for everyone. But I do believe that many of us have a version of my story about a part of our appearance that may distract others from seeing our actual strengths and should be taken to heart. For one of my writers, it was her under-eye circles. She insists they're naturally dark purple and black, that they have been since childhood, and that sleep doesn't help. I wouldn't know, because apparently I've never seen her without concealer covering them up.

Her story? A toxic boss asked her if she was hungover when she showed up to work one time with no makeup under her eyes. She's never done that in a work setting since. Is it fair or necessary that she cover up what's natural to her? Of course not. But like me, she realized there was something about her that distracted others from seeing her true worth, and it was something she could easily adjust to make her presence stronger. She simply asked the mirror.

## Wear Clothing That Fits

While I don't believe that someone's whole presence is determined by their wardrobe, or that "the clothes make the (wo)man," I do believe they make an impact. But only if they fit. Ask yourself these questions when getting dressed:

1. *Does it fit me physically?* No matter how high-quality or expensive an article of clothing is, you'll never look like a million bucks in it if it doesn't sit properly on your frame. So get to know your

body type, figure out what flatters you, find your favorite fits from your favorite brands, and stick with them. Or find a really great tailor.

2. *Does it fit my personality?* You don't have to compromise your identity to dress the part. If you've always been casual and suddenly find yourself working in corporate America, figure out an appropriate compromise between stiff slacks and sweatpants. If you hate gowns (like I do), don't wear one. People look their best when they feel their best. And we feel our best when we feel like our best selves.

3. *Does it fit the context and occasion?* Be sure to read the room, or at least the dress code spelled out at the bottom of the invitation. If you're still confused, use Pinterest or Instagram for outfit inspiration to help you understand the context and occasion. Then dress accordingly. (And when in doubt, better to show up overdressed than under.)

## Cover Up

This one's easy. Be appropriate, be modest, and be smart. Your chest—whether it's hairy or cleaved—should never be exposed on the job. Your thighs? They probably shouldn't be either. And bra straps should stay invisible. Basic, but too often bungled.

## Don't Fidget, Twiddle, Pick, or Twirl

Nervous tics are totally normal and nothing to be ashamed of. But when we give in to them at the wrong time, like a meeting or luncheon, they can be overly distracting. Unfortunately, picking our nails or tapping our feet can make us seem less confident, competent, calm, and composed. What we do with our fingers while we're talking can, in fact, impact what someone hears. It can also impact how interested we seem in what someone else has to say.

So, learn your tics and take steps to cast them aside temporarily—if not conquer them entirely. If you're a hair twirler, pull your hair back so twirling it isn't an option. If you tend to fidget with your hands, use them to take notes, even if you don't have something urgent to write down. Whatever your nervous tic is, find a way to distance yourself from it before it distracts—and detracts—from you.

## THE FINAL WORD

It's hard work to develop a presence that's memorable long after we leave a room—and cultivate a brand that people associate with us, and with good things, before we enter it. But as long as our outside is aligned with what's on our inside, a little concern about our presence—from head to toe—doesn't just go a long way. It's how we put our best foot forward and become our best selves.

# 5. You Can Have It All /
# You Will Have Choices

**What We're Told: *"You can have it all."***

A fulfilling career? Check. A loving partner? Check. Kids who are smart, social, and thriving? Check. A white picket fence and help around the house? Check, check. A great salary, personal time for yoga, girl-time with friends, and family time in the evenings, on the weekends, and for vacations? Check, check, check, and check. It sounds too good to be true, but for so many years (and to so many women), "you can have it all" has been sold as a fairy tale *and* a promise. The story goes that our mothers and grandmothers had to sacrifice and compromise in their lives—if they even could make choices to begin with. But that's the past, right? Women today can do, be, and have everything we want . . . right?

**The Truth: *"You will have choices."***

You could fill a library—literally—with all the books, academic papers, news articles, and magazine think pieces (not to mention the entirety of the internet) that have been written on the question of whether women can have it all. But I'm more interested in asking another question: What the hell does "all" even mean?

Today, "all" is shorthand for successfully balancing the demands of career, motherhood, and partnership—for pursuing professional ambition, maternal instinct, *and* marital or romantic bliss, all while feeling fulfilled. But that's not what it always meant. Not remotely. Not even close.

Back in 1982, the legendary longtime editor of *Cosmopolitan* magazine, Helen Gurley Brown, sparked a cultural revolution. At the time, *Cosmopolitan* was *the* women's magazine—the one that dominated the market and pushed the envelope. And Helen Gurley Brown was the woman behind it all. When she published her book *Having It All: Love, Success, Sex, Money (Even If You're Starting with Nothing)*, she launched the term into the mainstream. To women today, though, *Having It All* might be even more shocking for what it omitted—both in its subtitle and in the book itself: almost *any* mention of a balanced personal life, including family and kids. (While we're at it, we should also define whom "having it all" was promised to—even falsely—in the first place: middle-class-and-above females. While the target demographic for this type of empowerment was select women in corporate America, it was decidedly *not* most of the women in this country.)

To the woman who quite literally wrote the book on the topic, having a nurturing homelife chafed against her vision of emboldened, empowered womanhood. About the prospect of having children, she wrote, "Isn't that a hard sell if you ever heard one?" But it wasn't just Helen Gurley Brown's message. After millennia during which women were bound to the home and defined by our caretaking, figures from Gloria Steinem to Carrie Bradshaw came along and encouraged us to get out of the house, get to work, and get into bed with whomever we wanted—without ever feeling obligated to settle down and create a family with our bedmate(s).

Today, "having it all"—originally meant as a rebellion against traditional societal expectations, in defiance of familial norms—has become a new set of heightened expectations and expanded norms. We shouldn't *just* be the perfect mother; we *also* have to be the consummate, ambitious working woman. Anyone who says that being both is too hard a balance to strike is considered retrograde, even if they're just being realistic.

I'll say it anyway. The truth is this: Being a doting mother, a devoted partner, and a dedicated career woman—and being our best and most present self as all three—is the very definition of being off balance. Factor in other realities, most of which haven't changed in decades, like our biological clocks, no federally mandated family or medical leave, maternity policies that are left to the whims of our employers, and the assumption of that "second shift" of PTA and school board meetings, household chores, doctor's and dentist appointments, and childcare as women's work—or at least our responsibility to figure out—and "having it all" isn't just a hard sell. It's nearly impossible.

The pressure alone is enough to leave women feeling stressed, dissatisfied, and burned out. Even if we manage to succeed on all these fronts, there's very little chance we have time left over for ourselves.

At the risk of sounding like a bad feminist, let me stake my claim firmly on the negative side of this debate: No, women *cannot* have it all—at least not as "all" is currently defined, so broad that it encapsulates everything and therefore means nothing. I'm not saying women should go back in time. I want us to live in the present and face reality. That requires opening our eyes and seeing the world as it is, not just as we wish it would be.

That doesn't mean nothing's changed for women since the Stone

Age, or even since the dawn of the feminist movement or the sexual revolution. It doesn't mean that the idea of having it all didn't capture a real shift in society. It did! But we've been using the wrong phrase to describe it. What makes us different from our mothers and grandmothers isn't that we can finally have it all. It's that, unlike most of them and almost all women throughout history, we finally have choices.

A hundred years ago, most women were relegated to the home. Fifty years ago, well over 50 percent of working-aged women didn't work.[1] Having a job was one thing—having a career was another thing entirely. Today, almost twice as many women attend college as men.[2] The careers we fantasized about are all, for the most part, within reach if we choose them.

But these options and opportunities come with a cost, especially if we're trying to have families, too. There are the literal prices, like the exorbitant amount of a paycheck that childcare eats up. There are the financial penalties that come from taking time off for childbirth or caregiving—which compound over time and lead working mothers to make fifty-eight cents for every dollar made by working fathers. Then there are the less calculable emotional taxes: the guilt we feel when we miss hearing our baby's first word because we were at work, or the embarrassment we feel when we miss a deadline because our teenager was sent to the principal's office—and, of course, Mom is the one who gets called in for a meeting.

Like all the women who came before us, we have to make compromises and sacrifices, too. The difference is that today, we have a lot more say over what they are.

We can choose to focus on our careers and delay motherhood until we're established at work, until we're able to afford the costs that come with raising a child. But in doing so, we might be taking a risk and betting against biological reality. (Science may have made that choice a bit more tenable over the last two decades—from hormone treatments to fertility drugs to freezing our eggs and IVF—but these options are often exorbitantly expensive, on top of the nonmonetary emotional and physical costs. And they are never guaranteed.)

We can choose not to get married and live completely fulfilled and fantastic lives; still, we'll be reminded at nearly every turn that society—from our tax code to our carpool lanes—is a lot like Noah's ark: built for twos.

We can choose to put our pursuit of a family first, to settle down and have kids when we're younger; we just have to realize that our prime childbearing years overlap almost cruelly with the years we're meant to be finding our way at work, figuring out our professional interests and ambitions, and forging connections. It's just as Indra Nooyi, the pioneering female executive and former longtime CEO of PepsiCo, once said: "The career clock and the biological clock are in total conflict with each other."

We can choose to have careers. We can choose to have children. Or we can choose none of the above. We can settle down with four dogs in a house in the woods. We can adopt without a partner or spouse. We can have all types of relationships with all types of people. We can travel the world and work remotely. We can figure out what works for us.

But the expectation cannot be—and should not be—that we can and will have it all. First and foremost, because "all" doesn't exist. But even if it did, "all" is not the same for all of us.

The best we can hope for is that we'll have lots of options to choose from, that we'll get to make the choices ourselves, and that we'll be able to change our minds if our minds do change. This framing isn't a sexy book or essay title. In fact, it will hardly get us everything we want, but it *will* get us closer to our own definition of "all."

That may not sound empowering. But guess what? Telling women that we could have it all did *sound* empowering—but it never actually empowered us. Instead, it set society's expectations for us (and our expectations of ourselves) on Mount Everest, which only set us up for disappointment.

What's empowering is the truth. When women understand that we aren't expected to have it all, and that we have to make choices between the competing parts of our lives, we're able to prioritize what it is we actually want. Only once that happens can we finally throw away the impossible definition of "all" that's been spoon-fed to us, define the word for ourselves, and then go for it.

## MY TAKE

If you're a woman with a modicum of success in a male-dominated industry—which, to be clear, is most industries—you're bound to get asked the question: "How do you do it?"

The "it," of course, is a catch-all for "have it all."

Usually, I laugh in response. I make a joke like "The only place a woman can have everything is on a bagel!" And then I explain that, from my perspective, I don't. At the office, I've felt like I'm cheating on my family; on vacation, I've felt like I'm cheating on my team and my colleagues. I explain that I'm just like other women, struggling to balance work life and home life and regularly feeling like I'm failing—or at least flailing—at both.

And yet, I now realize that answer is a cop-out. Most answers to this question are. Because, if you're a woman with a modicum of success in a male-dominated industry, you've probably done *something*

differently from the many women who didn't make it. You probably have *something* to share, beyond clichés and catchphrases, with
younger generations who are looking to follow in your footsteps—
and who are therefore looking for the truth.

My truth: At age seventy-two, I can look at my life and tick off
those three general boxes: great career, great marriage and partner,
great kids. But the only time I've ever "had it all" was in hindsight.
In the moment, at every stage of my life, what I've actually had were
choices.

And while every choice counts, there are three in particular I believe had an outsized impact on my career and my life trajectory.
While I didn't make any of them strategically, I also realize in retro-
spect that I also didn't do what many women in my position might
have. In many ways, I made choices that a lot of people, even women,
would have scoffed at. I took roads less traveled. (It should go without
saying: What worked for me won't work for everyone. What worked
for me didn't even always *work for me*—because for everything I chose
in life, there were other things of value that I gave up.)

The first big choice I made was deciding to get divorced at age
thirty—and not getting remarried for another decade.

At the time, I was working in Boston, living with a great guy whom
I'd met at sixteen, started dating at seventeen, and married at nineteen. We got together when we were still kids, and as we grew up,
we simply grew apart. I knew something had to change, so I called
a friend's therapist one day for advice. He said he was booked for
months and probably couldn't fit me in, but asked what was going on.

"Okay, I'll make it quick," I said. "I'm about to turn thirty. I want
to quit my job. And I think I need a divorce."

He replied, "How about tomorrow at ten?"

To be crystal clear: I did not get divorced to advance my career, and I never believed that my relationship was inhibiting my professional progress. The reason I chose to end my marriage had nothing to do with trying to have it all. (If anything, it pushed me further from having the family that society expects every woman to want, *especially* those who "have it all.") It had everything to do with the fact that the life I chose at nineteen was not the same life I would have chosen at twenty-nine.

And yet, in hindsight, that choice impacted my career tremendously.

In the conflict between career clock and biological clock, as Indra Nooyi put it, many women in my generation chose family. But because I knew I didn't want to have kids alone—and once I got divorced, I wasn't going to settle down with the wrong person just so I could have them—I spent my thirties free of any sort of procreation pressure.

Instead, I was able to channel all my time and energy into work. I moved where the industry and opportunities took me, from Boston to New York to Los Angeles to New York again. I traveled, woke up at the crack of dawn, worked long hours, and often ate dinner on the fly—unencumbered by logistics or guilt or shame or the burden of the dozens of decisions that women with children and partners have to make on a daily basis.

When so many of the women I knew took steps back from work to focus on their families, I could—and did—move my career forward. Being untethered, I never had to think about putting anything, or anyone, above my ambition.

Professionally, it's hard to deny the impact that being childless and spouseless in my thirties had on my career.

Still, as someone who *did* want to have a family—it was also a huge risk. While I never thought of it in these terms, choosing to get divorced at thirty while hoping the right person would come along later meant, essentially, that I was okay running out my biological clock. I may have wanted it all, but every year I put off pregnancy, I increased the possibility that a biological child would eventually be impossible. Had I not gotten lucky and married my husband before it was too late, I might never have had kids at all.

That brings me to the second big choice I made: to marry a man, when I finally remarried at age forty, who was willing to put my career above his own.

My husband, Dale, is my best friend and partner. If he's not mentioned in every single chapter of this book giving me some piece of wise and relevant advice or helping me see a situation from another perspective, it's only because I didn't want to overdo it.

He's one of the smartest and most interesting people I've ever met—and over the course of my life, I've been privileged to meet a lot of smart and interesting people. He's attended more than a third of the Ivy League, yet he's the first person to say that a piece of paper from a prestigious institution has absolutely zero bearing on a person's intelligence, talent, or worth. And he means it. He's also confident enough in himself, his brains, and his looks to not easily feel insecure or threatened.

Who he is is part of why I decided to marry him. But what I didn't know was that if one of us had to step back from our professional lives to be more present at home, he'd be willing to do it. For the record, I don't think he knew it either. But that's exactly what happened.

In some ways, it was the obvious decision. As an undergrad at Dartmouth, Dale had studied philosophy and religion, and then enrolled in Harvard Divinity School for a master's degree. His goal was to become a professor. But after he married his first wife, and they had a daughter, he felt obligated to abandon that path and pursue a more practical and lucrative profession. So he left academia and took a job at a consulting firm.

It must be noted: If the burden of the middle-to-upper-middle-class woman is that we feel pressure to have it all, then the pressure on a vast number of men is almost the opposite—to be the breadwinners and make the most possible money, often sacrificing everything from time with their families to a passion for what they do.

By the time Dale and I had to have that conversation, Dale said he would invest less of himself at work—not only because the earning potential in my industry was higher than in his but also because I loved my job and he, a would-be professor working a corporate job, didn't.

I got extremely lucky that I married and started a family with a man who actually saw me as his partner, and who often believed in me and my career more than I did myself.

Dale didn't quit his job. It was more that he stepped back at work—he didn't pursue promotions, gun to make partner, or seek other exciting opportunities—so he could step up at home as our son, Jesse, got older. Had I married a man unwilling to be *that* parent, it probably would have been my role, and my career would have stagnated as a result.

Speaking of our son, Jesse, he—in essence—is the third big choice I made: to have only one biological kid.

To be completely transparent, this decision was largely made *for* me. I had Jesse when I was forty-three, after struggling with infertility, and I often joke that he was my last egg. It may well be true. But I'm not sure I would have chosen differently if I could. (And again, the partner I ended up with was critical to the life I ended up with, because he supported my decision to have just one kid—and was happy to become a father all over again when other men who already had a child well out of diapers would have felt like the fatherhood stage of their life was behind them.)

When Dale and I got together, he already had a daughter, Ki Mae, from his previous marriage. She was eleven when we married, and I consider her a daughter in every way—but because she already had a great mother and a great stepfather, and because she was older when she entered my life, my role in her life was fairly straightforward. I was there for heart-to-hearts, shopping trips, voice lessons, graduations, first dates, the college application process, summer internships, first jobs, and her wedding. But I didn't have to deal with many of the downsides that sometimes accompany motherhood—the parts we're usually ashamed to admit out loud that we resent. From the start, I truly lucked out to have such a wonderful young woman in my life.

With Jesse, the son Dale and I had together, I also lucked out, but I had to deal with all facets: not just the disciplining and misbehaving but also the dirty diapers and the nonstop crying through the night—as well as morning sickness and a pregnancy that felt like it went on forever. While I was fortunate to be able to take maternity leave, I also experienced the anxiety that comes from taking it when most of my male counterparts never did. And I had uncontrollable hormones that made tremendous guilt even worse.

Leading up to Jesse's birth, I worked until the very last second— past my due date, until I could literally no longer walk. I got lucky and found someone I knew and trusted to freelance my job at USA while I was out . . . which ended up being longer than I'd expected, because by the time my maternity leave was over, I was still not ready to return. (I was incredibly lucky, too, that my boss allowed me to extend my leave for another month, and that the person who was freelancing my job agreed to stay on.)

When I finally went back to work, I abided by a strict schedule that was antithetical to the way I've always operated—before and since. I would arrive at the office at 9:00 a.m. sharp and take no breaks (not even for lunch) and rarely if ever socialized, so I could make the 5:20 p.m. train back to Connecticut every day. As someone who believes that workplace friendships are critical—not just to enjoy work but to move up on the job—this schedule was incredibly out of character for me. But as all new moms know, I wasn't thinking about how to thrive; I was just trying to survive.

It took time for me to really recalibrate, catch up, and let go of the anger I had toward myself for missing the first time Jesse ate solid food, or the guilt I felt when I boarded the train each morning—a guilt that never really went away. Yes, Dale did everything he could to help. He was as amazing a partner as anyone could be, especially in Jesse's later years when I was taking on more and more responsibilities in the corporate ranks of cable TV. But when you're a mom, all the help in the world doesn't change the fact that your career is impacted. And I'm truly not sure what mine would look like if I had to go through that again. All I know is that my career is what it is, and I have one biological child.

That doesn't mean I have no regrets. At times, I've wondered if I should have chosen differently. I'm pretty positive I would have loved to have had a daughter whom I raised from birth, or another son, whom Jesse could have played with. I don't have that and never will—which means, even if I have it *really, really good*, I don't have it all.

My choices also left me lacking in other key areas of my life. As one of the very few working moms in our suburban Connecticut town, I had almost no local female friends in the early years. At the Saturday Little League games that I was able to attend, I would show up with my camera and use it to ingratiate myself with neighborhood moms who were skeptical of my choice to keep working full-time but were appreciative of the photos I took of their kids. Still, those relationships rarely left the ballfield.

As for Jesse, I did what I could to seem present during his childhood even when I was absent—which was often—by setting up scavenger hunts around the house right before I left on a work trip, with a new daily clue that we'd discuss by phone each night. It almost made him look forward to my departures, but of course, to me, it never felt like enough.

At every stage of my life, with every choice I made, I've always felt like I was coming up short. So how could I possibly have it all? The answer is, I couldn't, and I don't. What I have is the same thing every woman has: choices. While mine have gotten me to where I am today, they definitely didn't get me everything, and they definitely involved some plain old good luck.

## NAIL IT

Women can't have it all, and society should stop telling us that we can. But we do have choices, and most aren't all or nothing, right or wrong. To make our choices, then, we have to work backward: We have to first define our version of "all," and then figure out what we can do to have as much of it as we can—while remembering we'll never have all of it.

So . . .

### First, Define Your "All"

Even if "all" as society defines it were possible, it's actually not what a lot of people aspire to! Some people don't want to have kids. Some don't want marriage. Some dream of a house in the suburbs. Some have nightmares about ever leaving a big city. Some hope for a career that allows them to put down roots. Some prefer the thrill that comes from finding and then leaving jobs. Some love to travel. Some are afraid of flying. You get the picture.

While "all" as society defines it isn't possible, it's good to have goals to help you determine the choices you prefer to make at certain junctures of your life. That's what your "all" should be—but it only works if it's really *yours*, not someone else's. So, take time to meditate on what it is you need, want, and would love to have to live a happy life. If your list is long, take time to prioritize the items on it. If two items are in conflict, figure out which item is more important to you (and realize that the one that isn't may very well become the one that got away).

And if your "all" is completely different from everything you've been told and the definitions of everyone else you know, people you grew up with, people you work with, people you live around? Not only is that okay—it is a good thing. It means you've done your homework. The more you've thought about what "all" means to you, the more likely you are to actually achieve some of it.

## Second, Let Your Definition Change

If you've done your homework, then your definition of "all" shouldn't just differ from other people's. It should also change over time.

In her legendary commencement address to Wellesley College, the author and screenwriter Nora Ephron described a game she and her friends would play when they were waiting to be seated at restaurants. On a piece of paper, they had to jot down five things to describe themselves. "When I was your age," she told the graduates, "I would have put: ambitious, Wellesley graduate, daughter, Democrat, single. Ten years later not one of those five things turned up on my list. I was: journalist, feminist, New Yorker, divorced, funny. Today not one of those five things turns up in my list: writer, director, mother, sister, happy. Whatever those five things are for you today, they won't make the list in ten years—not that you still won't be some of those things, but they won't be the five most important things about you."

Ephron's point? In her words, "You are not going to be you, fixed and immutable you, forever." And your definition of "all" shouldn't be fixed and immutable, either. As it changes, so can—and should!—the choices we make. If having it all once meant wedded bliss and now it means being single and free, great. Make a choice that reflects that change. If it meant climbing up a corporate ladder and now it means staying home with a family, amazing. We are allowed to change our goals and our minds. Trust me, all of us will. We just need to make sure our choices reflect that.

### Third, Own Your Choices

At the end of the day, what matters is not really *what* we choose. It's that *we* choose. Once we've decided what works for us, we need to go for it with gusto, and not allow the doubts, judgments, and negativity of others to impact us. Of course, that's easier said than done. But we're the ones who have to go to sleep with our choices and wake up next to them every morning. We're also the only ones who know what will make us happy. So be yourself. Be kind to yourself. Make your own choices—and then own them.

## THE FINAL WORD

Energy is a finite resource. And every minute we spend trying to have it all—rather than trying to have the life that we actually want—is a minute we'll never get back. So it's critical to define what will make us happy . . . and then make choices that get us closer to it. Anything else isn't just a waste of our time. It's a waste of our life.

part two

# STANDING OUT

### TO SET YOURSELF APART

- Stay authentic; don't fake it

- Embrace your gender in a "man's world"

- Use your words; find your voice

- Take action; don't wait for things to happen

- Hop off the career ladder instead of climbing it

# 6. Fake It 'Til You Make It /
# Face It 'Til You Make It

**What We're Told:** *"Fake it 'til you make it."*

The mantra entered our workplaces innocently enough—a feminist battle cry to help combat "imposter syndrome," the feeling that women don't belong in certain spaces, have somehow conned our way in, and might at any moment be exposed. Not only does it rhyme and roll off the tongue but, given that women are statistically more likely to doubt themselves and underestimate their abilities, it also sounds like a simple and sensical solution: Imitate the competence (or confidence) we wish we had—fake it 'til we make it—and eventually, like some sort of self-fulfilling prophecy, we can will whatever we believe we're lacking into existence.

**The Truth:** *"Face it 'til you make it."*

According to the latest surveys, 75 percent of female executives across America have experienced imposter syndrome at work, meaning that they struggle with feelings of inadequacy and self-doubt.[1] The official number has been climbing for years, but in my experience, the unofficial number is even higher (and both genders experience the syndrome). One thing, however, is undeniable: For ambitious and objectively competent women, feeling like an imposter has become the rule and not the exception.

Understandably, "imposter syndrome" is identified as yet another way low self-esteem rears its head and works against us. And some downstream effects have been documented: Feeling insecure and out of place can impact our performance on the job, decrease our overall job satisfaction, and eventually cause us to burn out. It can even prevent us from getting a job in the first place. Studies have shown that women apply for roles and promotions when they feel they meet a full 100 percent of the qualifications, while men will generally apply when they meet just 60 percent of them.[2]

Our delusions of deficiency may lead us to screen ourselves out of opportunities—and sell ourselves short in the process.

The anxiety and depression that occasionally accompany feeling like an imposter can be serious—and should be taken seriously. But imposter syndrome is very different from the far more common imposter *phenomenon*, the name given by Pauline Clance and Suzanne Imes, the authors of the 1978 academic paper, to this low-level feeling of anxiety.[3] "Imposter phenomenon" isn't a nothingburger, and almost everyone experiences it at some point in their life and career. I wish everyone—me included—would be more confident about who they are and what they bring to the table in the workplace. But from my perspective, this imposter phenomenon is far less damaging to women than the advice we've been given to deal with it: to fake it 'til we make it.

When we're feeling underqualified, underconfident, or bound to underachieve, we've been told to simply act like we aren't—and that doing so will help us become someone who isn't. And look, a little ego boost isn't a bad thing. Acting with confidence when we lack it won't get us sent to the principal's office.

But there's a difference between convincing ourselves we're capable of something and misleading someone else about what, exactly, we're capable of. There's a difference between telling ourselves "I'm a good cook" and telling someone else "I've studied at the Culinary Institute of America."

The former is a dose of self-assurance in the face of possibly unwarranted self-doubt. The latter is deception, plain and simple. And all too often, "fake it 'til you make it" is taken as an allowance to engage in exactly that. Even when our intentions are innocent, the outcome is anything but.

Let's start with the obvious. Every time we pretend that we've done something we haven't, that we are capable of doing something when we aren't, that we know something we don't, or that we're better at something than we really are, we're arming a ticking time bomb that can blow up in our faces at any moment. From embellishing our resumes to include management experience we've never had, to exaggerating how involved we were with a certain project, to professing our love for an author we've never read, to claiming we possess a working proficiency of French when we only took one beginner's course, each distortion of the truth is actually a *lie*.

From a moral perspective, it's wrong. From a legal perspective, it can be criminal; just look at the many Silicon Valley founders who fudged the numbers on their balance sheets and ended up committing fraud because they believed they had to exaggerate the size of their assets or user base to be taken seriously, and that their dishonesty would only be temporary. From a practical perspective, it's foolish—because each lie invites the possibility of being found out, if not immediately then eventually.

Once that happens, we open a Pandora's box of distrust and skepticism that tinges everything we do and say going forward. Coworkers, bosses, the people who report to us . . . they may never look at us the same way again. Even the total truths we tell later will seem suspect. We discredit ourselves forever.

Even if we're never caught in our lies, faking it sets us up for failure, because it limits our growth in real, concrete ways. When we feign knowing about (or how to do) something because we want someone to believe we know more, we erect a wall around ourselves. When we refuse to be vulnerable out of fear that someone will spot our weaknesses, we close ourselves off to the world. We forfeit the opportunity to learn from others and ask for their help.

That's especially unfortunate because most people do want to help others out. It makes *them* feel good and gets them invested in our progress. But they can't help us if they don't know we need it. And they won't know that we need help if we pretend to know something we don't or refuse to ask for assistance.

Then there's this kicker: While faking it is framed as a fix to the problem of imposterdom, it's actually a cause. The more we fake who we are, what we've done, and what we're capable of, the more convinced we may become that our true self *isn't* worthy, qualified, and capable of a task at hand. Even if we succeed, the insecurity that pushed us to lie in the first place will tell us that our success is a fluke—that we only got to where we are because we were dishonest, and that our truest selves never could have done it. To ourselves, the fraudulence we feel isn't a delusion or a distortion. It becomes the truth; it's merited. And the next time around, we'll feel like we have no choice but to fake it yet again.

So when we feel like an imposter at work, faking it is the *worst* possible solution.

Instead, we should recognize that everyone feels like an imposter at least some of the time . . . even those of us who have objectively *made it*. Success isn't a cure, according to Clance and Imes, the founding mothers of the theory. A long list of luminaries have admitted to experiencing it even as (and even though) they reached the pinnacle of success and recognition in their fields—Maya Angelou, Tina Fey, Michelle Obama, Natalie Portman, Barbara Corcoran, Tom Hanks, Howard Schultz, and Albert *Freaking* Einstein, to name a few.

But here's the upside: If even geniuses can feel as irrationally inadequate as the rest of us, then self-doubt must *not* be the barrier to success that we've been led to believe. In fact, perhaps feeling insecure, at least in small and manageable doses, can even *contribute* to our success.

For starters, when we feel inadequate, most of us tend to overcompensate. But if we do so by working harder, learning more, and improving ourselves in the process, that's a boon to our professional lives. If our insecurity leads us to ask a colleague to look over a proposal before we turn it in, that makes us more thorough and leaves less room for error. If our nerves lead us to rehearse a pitch multiple times before we present it, that makes us more prepared. If our fear of being seen as ignorant or unaware leads us to consult experts or do additional research on a topic before opining on it, that makes us more informed. If our self-doubt leads us to wait until after a meeting to decide whether the ideas that we had are worth sharing, that makes us more thoughtful and less impulsive.

Almost by definition, when we feel like an imposter—even if the feeling is unwarranted—we're bound to possess more humility than we would if we were entirely self-assured. That means we're likelier to second-guess our instincts and invite other people into our decision-making processes, which makes us better listeners and more collaborative.

As for the data on imposter phenomenon hurting us and our performance at work? According to some experts, it's only damaging once it crosses a certain threshold. Up to a point, a few nerves can *improve* our job performance—for all the reasons I just listed. The challenge is to let those nerves drive us, not drown us. My old boss and friend Michael Rice, the former general manager of WGBH in Boston, clearly thought that a bit of imposter phenomenon was useful. He prided himself on hiring people before they were technically qualified for a job if he believed they could grow into the role in a year or two: Someone who felt like they still had something to prove would probably work harder than someone who felt like they had already proven themselves.

As long as a potential hire was honest about what they knew, what they'd done, and what they could be doing better, someone with a little imposter phenomenon was always more valuable to him than someone who faked it and acted like there was nothing left to learn.

## MY TAKE

In a way, I'm lucky. The first time I was asked to do something on the job, and I knew that I couldn't, it was 1976. Women made up just a quarter of the workforce. No one was suggesting we fake anything to get anywhere.

I was working in Boston as a production assistant on *Infinity Factory*, where I was picking up dog poop, babysitting the kids in the cast, collating scripts, and generally doing whatever was asked of me. When the show's shooting schedule fell behind, our director requested that I fly out to Los Angeles. He needed me to oversee the postproduction of four episodes—normally his job—while he stayed in Boston and kept filming.

I was shocked. I was twenty-six. I was brand-new to the TV industry. I knew none of the technology—or even the technical terms. Until then, I'd never even been on a work trip. The director trusted *me* . . . to do *this*?

I flew to LA to "edit."

I was so nervous I'd be late that I rehearsed the drive from my hotel in Hollywood to the editing facility in Burbank to time the route and make sure I knew where to go. After a restless night, I showed up to the editing studio—where the reels of raw footage were waiting—an hour early.

When Jim, the hip video editor at least a decade my senior, drove up in a Porsche, my nerves spiked. I introduced myself, he did the same, and then he asked, "Whatcha got for me?"

"We have four shows to edit," I said. Then, still nervous with a somewhat forced smile plastered on my face, I added, "I've never edited a piece of film in my life, and I've had zero exposure to computer editing. But I know the material well and I'm here to learn."

It never crossed my mind to pretend otherwise. I knew what I knew and what I didn't, and there was no Wikipedia page or YouTube video (or internet, period) I could turn to on short notice to help fill in the gaps in my knowledge so I could pretend they didn't exist. If I wanted to get the job done, my only option was honesty.

What I learned then, and in the decades since—especially when I've been on the other side of the table—is this: People respect honesty, especially when it's paired with humility and vulnerability. We feel good about ourselves when we have an opportunity to teach others who are curious and eager to learn. When we become part of their professional story, we become invested in their professional growth. Perhaps, counterintuitively, we think more highly of them than we do of the people who arrive knowing everything (or at least seeming to) from day one.

Case in point? Jim's response to me: "Thanks for being honest. I'm gonna make you a star."

Over the next week, that's kind of what he did. I had started as a bona fide editing ignoramus, but I quickly became comfortable with the process and language of editing. I learned (and genuinely understood) what it took to put a show together. In hindsight, my transparency and attitude made the difference.

My vulnerability and earnestness allowed Jim to loosen up and take me under his wing. He had no interest in testing what I already knew, because we'd already established that I knew nothing. Instead, he was interested in teaching. It allowed me to loosen up, too. All my cards were on the table from the very beginning, so I didn't have to worry about being found out later. Instead of planning what to say next, I was able to sit back, observe, and ask questions. Instead of controlling the journey, I enjoyed the ride. I empowered him to teach me, and I empowered myself to learn. By the end of my week in Los Angeles, I was able to measure my progress honestly—and feel proud of everything I'd picked up rather than obsess over everything I wished I'd already known. That couldn't have happened had I faked it from the get-go.

This experience taught me that experience, as great as it may be, is only one tool in my professional toolbox, and that it's not always needed to build something great. I've never forgotten that lesson, and nearly twenty years later, it's what I turned to when I was called to take on a role that I couldn't have been less qualified for or, frankly, less interested in.

In the fall of 1995, I was an ambitious forty-something working long hours as the VP of original programming at USA Network, as close to a dream job as I'd ever thought I'd have . . . until my boss Rod Perth, a talented CBS veteran and all-around good human who was now the network's president, asked me to drop what I was doing and take on a new task: overseeing the network's professional wrestling franchise (then known as the World Wrestling Federation, or WWF, now known as WWE). Its live shows were (and still are) legendary. But back then, there wasn't as much storytelling or character development. The production value for TV viewers wasn't great, either. And it was up against a franchise on a rival network. Of everyone at USA Network, Rod somehow thought *I* was the solution.

At the time, I was responsible for heading up many projects at the network, including the Emmy-winning "Erase the Hate" initiative, a series of documentaries and thirty-second TV spots promoting racial and religious inclusion. This assignment came from left field, literally. Rod had given it to me with no warning on a call with other people. While it was framed like an offer, it was really an order. I felt completely miscast, misunderstood, even mismanaged. I wasn't just underexperienced; I'd never even seen a wrestling match in my life. Honestly, I never planned to, and I think everyone knew that.

I almost quit. But my husband, a former high school wrestler, convinced me to give it a try. I agreed, figuring I could always quit later if I hated it.

To say I felt like an imposter walking into that first meeting at the surprisingly corporate-looking WWE headquarters in Stamford, Connecticut, with professional wrestlers who doubled as C-suite executives and managers, would be the understatement of the century.

It didn't help that the three people who'd overseen WWE from USA before me were all men with sports management or acquisitions backgrounds, who all knew at least something about wrestling.

I had absolutely no idea what to expect, except for the fact that I would stick out—if I was seen at all.

But with the memory of that week in Los Angeles in my head— and the knowledge that men who looked and acted like better fits hadn't managed to win the wrestlers over—I shook hands that could have crushed mine completely and sat down around the conference table. When WWE's chairman and CEO turned to me and said, "So?" I introduced myself. Then I took a deep breath and gave my spiel.

"I have to be honest. Until Rod asked me to do this, I had never watched your show. I've still never been to a live match. I know almost nothing about wrestling except what I've learned in the past two weeks. I know almost nothing about your business—except that you make your money on live events and merchandising," I began. "What I do know is how to produce good television, tell good stories, and create good characters. And I know you want to beat the crap out of cable competitor Ted Turner's WCW [World Championship Wrestling] in the ratings, so I think I can help you there."

The CEO's response to my honesty was like the professional-wrestler version of that LA editor's two decades earlier: "Okay," he said. "Let's go."

Over the next hour, I sat quietly and listened as the CEO and his panel of executives, writers, wrestlers, and ex-wrestlers delved into the challenges at hand. I didn't cower in the corner, but I also didn't interrupt to make myself seem more informed than I was. Free of the pressure that comes with faking it, I was instead able to observe and ask tons of questions. Because I'd made it clear that I knew almost nothing, I had almost everything to learn—especially from the CEO, who'd grown up in the wrestling business and knew every inch of his turf, from the economics to the choreography to the audience, better than anyone.

And I learned *a lot.*

But I was also able to teach. Because I never claimed to be an expert in something I wasn't, the expertise I did have—and did stake claim to—was trusted and never doubted.

When I suggested that the CEO hire professional TV writers who could help develop storylines to make the WWE more like a male soap opera—so viewers would keep watching night after night to find out what happens next and feel invested in more than who wins or loses a match—those writers were hired. When I recommended that female WWE wrestlers move beyond "arm candy" status and have actual character development and story arcs—not just because of equality but because there was an entire demographic missing from the audience—it happened. When I was on the phone with the director during a live show and told him exactly when to cut to black—upping the intrigue quotient right before something too naughty and gory for TV viewers—he listened. When I wanted to cast some big WWE faces as guest stars in USA Network shows to raise their profiles, they happily obliged.

I started out with little experience, knowledge, interest, or confidence. But I was able to make up for it all with an outsized willingness to listen and learn from men (and women) with necks the size of my waist. I never pretended to know more than I did. What I did know, though, I shared widely.

Almost thirty years later, working with WWE is still one of the highlights of my career—and one of the craziest and most fun experiences I've ever had. I've learned that long after, during a chaotic corporate transition, part of why I got a promotion when many of my colleagues got axed was that the new boss was fascinated (and amused) by a five-foot-four chick who could hold her own with the world's biggest wrestling stars. He was impressed that I could make it in an environment that was anathema to where I'd come from—and thrive creatively and financially. From this one experience, for which I had no prior experience, he could see my range and my value.

What's more, I managed to fulfill my original promise from that first meeting. Not only did the ratings pop, WWE's status as a male soap opera completely transformed the franchise. At the height of its ratings popularity, WWE reached nine million viewers a night. Eventually, we even drove Ted Turner's wrestling shows off the air.

And if you enjoy superstars John Cena and Dwayne "The Rock" Johnson, well, their careers first took off thanks to WWE.

## NAIL IT

There's a little feeling of being an imposter in everyone. It's natural. But the worst approach—on the job or off—is to hide our insecurities by lying about who we are, where we've been, and what we can offer. Instead, we should realize that even when an opportunity or position feels far out of our league and we feel that we don't belong, there's still a lot we bring to the table. Contrary to popular belief, there *are* substitutes for experience. While we may never conquer our feelings of imposterdom entirely, we can use them to our advantage and find success.

So . . .

### Acknowledge Your Imposterdom (to Yourself and Others)

While it's impossible to fully solve the imposter phenomenon (every CEO and board chair I know, female and male, still admits to suffer-

## Are You Out of Your Depth or Just Afraid of Heights?

Insecurity hits all of us—but it's not the same thing as inability. The worst thing you can do is dismiss your real shortcomings, gaps in knowledge, and lack of skill as issues of confidence if the real issue is competence. When you aren't certain which one you're facing, ask yourself:

- Are there any absolute requirements I don't have—a language I don't know, a degree I never earned, a technical skill I need time to master?
- What are the qualifications of the person or people who've done this work before?
- Is this more than a one-person job?
- Have I surpassed expectations—of others and myself—before? What were the conditions that led to my success?
- Am I prepared to manage the situation and the team, even if I haven't mastered the details?
- Do I know where to go for the answers and how to ask the questions?

While it's important to power through a crisis of faith, it isn't great to make promises you can't keep or take on tasks you can't complete. If you've done either of those, be honest and admit it—to yourself, and to your boss.

ing from it at least on occasion), one thing has been proven to *lessen* our feelings of inadequacy and inferiority: learning there are other people who feel the same way. To get to that point, though, we need to be self-aware and identify it in ourselves in the first place.

So when you're feeling like you don't know what you're doing, don't shove the discomfort aside or try to fake your way out of it—because neither will work. Instead, understand and then own how you're feeling. Try to use rational thought to determine if your insecurity is merited, or if it's just striking you because it's bound to strike everyone at some point. Accept that you will occasionally feel out of your depth even if you aren't. Then be open, be vulnerable, let others in, and share what you're feeling and experiencing with some trusted confidants. Chances are, they're going through it, too, and talking about it with them will make you feel less alone *and* less out of place.

## Come In with a Can-Do, Curious Attitude

It sounds trite, but attitude really is everything. If you feel like there's something missing from your skills, capabilities, or knowledge, compensate for it with a can-do approach. Treat every opportunity like an opportunity to learn. Make curiosity your brand. Act like you're starving for new skills, thirsting for new information, and desperate to grow—because that's exactly how you should be, especially when you're unsure of your place in an organization or the value you bring to it. You don't have to be one of the smartest or most experienced people in a room to become one of the most appreciated; you can do that by becoming the person who says yes to anything you're asked, sounds excited about the opportunity, and poses great questions along the way. Even if you are an amateur, the right attitude is an asset that can turn you into an expert fast.

## Do Your Homework

I've long said my secret to success is that I've never needed to be the smartest person in any situation. But I always made sure to have that person, or people, on speed dial. And I've never pretended to know more than I did. But I *always* did my homework to learn more. Sometimes that means reading (and, more recently, listening to) books on subjects I never thought I was interested in, or going down rabbit holes on Google to understand topics I would have otherwise never tried to tackle. Even more often, it means talking to people who know way more than me to establish a baseline understanding of whatever it is I need to understand.

So do your homework. Be sure to get a feel for the world you're operating in . . . ideally before you start operating in it. You don't need to use whatever information you learn to pretend you now know exactly what you're doing. (Because unless you've done it, you don't.) But at least you'll know what questions to ask.

## Offer an Outsider's Perspective

Occasionally, certain insecurities can become strengths. Being an outsider is one of them. After all, if you think about it, coming into a situation blind—whether it's a new industry, a new company, or just a new role—is just coming in with a fresh perspective. But only if we look at it that way. Back at WWE, I succeeded not only because I had a different background from those in the wrestling world but also because I wasn't mired in old ways of thinking or unwilling to try different solutions or to shake up the status quo. I was able to see the pros and cons of the franchise—like the fact that the stars were characters before they were even athletes and that people will watch anything (literally) if they're invested in those characters and their stories. Then I was able to use that expertise to improve what wasn't working and further improve what was.

So don't be afraid of offering an outsider's perspective. As long as you take time to observe and then deliver it with humility, you won't be hurting anyone, no matter how wacky or outside the box your ideas are. You'll be helping. And who knows? Maybe, like a soap opera starring three-hundred-pound men in underwear, those ideas just might work.

## THE FINAL WORD

Feeling less than your best at work can be demoralizing, whether that feeling is rooted in a lack of experience or confidence (or both). But our insecurity, insufficiency, and inferiority complexes don't have to hold us back, whether they're merited or not. The more we're willing to honestly acknowledge our deficits, put in the work, make ourselves a pleasure to be around, and compensate for what we don't know by always being eager to learn, the less our prior experience—or lack thereof—will matter. The more we *face it* 'til we make it, the less we'll need to fake it.

# 7. It's A Man's World /
   Only If You Let It Be

**What We're Told:** *"It's a man's world."*

Shelves we can't reach even on our tiptoes. Arctic office temperatures that freeze us in the summer. A tax on tampons. Laws that restrict access to abortion—and none that regulate the right to a vasectomy. In countless ways, society is set up for men. While things have gotten better over time, in the corporate world—where women are still the minority, especially at the top—the odds are still stacked against us. It's a man's world, it seems, and we women are just living in it.

**The Truth:** *"Only if you let it be."*

Have women been treated fairly in the workplace? The question answers itself. And yet . . . that doesn't mean that being a woman is an impediment to success. In my experience, the opposite can in fact be the case. Even at work. Even in male-dominated industries. Although it may sound dubious at first: All other things being equal, women can even enjoy an advantage in the workplace—if we play the game right.

But catchphrases like "it's a man's world" or "we live under the patriarchy" have partly become self-fulfilling prophecies. Think about it: When you tell women we're destined for a lifetime of second-class citizenship in a man's world, a lot of us end up believing it. As a result, many never bother learning how to navigate that world. Convinced that the game has been solidly rigged against us, we all too often forfeit before we even get to halftime.

I want more women in the game. I want us to win. But some women believe that the only way to succeed is to act less like themselves. And that's what I've seen many women—especially ambitious ones—do. Afraid of appearing weak, meek, or God forbid girly, they abandon who they are and try to become someone else. Scrutinized for the way they look, talk, dress, and even carry themselves, they deign to change it all. At the now-imprisoned ex–Theranos head Elizabeth-Holmes-ian extreme, some even deepen their voices intentionally. Maybe a few of these women make it to the top. But more likely, they don't. Because the way to succeed in a man's world isn't to become a pseudo-man. The way to succeed in a man's world is to stand out *as a woman.*

Having spent decades often being the only—and almost always the most senior—woman in a room full of men, in an industry known for its lengthy Me-Too rap sheet, I've had to compete or collaborate—or both—with men at every level. Here's what I've learned: Men and women are often different at work—we may gravitate toward different skill sets or different approaches.

But in a race toward the top of the equality mountain, our culture has overcorrected. We've made these differences, and this discussion, too taboo to even talk about—when the real impediment to progress isn't pointing them out. It's painting them as weaknesses when, in fact, they can be unparalleled strengths.

Tapping into those strengths is what I call the XX factor.

A line from *Grey's Anatomy* sums up the je ne sais quoi of the XX factor well. Watching a bunch of men compete to become chief of surgery, Dr. Addison Montgomery is asked if she plans to "get in there" and join them. Her response? "Oh, I intend to fight like a girl. I'll let them kill each other and then I'll be the only one left standing."

The XX factor starts with our ability to communicate. Women often use conversations to forge emotional connections, which helps draw in others rather than turn them off. And we don't just hear what people say to us—we listen empathetically. Some experts think this is because, on average, women are literally more sensitive to sound than men.[1]

That leads to our knack for collaboration. The higher oxytocin levels we release compared to men increase our tendency toward bonding, trusting, cooperating, and, yes, empathy. The way women communicate and collaborate also influences our approach to arguments, conflicts, and full-blown crises. While men tend to seek victory at all costs, we tend to seek resolution; they want to win the war, we want to end it.[2] We don't just *seem* less threatening, we really are.

There's more. In business, research tells us that in stressful situations, men tend to take more risks, even when the odds are long, while women think long and hard before making decisions, even when anxious. We tend to exhibit more self-control and keep our cool rather than act aggressively or react impulsively—which may be why women-run hedge funds perform three times better than those run by their male counterparts.[3]

In the face of distractions, too, women are adept at juggling multiple things at once. Don't just take it from me—the former head of Israel's national intelligence agency, Tamir Pardo, has singled out female spies for their ability to multitask. He also homed in on another trait that sets women apart: our intuition. "Contrary to stereotypes," Pardo said in a 2012 magazine interview, "you see that women's abilities are superior to men in terms of understanding the territory, reading situations, and spatial awareness."[4] That tracks with other research, which has proven that women are experts at picking up on both verbal and nonverbal cues.[5]

And who can forget our ancient orientation as caregivers? Our inner caregiver helps us comfort, nurture, and inspire the best in people, in good times and bad. We look out for and protect those around us, even at our own expense. In return, people trust us and even tie their fates to ours.

All these factors come together to form our XX factor. The benefits it provides, especially on the job, should seem obvious.

But a lifetime—no, an eternity—of being told that being a woman is a weakness has gotten into too many of our heads and confused women into believing we should suppress the very traits and qualities that make us valuable employees and strong leaders. It's gotten to the general public, too. Every year from 1982 to 2016, Americans of *both* genders reported preferring male bosses to female ones. That's confounding when you look at the data: Female-led companies tend to outperform those led by men and fare better in crises, while employees with female managers tend to feel happier at work. It makes a little more sense, though, when you remember that female leadership at work is still a relative rarity—which means the sample sizes in these data sets have been so small, and most respondents likely formed their opinions through conjecture and stereotype, not personal experience.[6]

Fortunately, as more people experience the benefits of female leaders and leadership, those numbers are changing. In 2017, for the first time ever, a majority of Americans said their boss's gender made no difference to them.

I'll take it, but with one added caveat: The XX factor is a working woman's best friend. It's high time more of us tap into it. The more we do, the more great female leaders there will be, and the more people will see our gender as an asset at work—something to embrace, not evade. Who knows what happens after that? In a few years, perhaps a majority of Americans will even want to call us boss.

Making these changes might not be enough to change *the world.* But it is progress—and it's the only way we start to transform a man's world into one that is built for all of us.

## MY TAKE

Let's start with the obvious: I've been a woman in television for the past five decades, in and around Hollywood for the past four. I don't just know the man's world—or the old boys' clubs within it. I've lived them. I'm under no illusions that women have it easy, or equal, at work.

With very few exceptions, corporate America is designed for and controlled by men. We're learning that even in ancient societies, women weren't just "gatherers," they were hunters, too. A tomb found in Peru—which archaeologists initially thought was a high-ranking hunter surrounded by *his* weapons—turned out, when the bones were analyzed, to belong to a woman. Today, women may be equipped to "hunt," but too often they are not given the opportunity, even if they have the sharpest, most advanced weapons.

Yet I learned early on that being a woman was a superpower, not a source of weakness the way so many of us have been taught. I learned that my gender could be a boon to my career, not a burden. On my worst days and at my lowest points, I learned that sexism is a powerful foe—but if we embrace our XX factor, we can achieve in spite of the obstacles in our way.

A story that illustrates my point: When I was thirty, I became the executive producer for a local morning talk show in Boston called *Good Day!* My boss at the time was a textbook jerk whose actions, attitude, and as-loud-as-could-be yelling were bringing down our morale.

The work was grueling: six days a week of crack-of-dawn wakeups to make ninety minutes of live TV five mornings a week. On the seventh day, like God, we rested. I often joke that I was the smartest I'll ever be during my years at *Good Day!* After all, there's no better way to learn about the world than to pitch, produce, and edit an endless stream of four-minute segments about anything and everything—from a new drive-through steak house to a high-profile murder trial to the latest advances in heart transplant surgery to a shrink interviewing movie, stage, and Broadway star Carol Channing.

Fortunately, I had an extraordinary staff, specifically my all-female team of associate producers and a director, a rarity then and even now. The proof was in the ratings. At the time, we were the number one morning talk show in Boston and in the top five or ten in the entire country. (When *Good Morning America* eventually debuted, they even tried poaching our talent. I don't blame them.)

But none of that mattered to my boss. The only thing that seemed to put a smile on his face was taking the smiles off ours. He gave no compliments and showered us with abundant criticism. When a segment didn't go perfectly—with fifty-plus segments a week, it was bound to happen—he'd demand to know which producer was to blame. He wanted me to throw my people under the bus. I'd refuse to do it. To me, the calculation was simple: I'm the executive producer, I let it go on the air, so I'll be the one whose face he screams in.

I endured those screams a lot.

But my boss actually isn't the antagonist in this story. That title belongs to *his* boss, one of the senior executives at the company. Eventually, I reached my breaking point and scheduled a meeting with him to explain that the work environment wasn't only crushing my team's spirit—it was threatening to hurt the show in the process, trying to pit my producers against one another when success depended on our collaboration. In hindsight, I'm not sure what I was looking for from this executive: perhaps a solution, a suggestion for how to handle the situation, even just a little moral support. Instead, he gave me advice that still echoes in my ears from time to time.

"Bonnie," he said, looking me up and down and then staring straight into my eyes, "you need to learn one thing: In this business, if your boss tells you to suck dick, you suck dick."

I still haven't forgotten those words. I never will.

I remember walking out of his office in shock, my face pale and frozen. I could barely breathe. I'd never experienced such a combination of emotions. I was angry and humiliated. And I was mortified for being so naïve as to have approached him in the first place. I wanted to quit, and when I first got home, in between tears and hyperventilating sobs, I made up my mind to do just that the very next day.

In tough times, we often tell people to "man up." But instead, I handled the situation like a woman. After I cried it out, I cooled off, calmed down, and considered what I'd be giving up—and what would happen to my team if I did quit. I showed up to work the next day. I realized what was in my power and what was out of my control, and I chose to focus on the former and forget the latter as best I could. The truth is I loved my job and my team, even if I didn't at all love or like my bosses. While I didn't recognize it at the time, all of that was my XX factor in action. In the long run, I came out ahead.

I often say that being a woman at work is an exercise in resilience, and it's true—I didn't know how tough I was until I realized I could come into the studio day after day, look my bosses in their eyes, and no longer flinch. If anything, the experience made me stronger and even more committed to protecting the people around me. It also smartened me up to the reality of corporate politics. I realized there was no Prince Charming (or even an HR department as we know it . . . it was the early eighties, after all) coming to save me or my team. I had to do it myself. So that's exactly what I did: without burning any bridges, betraying anyone's loyalties, or sabotaging my own career because I couldn't see the bigger picture.

Sexism is a fact of life. Sometimes, it's blatant: like a male boss who makes comments to you about genitalia. In the time since I left *Good Day!*, it's also been more subtle: like the fact that, over the course of my entire career, I have only worked under one female CEO (my boss's boss at the time). Or the fact that I know for certain I've been passed over for jobs given to less competent and qualified (and often younger) men.

But in so many other ways, my gender helped lift me up. By harnessing my XX factor and acting on my more stereotypically female instincts, I was actually able to propel my career forward.

Here's what I mean. The leadership style I practiced at *Good Day!*—compassionate, collaborative, eager to give credit where and when due—was, and mostly still is, seen as stereotypically female. But it paid off in spades and dividends, engendering a sense of trust and loyalty that made everyone on my team work longer, harder, and better. They wanted the show to succeed at all costs, because they knew the success would be theirs, too. They knew that if they held up their end of the bargain, I'd never let them fail—or take the fall—alone.

In all the roles I've held since my time in Boston, I've never bothered with trying to lead—or do anything else—like the men around me. Instead, I've continued to embrace and utilize my XX factor in ways big and small.

I've navigated seven corporate mergers and takeovers and came out with a better job each time because I've become adept at picking up on body language, reading a room, being flexible, knowing when to compromise, and intuitively understanding how to match what I can offer with what someone needs—all skills that come more naturally to women. For decades, I've built and led teams that people genuinely want to be part of. Even when they exceeded two-thousand-plus people, my teams boasted disproportionately low turnover rates. And I did it not by abandoning my distinctly "female" brand of leadership but by doubling down on it.

When I'm hiring, the XX factor has always been one of the first things I look for—regardless of the candidate's gender. I want to know that someone is a collaborative team player. When they talk about past projects in interviews, I listen closely to hear if (and how) they credit others. I look for proof that they care for their colleagues and see them as more than professional automatons. While I'm always on the hunt for people who are well spoken, I'm just as focused on someone's ability to listen. Do they interrupt my questions to give an answer before I'm done asking? I'm interested in their personal lives—and I'm less impressed by the people who don't have them than I am with the people, especially parents, who are forthcoming about the challenges that come with balancing a career and a family. My own experience as a working mom has taught me that nothing better prepares a person for managing competing obligations and meeting tight timelines.

Some might say I've broken the rules to get where I am today;

I'd simply say I've bent them, like any smart woman knows how to do. Case in point: Whenever one of my employees has a newborn, I've allowed them to take four-day workweeks (even when that meant dancing around company policy). I trust they'll get the work done—they always have—and they trust I'm looking out for them. It's a win-win situation that has won me immense loyalty over the years.

I've taken the same approach to money and salaries—one vital area where women still significantly lag behind. Here, I learned from the master, Barry Diller. When Barry took over USA Network and Sci-Fi, I was running Sci-Fi and a man was running USA. Although USA had more viewers, the jobs were identical and entailed the same amount of work. But the male president in charge of USA was being paid twice as much as me. I didn't know my worth, but Barry told me exactly what it was. He doubled my salary in one day so that I was making as much as my peer.

Later, I followed a version of Barry's rule when I spoke to a woman who was taking on a similar role to mine at NBCUniversal. I introduced her to my lawyer to help negotiate her contract, and I also instructed my lawyer to tell her exactly how much I was making, so she would know what to ask for. In my view, it was only fair.

As for my original bosses at *Good Day!*? It's safe to say that being a man in the industry did neither of them any outsized favors in the long run. One of them never left local Boston television, and the other transferred to a far smaller TV market in Tennessee.

No thanks. I'll take being a woman—even in a man's world—any day.

## NAIL IT

At the end of the day, none of us alone can change the rules. What we can do, though, is use our XX factor to bend them to our advantage. After all, Sarah Jessica Parker's character Carrie Bradshaw was right: "Trying to be a man is a waste of a woman." Not because women are better than men but because there are certain things we *do* better, things that come more easily or naturally to us. Failing to take advantage of them is a fatal error, especially at work. But the flip side is even more true: Embracing the traits and attributes that set women apart, and using them as strengths instead of weaknesses, isn't just how we make it through a man's world—it's how we make it to the top.

So . . .

### Care Like a Woman

Women tend to give a crap about the people around us. Quite simply, after our millennia of performing caregiving roles, we care. And while it's often overlooked and undervalued on the job, caretaking is actually the secret sauce that makes female leaders so effective. So unleash your inner caretaker that makes you attuned to others and alert to their needs—even in professional settings.

Stay attuned to how people feel on any given day—whether they report to you or you report to them—and check in if something seems wrong. If someone's having a rough time, offer to help. Drop the tough exterior and remain approachable even as you rise in your career. If someone is coming to you—for advice, with feedback, or simply to share an idea—it means they trust you, and trust is foundational for any good leader. It also means they're being vulnerable, so you owe them that back.

Above all, don't confuse warmth with weakness. Never let the fear of seeming soft keep you from showing you care, because when everyone feels protected and cared for—that their talent is nurtured *and* the totality of who they are matters—everyone wins.

## Communicate Like a Woman

For the past half century, conversations about language have centered on the ways women mess up when we open our mouths. And yet we often overlook a simple truth: Women have inherent strengths when it comes to communication. So talk like a woman. First, talk *with* people, not at them. While men tend to utilize a "command and control" approach to dialogue, women invite participation and interaction. On the job, that's a great thing—permission for others to open up and suggest their own ideas.

Second, no one likes the loudest person in a room. In team meetings, board meetings, and everything in between, there will always be people who like the sound of their own voice and conflate saying something with contributing. But it's the quality of your words that rewards you with credibility—not the quantity or quickness of them. It's a mistake to feel like you have to say something if you don't have something to say. I realized early on in my career that my voice was my value—I wasn't going to waste it on a worthless or unrefined idea. Instead, I've made a habit of taking notes during meetings, confirming to myself *afterward* that what I had to say was noteworthy, and only then approaching the relevant party privately with my thoughts. It's always well received, and it's gained me respect and trust in the process. When I *do* speak up in meetings, people know to listen.

Finally, remember that what makes women good communicators—and what makes good communicators *great*—is the ability to listen well. In general, women are better able to stay present in conversations: to not just hear but listen with empathy, to wait until people finish their sentences without interrupting, and to even summarize the points that have just been made to make sure they've understood. So don't just talk like a woman. Listen like a woman, too. And listen like an early 1990s woman: put away your phone.

## Collaborate Like a Woman

In most workplaces, collaboration and teamwork tend to feel forced—or, worse, like afterthoughts (if they're thought about at all). But I've learned that it's collaboration—more than creativity, efficiency, or even talent—that determines a project's or team's success. In TV, most divisions are siloed. Marketing doesn't greenlight scripts, sales doesn't have a say in casting, programming doesn't do marketing, research doesn't join us on set. Everyone sticks to the job in their job description. But at USA, I'd make everyone in leadership read the scripts, discuss casting, talk about scheduling, watch the pre- and postproduction edits, and contribute ideas to the marketing plan. That way, we had the broadest spectrum of input on every project. A win for one of us was a win for all of us.

We moved on from losses quickly rather than pointing fingers, since we were all responsible and equally invested; "not my job" and "not my fault" weren't in our vocabulary. Thanks in no small part to that collaboration, USA became the most-viewed entertainment cable channel for a record-setting thirteen consecutive years under my watch—and we grew the network's profitability by billions.

That's what it means to collaborate like a woman. Stop focusing on your needs alone and start seeing the bigger picture. Forget the idea that you alone deserve credit; if you do, you'll get it from the reputation you build as a leader. Step up your effort and send your ego to the back of the line. Get involved in other people's business—and invite them into yours.

Collaboration isn't just a cutesy corporate catchphrase—at least it shouldn't be. It's a proven tactic to get the best possible results.

## Fight Like a Woman

When it comes to fighting and conflict, men and women tend to have opposite approaches. Men bring guns to knife fights, while women bury the hatchet. By which I mean: While men are looking to win at all costs, women are looking to resolve things. As a result, even in today's politically correct culture, we associate fighting "like a girl" with fighting poorly.

But when the conflict is corporate, cultural, or even interpersonal, fighting like a woman can give you the upper hand. Even though both men and women want to come out on top, women realize that victory in a short-term battle isn't the same as winning in a long-term war. We know that compromise isn't a crime, and making up isn't the same as giving in. At work, after all, as in most parts of life, you *do* want to resolve conflicts rather than prolong them. You want to maintain friends and make allies, not create enemies or embolden rivals.

That doesn't, however, mean that every female tendency in conflict is positive. Too often, we're overly accommodating, willing to compromise our own needs or goals for someone else's wants and wishes. So don't kiss and make up if you're still pissed and fed up. Anger and hurt are infectious; if left untreated, they'll spread. Instead, work through your emotions before you promise you're over them: Take time to think, write down your feelings and what's still upsetting, talk it through with a friend, take a walk outside. And don't settle on a solution that unsettles you. Instead, figure out a Plan B or Plan C that you can live with—that will still feel like a victory to you—and aim for that.

---

### Before You Go to Battle, Make a Plan

---

- Define victory; identify two other solutions you could live with
- Understand your opponent's agenda: their goals and intentions
- Know what you'll compromise on, and know what you won't
- Ask, why am I doing this? Why is it worth it? Why do I care?

## Cry Like a Woman

Crying is a sign of weakness . . . or is it? No matter your gender, you've probably been cautioned against "crying like a girl." The truth is that there is truth to the stereotype. On average, women cry around four times more each month than men do. It's a trait that's seen as distinctly female—and entirely negative. But even and especially in our professional lives, there are upsides to tearing up.

For starters, scientists have shown that crying releases oxytocin and endorphins, which act like painkillers and help ease emotional *and* physical pain. When you get hit in the face with a baseball and can't help but bawl, you aren't being overly dramatic or emotional: That's your body's way of self-soothing. If you're hit with an unbelievably offensive or insulting comment at work—or even if you simply have a hard day—and can't hold back the tears, don't be too hard on yourself either. It turns out that we can often get over bad experiences, move on, and pick ourselves back up not because we aren't impacted or don't cry—but because we *are* and we *do*. In hindsight, crying about what happened at *Good Day!* forty years ago likely helped me process it and then put it to rest.

That's not to say crying at work is professional, and it's definitely

## Pay Attention, Then Pay It Forward

Getting that XY paycheck isn't as easy as ABC. But there are ways to determine your value, get paid what you deserve, and then—literally—share the wealth.

**PAY ATTENTION:** You can't go into a salary negotiation ignorant. So do your research beforehand. Figure out what previous people in your position were paid by your company—especially the men. If it isn't publicized anywhere, ask around. If your job is new, or you feel uncomfortable asking future coworkers about their salaries, reach out to people at rival companies and figure out what those companies pay employees with your experience.

Once you land on a number to ask for, ask for it the right way. Come equipped with a list of your qualifications and contributions to the company. Have you landed big clients? Have you launched any products or spearheaded any critical projects? Have you been doing professional development on the side—maybe a skills course or leadership training? Are there teams you manage or junior employees that you mentor? Keep track of these whenever they pop up. Maybe the person determining your pay doesn't know why you deserve it, so you better be prepared to tell them.

**PAY IT FORWARD:** As women, it's tempting to view each other as competition. After all, history has forced us to fight over the same meager slice of pie—but today, there's enough dessert for all of us. One woman's success (or salary bump) doesn't hurt the rest of us; it helps. So when you get paid, pay it forward. Share your salary with your female coworkers. Let more junior employees know what their going rate should be. If you've reached a senior level in your organization, encourage a culture of pay transparency.

not recommended by yours truly. You want to cry like a woman, not "like a girl"—which means controlling your emotions instead of letting them control you. But crying *about* work has my full endorsement. It's a physical release that allows whatever's been building up inside us to get out. Just try to save the waterworks for home, or at least your favorite bathroom stall. And then move on.

## Earn Like a Man

The one area where women need to emulate men is their paychecks. Women are still paid less than men—82 percent of what men earn, according to the Pew Research Center—and they often make less than the guys for doing the exact same job.[7] A 2022 study published in the journal *Nature Human Behavior* found that U.S. women, working basically the same jobs for the same employer, were paid roughly 14 percent less than their male counterparts.[8] For women entrepreneurs, the numbers are shocking: Women founders receive a paltry 2 percent of all the venture capital invested in the U.S.[9] So embrace the XX factor, but insist on the XY paycheck.

# THE FINAL WORD

Out of the blue, forty years after we'd worked together, an old colleague from my time in Boston, Burt Dubrow, reached out to me. During our conversation, which started on Facebook and ended up on Zoom, we caught up on each other's life. Then he mentioned how, even back then, he knew I'd find success. Why? Because, as he put it, I was always very "ladylike." At first, I was taken aback. People don't say that word anymore, I remember thinking to myself. And when they do, they don't say it as a compliment.

But here's the thing: Burt *did*. His verbiage was outdated and clumsy, but he didn't mean to imply I was ever dainty, fragile, or soft. Quite the opposite—I think he saw power in the fact that I never tried to be one of the guys. I think he saw strength in how I put the traits that made me a friend, wife, and eventually mother to work on the job. Burt called me ladylike, but he was in fact talking about my XX factor. And he's right. I've lived my entire life—and made it to the top of my industry—proudly embracing my gender. I succeeded not in spite of being a woman but because of it. This man's world be damned: If Burt wants to call me ladylike, I'll welcome it.

# 8. Talk Is Cheap / Talk Is A Valuable Currency

**What We're Told:** *"Talk is cheap."*

Almost as soon as we learn to talk, we're taught that language has limitations. Our actions speak louder than our words—or our actions simply speak for themselves. We shouldn't just talk the talk; we should walk the walk. Sticks and stones may break our bones, but words will never harm us. It's what we do that matters, not what we say. And on the surface, these catchy catchphrases make some sense. When anyone can say anything, it's easy to understand why words alone can feel weightless.

**The Truth:** *"Talk is a valuable currency."*

Deep down, I think most of us know that. After all, political campaigns are often won and lost on debates and stump speeches. The dialogue in a movie—and the chatter around its release—can make or break it at the box office. And "we need to talk" are the four scariest words in any relationship for good reason.

We understand that words carry weight. But in my experience, most of us don't understand just *how much* weight they carry. If we did, we'd treat what we say (and how we say it) with a lot more care, consideration, and concern.

For the most part, we know not to flat-out lie. Instead, we throw around compliments we don't mean—think Regina George facetiously saying "I love your skirt!" in *Mean Girls*, before calling it "the ugliest f-ing skirt I've ever seen" to someone else. We propose plans we don't intend on keeping—from casual coffee dates to cross-office catch-ups. We promise to follow up and then forget, or simply fail, to follow through. We say we understand a subject we still don't grasp. We sugarcoat the stories we tell and the suggestions we give—well-intended attempts to safeguard ourselves from criticism, to shield another person from discomfort and disappointment, to make someone or something look good or feel better.

To some extent, we're all guilty of occasional exaggeration and empty rhetoric. We might not erase the truth, but all of us have, at some point or another, likely papered over it. The problem, though, is that talk *isn't* cheap. The times we say something that isn't entirely accurate add up. Taken together, they can eventually cost us our integrity. If our word can't be trusted, neither can we. That's why, in business as in life, our word is everything.

What's more—our words can also get us (almost) anything. They really *are* a currency.

But at work, women especially often fail to capitalize on the power of our words. Perhaps most of us know how we can't and shouldn't use our voices: don't lie, don't scream, don't curse out the boss or condescend to coworkers. But many of us don't understand all the ways our voices *can* and *should* be used. I'll listen to people complain about a problem or contemplate an idea or catastrophize a worst-case scenario without them realizing that their words can provide them a way out, a way up, or a way through. Or they do—but they still find themselves struggling over what to do next.

What I tell them is this: Our voices are vehicles that can get us from point A to point B and help us cross the finish line. (If we use them recklessly or lose control over them, they can also derail us, get us into accidents, and cause us to crash and burn.) They don't just win us trust, respect, and recognition. With the right tone and tactic, they can also get us raises, promotions, and access to otherwise unreachable individuals and opportunities; they can get us upgrades at hotels and on airplanes, and dinner reservations at a fully booked restaurant; they can get us out of trouble and into someone's good graces; they can get us closer to whatever it is we want—or at least get us an answer for why we can't have it. Closed mouths don't get fed.

Forget about our actions speaking louder than our words—sometimes, the only way we'll even get the chance to act is if we first seize the chance to talk. Too often, though, we assume that the absence of yes means no. Too often, we let our fear of hearing no sabotage our chance of hearing yes. And all too often, we hint rather than ask.

That's no way to live. If we want something, we have to follow the toddler dictum: Use your words and ask for it. But it's not enough to simply say something out loud. We have to say it *right*. After all, if our words are our most valuable currency, then the way we spend them matters a great deal. For good and bad, they echo long after we leave a room. They tell whomever we're talking to a lot about our personality, priorities, even our potential; about our capabilities, concerns, cares, and creativity; about our values and our vulnerabilities. If we string them together the right way, we can increase the odds they resonate and get us the results we're looking for. If we say them with warmth, enthusiasm, energy, confidence, and clarity, we allow ourselves to truly be listened to and heard, to be engaged with and taken seriously.

But while talk is hardly cheap, there are three reasons why, occasionally, the weightiest words we can utter are none at all. First: When we overuse certain phrases—think *I'm sorry*—they lose their meaning and ability to impact; the way to retain their value is if we utter them only when necessary and genuinely felt. Second: In the heat of a fight or acting on impulse, what we say can hinder us from getting what we want and haunt us down the line—to say nothing about how it can hurt other people. Finally: Even the greatest of talkers, the ones who know how to wield words like scalpels and not hatchets, know that great talking alone is only one half of the puzzle.

After all, we can't connect with someone—our boss, our employee, the client we've had for years, or the one we're trying to land, our partner, or our kid—if we don't know what *they* want. That's why sincerely listening to, and truly hearing, what people are saying (and what they aren't) is just as important. On certain occasions, the AMC movie theater screens at the start of the show are right: Silence really *is* golden.

## MY TAKE

In their own words, this is how some TV producers have described their jobs to me: "air-traffic controller," "circus master of ceremonies," "coach of a major-league sports team," "one-person band," and "conductor of a one-hundred-piece symphony." That's because, in TV, a producer's job is almost anything and nearly everything. From conceiving segments and stories to securing experts and talent to scouting out locations to cementing logistics to scheduling and rehearsing and shooting and editing, they do it all.

In my late twenties and early thirties, I would have said *we* do it all. Those were the years I spent working as a supervising producer (and eventually the executive producer) of the morning talk show *Good Day!* But while the scope of my responsibilities was truly boundless, the entire premise of my job could have been boiled down to five words: Get them to say yes.

That's what I had to do when I was booking talent for our show, and when I was trying to get that talent to do something out of their comfort zone. It's what I had to do when I was convincing an expert to agree to an interview, or a local hospital to allow us to film inside a cramped operating room. It's what I had to do when I was persuading a team of overworked set designers to spend nights and weekends wrapping up a project. And it's what I had to do when I was looking to hire someone who already had a competitive offer from a competing network.

I had to get them to say yes, and the most powerful tool I had was my words. (In the case of booking talent for morning news, it was also the only currency I had—literally—since guests legally couldn't be paid to appear on the show.)

As a result, I developed a playbook of sorts to follow, if I needed to ask for a favor, persuade a skeptic, apologize sincerely, or even confront someone, or if I needed to talk my way into a room or out of trouble and I didn't know where to start. It wasn't about having the broadest vocabulary or the perfect grammar. It wasn't about being an unrivaled public speaker. It was about using my voice to make things happen on the show. It was about, well, producing.

What does "get them to say yes" look like in practice? In 1982, my Boston morning show team had to convince the town manager (the closest thing they had to a mayor) of Provincetown, Massachusetts, to close the main street for a week of live outdoor shows. We couldn't pay Provincetown or the shops that might lose out on business, but we talked up the exposure we offered in terms of viewers (and as the number one morning talk show in New England at the time, it was a lot), which got him to agree to our request. Then came the second part of our challenge. One of my producers had booked Peter Allen—a star musician at the time and my generation's Harry Styles—for a live, on-air performance. He had just one stipulation: He would only play on a white baby grand Steinway piano, his signature, which sold for $100,000.

In case you don't know about pianos: It's hard in general to find a white one. It's harder still to find a Steinway, no less a white Steinway. And getting to use it for free, outside, exposed to the elements? Forget about it.

But my producer said she would make it happen, and then she worked backward. She called up every piano store and supplier in New England and finally convinced one in New Hampshire to loan (and transport) the piano at no cost to us, in exchange for incredible exposure—again, that word producers often use as currency when actual currency can't be paid. "If you help us out," she said to the owner, "I'll make sure the name and phone number of your store are plastered on TV screens all across the region. This isn't just free advertising. Hell—it's the kind money can't even buy! Do you know how many moms with kids who are just starting piano lessons watch our show every morning?"

The store delivered, literally and figuratively. Peter's outdoor performance was the highlight of our week. When he was wrapping up and it started to drizzle, our entire team sprang into action and pushed the Steinway to safety. While our words had gotten us a hundred-grand baby grand for the day, I'm not quite sure they would have gotten us off the hook had we destroyed it.

Occasionally, however, the promise of exposure works against producers. It can be a deterrent, not an incentive, in which case we have to work (and talk) our way around it. Back in 2016, one of my former *Good Day!* associates and her team at CNN needed permission from the head of a children's hospital to film a twenty-seven-hour operation to separate conjoined twins attached at the brain. Oh—she also needed the parents' okay to stay in the OR the whole time and keep filming, no matter what happened. She couldn't pay, and she knew "exposure" wouldn't appeal to a family afraid for their children's lives.

But rather than hope they'd be neutral about it, the producer framed the situation as a win-win for all involved and gave everyone an incentive to participate. She promised an honest portrayal of the emotionally and medically exhausting experience that both humanized the twins and showed the heroism of the countless doctors and nurses who'd be involved. One Emmy-award-winning documentary later, that's exactly what she had delivered.

I left producing decades ago, but I've succeeded in every job since then precisely because I've kept a producer mentality. The show must go on—whether it's a Boston morning talk show, a wrestling show, a reality show, or an entire network of shows. I'm not afraid to speak my mind or ask for exceptions to arbitrary rules that don't fit. And if I can't say it in person, I will always, always, always pick up the phone and make a personal pitch with a personal touch.

As I rose up through the professional ranks, I gained lots of other tools to help me get what I wanted, including top-notch actors, writers, and set props, competitive salary offers for new hires, and, eventually, a fancy chairman title and flashy C-suite office. But I wouldn't have gotten any of that without my voice. And throughout, it's always remained the most powerful tool I have. The rest are just trimmings.

My voice—knowing where, when, and how to use it—isn't just a professional asset. It's served me off the clock, too. Years ago on a family vacation, when we were given a dinky old sedan instead of the SUV we'd reserved and paid for, my husband Dale insisted we could squeeze in and make it work. He said the car didn't matter. I said it certainly did; more than comfort, we had a long ride ahead of us on snowy, curved roads with lots of bulky luggage and ski equipment, and we'd barely be able to fit it all (or see out the back). To him, the word no is a cease-and-desist letter. To me, it's simply an obstacle to overcome. You can probably guess what happened next.

A short while later, as we pulled away from the parking lot in an even better SUV than the one we'd paid for, our then-ten-year-old son, Jesse, asked Dale, "Does Mom *always* have to get what she wants?" The answer, of course, is no. But I will *always* try.

These days, I may not need to convince the famous hairdresser Vidal Sassoon to milk a cow at the Topsfield County Fair on live TV. But when I need tickets to a sold-out premiere, a meeting with a writer who insists he doesn't have the time, or a doctor's appointment this week—not in three months—I speak up and try to change the story. When I need to apologize to a family member or have a difficult conversation with a friend, I remember that what I say and how I say it matter.

As a producer, I learned how to know what to ask for, and how to phrase those asks; how to read faces and speak to whatever was on someone's mind; how to use kindness, vulnerability, and even snark to my advantage. I learned how to smile and engender compassion to get what I wanted, and I even learned how to hold my tongue. I didn't just learn how to talk—I learned how to master my voice and make life happen.

## NAIL IT

Working in television taught me that talking was less an abstract art and more a science you could study. I also saw that this supposedly universal skill wasn't universal at all. But as a producer, I picked up on verbal tools, tactics, turns of phrase, and even tone-of-voice choices that everyone could use and benefit from every day. Choices that help our ideas resonate—and help us get what we want—empower us to be the producers of our own lives. If our words are our most valuable currency, this is how to spend them and make them count.

So . . .

### Don't Inflate the Truth

If your voice is a currency, it loses value each time you aren't honest. This goes for the big lies, of course. Getting caught in one of these is a surefire way to get fired (or broken up with). But it also goes for the small stuff: the truths you omit, the details you gloss over or exaggerate. And it goes not just for the words you speak but for the ones you write.

People at all levels have pretty sophisticated bullshit meters. And even the littlest white lies can lead to a great big bite in the ass. So don't write that you have working proficiency in Finnish (like novelist Sophie Kinsella's character Becky Bloomwood in *Shopaholic*) on your resume if you dropped the language in the middle of the first semester. Don't overstate your role on a project during an interview if your supposed supervisor, when contacted, wouldn't remember your name. Definitely don't tell your boss you're almost done with a presentation if you need another week. Better to keep a timeline tentative than agree to a deadline and then miss it entirely. Once your trust is tarnished and someone's confidence in you is compromised, it's hard to earn them back. Your words become worthless. If you don't have that, you have nothing.

## Buy Yourself Time

As children, we say "I don't know" all the time. As adults, we still feel that way. (Trust me, I still feel uncertain about something every day.) But at some point on the path to growing up, we forget that it's okay to admit we're stuck or unsure, or that we need to keep thinking about or understanding something to feel confident in what we say or do next. When that happens in conversations, we often find ourselves trying—and failing—to talk our way through the problem.

## Clean Up Your Verbal Bread Crumbs

Cleaning up the verbal bread crumbs we drop casually—our seemingly insignificant small talk—is critical. If we offer to facilitate a connection for someone, read over their resume, or send them a book recommendation, we better follow up. If we say we'd love to grab a drink with someone, we better initiate plans—even if we wouldn't love to at all. Especially today, with portable computers, planners, calendars, alarms, notepads in our pockets, forgetting is a lame and lazy excuse. While I almost never recommend using your phone in the middle of a conversation, this is my one exception. Whip it out, open your drafts folder, and write down whatever it is you said you'd do. (Feel free to say, "I'm writing this down, so I don't forget.") And then—when you get home, when you wake up in the morning, when you finally figure out your schedule or the answer—do the damn thing.

That's no solution—and at work, it might create a massive problem. So get comfortable with saying "I'm going to need more time to confirm," "I don't have all the facts in front of me just yet," or even something as simple as "I'd like to think this through before responding." On the job, phrases like this won't hold you back. They help you get ahead, because they show vulnerability, honesty, thoroughness, and drive—admirable assets for any employee of any level. That said, be sure to follow up and follow through.

## Put a Premium on Kindness

When the sun is shining on your face, a promotion falls into your lap, and a winning lottery ticket finds its way to your pocket—all on the same day—kindness is easy. When you get caught in the rain right after you've been fired and then come home to find that the power is out, kindness is a little more difficult to embrace. But when the world feels stacked against you and there's one person standing (or sitting) between you and whatever it is you want or need—a customer service representative, perhaps, or even a colleague—treat them like the solution, not the problem. A good rule to follow: The more frustrated and fed up you are, the more understanding, empathetic, and amenable you should be.

It may seem counterintuitive, and it will often require you to bite your tongue. But if your flight's been canceled, your airline app keeps crashing, you've lost all patience, and you're waiting in line with fifty other people who are equally peeved, try treating the agent at the gate like a victim of the situation rather than a villain who must be vanquished. If you approach them with an observation about how shitty their day has probably been—rather than a tirade about how terrible yours is going—a seat on the next flight is far more likely to magically become available for you. (An upgrade might appear out of thin air, too.) Debbie Cohen Kosofsky, who worked with me in Boston and is now a senior producer for NBC's *Today* show, helped teach me the value of a kind, empathetic word and a genuine smile, which are almost always the best routes to "yes." After all, the surest way to get someone to help you is to get them to *want* to help you—if they feel like it's their choice, and not a demand made of them. So empower them to give you a hand by being likable, vulnerable, and even sympathetic.

The logic is surprisingly simple for how rarely it's employed, disarming the person you're talking to and distinguishing yourself from the rest of the angry mob who wants the same thing you do. You're not shooting the messenger—you're killing them with kindness and capturing what you want.

## A Crash Course in Compassionate Conversation . . . and What Not to Do

THE RIGHT APPROACH

SEAT SEEKER: Hi. Bad day, huh? Bet you can't wait to get home.

*sympathy line*

AGENT: It's been a long day.

*flattery tactic*

SEAT SEEKER: I love your earrings, by the way. Did you get them in Santa Fe?

AGENT: I did, it's one of my favorite pairs. How'd you know?

*personal touch*

SEAT SEEKER: My mom actually lives there and just came to visit. She brought me a pin just like them.

AGENT: Anyway, what can I do for you?

**SEAT SEEKER:** I'm afraid I've got a typical problem, and I know how busy you are, so if you can't help me, I'll understand. I missed my flight this *— sob story* morning. I'd love to blame it on my eight-year-old who missed the bus, but I can't. *humility* It's my fault. This is the last flight today, and although I'm on standby, it's crucial that I get to Denver tonight for work. I would really appreciate your help. If anything opens, please keep me in mind.

**AGENT:** It looks full, but I'll see what I can do.

**SEAT SEEKER:** I'll stay out of your way. I'll be sitting over there in the blue chairs and will wait for whatever update you have. Thanks so much. *— the clincher*

**FOLLOW UP:** Ms. Seat Seeker sits neaby, always visible to the agent. She doesn't bother her and, indeed, gets a seat on board.

**MORAL OF THE STORY:** A little bit of understanding, humility, and patience goes a long way.

*Compare this to the wrong approach on the next page*

THE WRONG APPROACH

*obnoxious opener*

**SEAT SEEKER:** I'm having <u>the worst day ever.</u> You need to get me on this plane.

*a demand, not a question*

**AGENT:** I'm sorry, but the flight is sold out.

*false assumption*

**SEAT SEEKER:** That's ridiculous! We both know this airline overbooks flights. There must be something you can do. I'm a frequent flier!

*attempt to intimidate*

**AGENT:** Look, the flight is fully booked. An algorithm system assigns the standby seats and that is out of my control.

*insult to injury... you blew it*

**SEAT SEEKER:** I don't believe you. This is terrible customer service, and I will be telling everyone I know to never fly this airline again. Who's your supervisor?

**FOLLOW UP:** Ms. Seat Seeker did not get on board.

**MORAL OF THE STORY:** Arrogance never pays off. Even if the agent *could* do something more, the traveler has given her no reason to want to help her.

## Assess Your Options

The most common piece of advice I dole out, at work and in life, is this: *Just ask.* And if I had a dime for every time I was met with a dumbstruck expression in return, I'd be swimming in a pool full of dollars. There are so many ways our voices can serve us, and so many women don't know the half of it. In my experience, what holds too many of us back isn't just our fear of asking tough questions but our ignorance about the essential questions we can and should be asking.

If you feel stuck, stonewalled, siloed, suspicious, or sad, try asking yourself these questions: If I could have anything in the world right now, what would I want? What is blocking me from getting it? Who are the people in power who can help me get past that barrier? Have all of them said no already? Have any of them said no already? Have I not even asked yet? If I have, did I make the best case? If I didn't make the best case, can I follow up and try again? And if this door really is closed, is there a window I can crawl through?

## Joke . . . at Your Own Expense

Humor, sarcasm, and wit walk into a bar. Snarks fly.

Bad joke, I know. But not a bad way to communicate. In fact, humor is incredibly effective when it comes to making a point and leaving a lasting impression. It can help you tackle an uncomfortable subject or defuse tension in an uncomfortable situation. It distinguishes you and gives you personality. It keeps people engaged with what you're saying—and makes whatever you're saying more memorable long after. And though we think of the class clown as stupid, using humor actually makes you seem smart—which tracks, considering that funny people on average have higher IQs.[1] Research out of Harvard and Wharton suggests that using humor can even help you at work, by making you seem more competent and confident than you truly are.[2]

So joke on the job—during conversations with colleagues,

company-wide presentations, even performance reviews—with one caveat: Unless you work as a comedian and you're tasked with roasting someone for a Comedy Central special, joke at your own expense. Punching down is cruel. Punching up is foolish. Punching yourself in the face, though—that can be funny.

What's more, it shows that you don't take yourself too seriously and that you can ditch the formalities and have a little fun. On the job, *that* is a real distinguishing characteristic. *That* is what makes you seem relatable, vulnerable, open, and humble—exactly the kind of person other people want to be around. Again, unless you're an *SNL* cast member, you don't need slapstick humor or a perfected standup routine to succeed at work. Simply loosen up, and you'll lighten up a room while lifting yourself up in the eyes of others.

Some examples:

- Upon receiving a bottle of wine from a colleague, I wrote him a thank-you note telling him our friendship was bad for my sobriety.

- Every deck or presentation I've ever made for work has started off with a homemade, bastardized cartoon (adorned with cutouts of colleagues' faces) to defuse the tension in the room and help everyone—including and especially my boss—relax.

- My goals for the new year, term, or quarter are always laid out as colorful acrostics.

- I'm known to send work emails in Comic Sans typeface; make fun of me if you'd like, but when I'm delivering a strong message or news, it takes the edge off. No one can get *too* offended or hurt by something they read in Comic Sans.

## Check Yourself

As a woman at work, talking can feel like walking into a verbal trap. So much of how we've learned to use our voices when we were younger is looked down on by society—and gets judged as stupidity, self-flagellation, or lack of sophistication. The truth is much more complicated.

When we turn the ends of our sentences upward like we're asking a question, research shows we're subconsciously trying to project humility, discourage interruption, hold the floor, and seek reassurance. When we do the opposite and fry the ends of our sentences, turning them downward and letting them taper off, we may be engaging in unconscious attempts to deepen the pitch and alter the intonation of our voices. Both options—upspeak *and* vocal fry—work against us.

There are some other tics that women tend to employ. We use "likes" and "ums" as filler words in our speech to give us more time to space out our thoughts. We interrupt ourselves with "Do you see what I'm saying?" We pepper our emails, even the professional ones, with exclamation points and smiley faces—attempts to exude exuberance and soften the landing of any negative news or feedback we're delivering. We say sorry even when we aren't—it's a female addiction—and ask permission to ask questions, because we've been taught to be polite above all, shy away from asserting ourselves, and subconsciously doubt our actions even as we're performing them. Sometimes, we even say "Sorry, can I ask you a question?"—that double whammy of a verbal boomerang that flies back and hits every speaker of those seven words in the face.

You don't need me to tell you that the standards women are held to are unfair. But I'm also not going to lie and tell you they don't matter—because the truth is, they do. So, especially in a work setting, check yourself. Read your emails a few times before sending and backspace the unnecessary words or punctuation. If you have a big presentation to give, practice in the mirror or record yourself, with a focus on keeping the end of each sentence level with the rest of it. And talk extra slowly if it means you can better filter out the fillers.

I don't claim it's easy. Often, hardwired habits we don't even know we have are hardest to quit. The good news is that you don't need to do it alone. Today, anyone can use Google, YouTube, or even MasterClass to sharpen their presentation, communication, and delivery skills. If you're a mid-level executive or senior leader and you have a big conference or event coming up, see if your organization will invest in a communication coach or speech trainer for you. (If they say no, consider investing in one yourself.) Trust me, from politics and media to sports and corporate America, everyone who reaches a certain level hires a little outside help—including me. It works, and the payoff is well worth it.

## Don't Hedge Your Words

Open your eyes and ears and you'll notice that hedges are everywhere—especially when women are present. We use qualifying words and phrases like *just, sort of, kind of, you know, I mean, possibly, I think, you might, I could be wrong,* and *I feel like* to be polite and leave room for the possibility that we're wrong—or even that someone may

## The Subtle Art of Saying I'm Sorry

What's the best way to say "I'm sorry"? It depends. Did you do something wrong? If not, skip this section and don't say a word. It's the twenty-first century, after all—long past time for women to stop over-apologizing. But if you've done something wrong and you've hurt someone in the process, if your "I'm sorry" is a synonym for "I messed up big-time," then saying sorry isn't just a nice idea. It's nonnegotiable. But that doesn't mean any old apology will do. Here's a checklist to follow:

- Own what you've done wrong and the way it made the other person feel.
- Cut the "but." It's just another way to package excuses. And if you're using excuses, you aren't very sorry.
- Describe how you've learned from the incident and the efforts you're making to not repeat it.
- Don't vow to never do it again—vow to *try* to never do it again.
- Personalize and humanize the apology. Make it clear that you know and appreciate the person.
- Do it in a timely manner.
- Don't make it transactional or offer it at a time when you're asking for something in return.
- Don't go in with expectations of how the other person should respond.

simply disagree. Men, meanwhile, avoid these words and phrases because they're less inclined to convey uncertainty.

In this case, the ayes—er, guys—have it. While cockiness isn't the goal, confidence is, and hedging often undermines what we're saying before we even finish saying it. Worse, it often leads to us hinting at what we feel or want, which can get misinterpreted and misunderstood. Say what you mean and mean what you say. Trim your verbal hedges.

## Bonnie's Dictionary

**yes** ('yes), *adv.* Always means yes. Take it. And then stop talking.

**no** ('nō), *adv.* Often means not right now. Use the rejection as a challenge to get to YES.

**Ask yourself: What does this NO really mean? Not here? Not now? Not you? Not me?**

**but** ('bət), *con.* Amnesia. The second it's said, people don't remember or care about anything else that came before.

**sorry** ('sär-ē), *adj.* For genuine and necessary apologies only.

**Can I ask you a question?** ('kan 'ī 'äsk 'yü 'ā 'kwes-chən), *phrase.* You just did.

**hope** ('hōp), *v.* A passive verb, not a professional one. Save it for your fairy godmother. If you want something, ask for it explicitly. Don't hope that someone might come and save the day.

## Pay Attention

There's a reason why so many politicians and corporate executives start their tenures with listening tours—informal meetings or town halls with voters and employees who are empowered to speak their minds and share their ideas: The best leaders are the best listeners.

When leaders listen to the questions, concerns, and cares of others before leaping to action, they're less likely to do something that pisses off a whole bunch of people, and more likely to holistically understand an issue and make decisions that make people happy. At a minimum, good leaders make people feel seen and heard—which can minimize the damage or fallout from a decision they make that people don't support.

But just like talking, listening is a skill—and it doesn't come naturally to everyone. Fortunately, it *can* be learned. Here's the first and most fundamental rule: Pay attention. Put the phone away. Make eye contact. Follow what the other person is saying—not your own inner monologue—and then ask thoughtful, related follow-ups. If the occasion is right, ask questions about their jobs, families, and lives. If you have the opportunity, do your homework before entering the conversation; whether you're speaking to a crowded room or to an audience of one, equip yourself with a basic understanding of who they are and what they care about. Above all, be clear that there are no consequences for honesty—even and especially if it's coming from someone you report to (or supervise). You want to hear the truth. It might hurt in the short term, but it will only help you down the line.

### Ring 'Em Up

In our digital-first world, we're not just six degrees of separation away from anyone—we're one *click* away from *anything*. But in this age of apps, emails, and texting, we forget one simple thing about the devices we carry around (and freak out about if we forget anywhere): They were made for calls.

A lot of people today seem to think that function is outdated— ironic given that when telephones were first invented, a lot of people found them unnecessary since the telegraph could already send messages to people over long distances. In fact, Western Union (which had a monopoly on the telegraph industry at the time) declined to buy Alexander Graham Bell's patents for the telephone for that exact reason. Who, they wondered, cared about voice?

Well, I'm with Bell, then and now. It's easy to book a restaurant reservation online, and it's fine to Google "best shrinks currently taking new patients in Boston." But when you need a favor, an exception, or a special accommodation, remember that clicks will never convey your character or your need properly. And even the best-written words—when typed onto a screen or printed in black-and-white—can't capture emotion the way your voice will.

In our age of hybrid work, consider becoming a hybrid communicator. Use the apps like OpenTable when they work. Send the text when you're in a rush. But when you have the time, and the restaurant looks fully booked from the limited lens that your screen provides, pick up the phone and use your voice to ask for what you want—kindly—in a way that empowers them to say yes.

### Give Credit and Thanks

You should keep a close lid on criticism, but if you're doling out credit for a job well done, you should shout it from the rooftops.

The same goes for gratitude. When it comes to "thank you," it's hard to say it enough. It may seem obvious, but "great job" and "I'm so grateful" are never said enough, especially at work. That's because people tend to believe it's unnecessary to acknowledge or appreciate when someone does something that is more or less part of their job description. But if they do it well or go above and beyond, don't keep your feelings to yourself. Make them known and make them personal rather than generic. Say what the person did that stuck out to you, or how they went above and beyond. Not only is it the right thing to do but it's also strategic. After all, a person is more likely to help you the next time if you made them feel good about helping you the last time. You're also setting the tone for your organization's culture—and a precedent that will likely be repeated, perhaps to your advantage.

## Save It for Later

There are few things I regret more in life than not holding my tongue when I should have. In family board game competitions or corporate board meetings, I've been guilty of speaking before thinking about the consequences of what I was about to say. If you're like me—and if you're human, you probably are—the good news is that there are ways to control for chaos and tricks to help us hold our tongues.

So before saying something you might regret, slow down, take a deep breath, count to ten, and then ask yourself:

- Will it lower the temperature, or will it raise it?

- Will it waste people's time, or is it a good way to spend it?

- Will it derail the conversation, or will it get you back on track?

- Will it cause confusion or misunderstanding, or will it clear things up?

- Will it hurt someone, or will it help them heal?

- Will it start a fight, or will it resolve one?

Answer these questions, and you'll have your answer. It's never a bad idea to wait a little before saying something that might impact your life a lot. And if you're giving someone critical feedback, delivering bad news, or even asking a question that might be somewhat embarrassing—and you know it has to be done—remember: It should never happen in public. Do it privately, in an office or out for a cup of coffee, when you can talk alone.

## Don't Devalue Yourself

Women can be our own worst enemies and harshest critics. Alone and in the company of others, we pick out our flaws and put ourselves down for sport. We say things about our bodies, minds, and ideas that we would *never* say about another person's—that we aren't good enough, smart enough, pretty enough. But devaluing ourselves is dangerous: It distorts reality, diverts our attention from what really matters, and even discourages us from believing we can do better. It creates false limitations and causes needless conformity. It kills our confidence and feeds into failure.

Even if we never say the words out loud, thinking them is enough to make them real. Our inner thoughts don't stay inside forever— they manifest in what we do, and they help determine whether we succeed or self-sabotage. Silence your inner critic and get the voice inside your head on your side.

Years ago, when I was president of USA and SYFY, I had to take the elevator from my office on the twenty-first floor of 30 Rock up to the C-suite on the fifty-second floor for monthly meetings with my boss. Walking into the elevator, I didn't always feel my greatest, because I didn't always have great news to share. (Sometimes it was a show launching to soft ratings or receiving a crappy review from a critic. Other times, a problem with a cast member was slowing down production. Maybe we'd gone over budget for a series, or we hadn't made our budget for the quarter.) But I'd use the ride up to quiet my nerves, review my team's victories and achievements since our last meeting (because it's often easier for women to brag about others than ourselves), find a way to be honest and optimistic about everything else, and then exit the elevator with confidence and a smile.

What we think influences what we say, what we say influences what we do, and what we do influences who we are. If we want the world to open up to us, we have to think the world of ourselves and act like we deserve it first.

## Remember: There Are Always Receipts

Apologies to all the hermits out there, but in the twenty-first century, there's no such thing as privacy. At least that's what you should be thinking each time you open your mouth or put pen to paper (or, especially, finger to keyboard or phone screen). I've seen careers destroyed, relationships ruined, and lives upended all because someone said something and someone else who wasn't supposed to find out—or find it—did.

I don't care if you swear you've locked your X (formerly Twitter) account; the internet, along with everything you ever have and ever will put on it, lives forever. That confidential conversation you're having in a coffee shop? I've worked on enough TV dramas to tell you there are fifty-plus ways someone might be listening. You only meant to send that work email dumping on your boss to one colleague? Too late—you hit Reply All. Even if you didn't, your company server has a copy.

Am I being dramatic? Perhaps—but today everything is traceable and discoverable. When it feels like we're all one misstep, misspeak, or mistake away from being canceled, it's not a bad idea to live by this law: If you wouldn't scream it in public, perhaps you don't want to say it in private, either. You never know who will keep the receipts.

## THE FINAL WORD

There's a boundless upside to using your voice well. But when we use our words poorly or fail to use them at all, there's a high price to pay. That miscalculation or miscommunication can cost us precious time, once-in-a-lifetime opportunities, the trust of others, and the belief in ourselves that we need to succeed. It can cost us compensation, connections, and companionship. It can cost us our jobs and even our relationships.

Forget about putting your money where your mouth is. Simply put your mouth to use and watch as the money (and everything else) follows.

# 9. Good Things Come To Those Who Wait / Great Things Come To Those Who Act

**What We're Told:** *"Good things come to those who wait."*

Like a warm fire on a cold winter night, this phrase is a comfort when we need it most. When we're in a tough spot, up against some challenge, watching the people around move forward while we worry that we're falling behind, it's reassuring to think that everything will work itself out if we just sit back and relax. If patience is a virtue, then we don't have to be proactive. If good things come to those who wait, then we have permission to do nothing.

And who doesn't want to believe that life is like a board game, where everyone eventually gets a turn?

**The Truth:** *"Great things come to those who act."*

If good things come to those who wait, then great things come to those who don't. There's nothing stopping us from trudging along with everyone else. But if we want to distinguish ourselves, move faster, and go further, what we need isn't patience but chutzpah.

A Yiddish word with no direct translation in English, chutzpah roughly means "supreme self-confidence." One of my favorite defi-nitions adds a key qualifier: "Chutzpah is the confidence or courage that allows a person to do or say things that may seem shocking to others. It's having the nerve (or lacking the self-censorship) to sug-gest something, to opine on something, to ask about something, to go for something, to try and make something happen—or prevent some-thing from happening—rather than waiting around until it does."

In some circles, chutzpah gets a bad rap. There's often a gen-dered element to it: Chutzpah has become almost expected of men, a positive sign of being an ambitious and innovative go-getter. When associated with women, the word often carries a negative implication of arrogance or aggression.

Like carbs, cholesterol, and crazy, there are two kinds of chutzpah—good and bad. We want the good kind of chutzpah. We want to be audacious, not annoying. Bold, not brash or brazen. Self-assured, not self-entitled. Confident, not cocky. Impressive, not insolent. Refreshing, not rude. Direct, but never disrespectful. We want the chutzpah that wins people over—not the kind that turns people off. We want the chutzpah that gets us drinks on the house—not the kind that gets them thrown in our faces.

Good chutzpah, or what I call *goodtzpah*, is the only kind of chutz-pah worth having. It's not about feeling entitled to something better; it's about putting in the effort to get it. So, for our purposes, *goodtz-pah* is the only kind of chutzpah there is.

The word has roots in the Jewish tradition, and as far back as the biblical days of Moses in the Old Testament, it was considered an attribute to laud and applaud. While believers and nonbelievers alike often assume that religion demands absolute, unquestioning obedience to God, the late Rabbi Harold Schulweis explained things differently. He said it was actually the willingness to be contrarian and stubborn, the refusal to simply accept a decree or proposition on its face and instead push for a more desirable outcome, that made Moses a great leader. When he thought something was unfair, or if he had another idea, Moses would engage in fierce debates with God—and Moses's chutzpah often got God to change course.

So it's worth having some faith in chutzpah. But chutzpah transcends any personal faith. Call it moxie, courage, or conviction—all of us should have some of it, especially at work. While waiting our turn, knowing our place, playing it safe, doing what we're told, and following the rules probably won't get us in trouble, they usually don't get us ahead, either. It's hard to rise above the rest when we're intentionally putting our heads down. It's hard to stand out from the crowd when everything we're doing makes us blend in. If we want to achieve what others aren't, we have to act how others won't. That's chutzpah.

Chutzpah can give us the courage to voice a dissenting opinion rather than bury it—and thereby prevent a problem from occurring in the first place. It can give people the resilience to view rejection as nothing more than a pit stop on the road to success—and then buckle up and keep driving. It can drive someone to share an idea or give unsolicited feedback about a new product to their CEO in the elevator—and gain their respect, and maybe a promotion, in the process. It's what distinguishes those who see barriers to entry everywhere from those who understand that even corner office doors open for a reason. Chutzpah is the ingenuity and courage to find the right door to knock on. Chutzpah is saying or doing something others would shy away from—but saying or doing it with exactly the right words, tone of voice, and approach. If it won God over, it can work on our boss, the client we're trying to land, or a customer service representative who's having a bad day.

In practice, chutzpah can be difficult to harness. What looks ballsy to one person may look plain dick-ish to another. What we see as stepping up to the plate, someone else may see as overstepping. What we think is moxie, someone else might consider meddling. But with the right mindset, the right motivation pushing us forward, and the right parameters to follow, we can ensure our chutzpah comes across as thoughtful, not thoughtless; results-oriented, not performative; appropriate, not gratuitous; earned, not entitled; appreciated, not offensive. If we do all that, then chutzpah isn't just *an* asset. It's *the* most valuable one we've got.

Too many people live their lives and spend their careers waiting around for a permission slip that may never come. On the job and off, being patient often means being complacent, which is a vice, not a virtue. If we sit around, stay quiet, and hope something good comes our way, we'll often go nowhere.

If we want to go the extra mile, we have to get up, step (and maybe speak) up, and actually *go the extra mile*. We have to have some chutzpah.

## MY TAKE

Chutzpah is often defined as an attribute or a character trait—but to me, it's an action, an attitude, a mindset anyone can inhabit, and a set of behaviors that can set the tone for everything else.

I first learned about chutzpah from my father, a quiet, plainspoken, hardworking immigrant from Ukraine who didn't really embody it himself. What he had was mettle, a steely belief that there was no such word as "can't." "The only reason you *can't* do something," he'd say to me, "is because you aren't trying hard enough." He didn't cross lines, but he didn't toe them, either. Where my dad would put his head down and try to find a workaround, though, I've never hesitated to ask for one. While many people conflate conversation with confrontation, I never have—to me, the words that most people treat as the end of a discussion ("No," "You can't," "I can't," "I'm sorry but," "There's no way," among countless others) are simply the start of another conversation. At the very least, they're not lethal. Chutzpah has powered my career by empowering me to do a lot of things that others wouldn't even think of in the first place, starting at the very beginning when I applied to graduate school, which ultimately led me to work at WGBH.

When I decided to go to graduate school, I had two significant problems: I had missed the application deadline, and I didn't have enough money to cover tuition. The Boston University admissions office said it was too late. Acceptances had already been sent out, and there was nothing they could do. Apply next fall, they told me. But I didn't want to wait another year, so I decided to go straight to the person in charge of the entire university, President John Silber. I found his number on a form and cold-called him. Incredibly, he took the call and said if I could be at his office in half an hour, he would spare me a few minutes. I started our meeting by thanking him and asking him for his advice, given my situation. I was honest about having missed the deadline and even about why my request was outlandish. But while I was up-front about my goal, I never backed President Silber into a corner. Instead, I offered multiple ideas for how the school might work with me: allow me to enroll if another student withdrew, or start in a different program and then transfer, or begin my studies midyear. I also talked about why I wanted to complete this program and why I only wanted to study at BU, including how important my undergraduate years had been.

Most importantly, however, I was humble—I didn't act entitled to

President Silber's time, or to an exception to the rules, or to admission to the graduate program of my choice. I knew I wasn't owed anything by anyone. Except, I did owe it to myself to try. President Silber said he would consider my application—requiring transcripts, letters of recommendations, and essays—if I got all of it to him, completed, by Friday at 4:00 p.m.—only four days away. I did, and I was admitted to BU's master's program in media and new technology, with a work-study job on campus to help pay my tuition. And all because I had the chutzpah to go for it rather than wait around.

A few years later at WGBH, when *Infinity Factory* wrapped for the season, I applied for a production assistant role at another children's show called *Zoom*. A program for children who were aging out of *Sesame Street*, *Zoom* was almost iconic for decades—a show that was for kids and by kids, when most of the children's shows that preceded it (like the lovable *Mister Rogers' Neighborhood*) starred adults.

I had one interview, then a second, and thought they went pretty well. When I learned that the job had been offered to someone else, I was bummed but understanding—until I heard through the grapevine that WGBH had always planned to hire an internal candidate, and an outsider like me never stood a chance.

There's politics to hiring internal candidates—it's subject to legal or at least corporate requirements to publicize the job, open applications, and conduct multiple interviews in the name of, ironically enough, "fairness." Apparently, that's exactly what had happened. But at the time, I didn't know it. I just thought the whole process was unfair, unprofessional, and rather insulting. So—against the advice of nearly everyone in my life—I wrote a note to Henry Becton, the station's head of programming at the time.

Most of the note was gracious. I thanked him again for the opportunity I'd had to interview for the job and wrote about how impressed I was with *Zoom*. Still, I couldn't help but end with a question. If the show and network already knew who they were hiring, I asked, why involve me? I ended with the truth: I'd been excited about the possibility of joining *Zoom*, which was why I was so disappointed and disheartened to learn it had never been a possibility at all.

In the world of Boston TV and public broadcasting, Henry Becton was a big deal. And a letter like mine, to him, could have burned future bridges for me and made finding any job in the industry even harder than it was already proving to be. When I didn't hear back, I figured I'd made my bed and now had to sleep in it.

But two months later, Henry Becton called me up out of the blue and offered me a different job on *Zoom* as a postproduction supervisor—a slightly more senior position than the one I'd originally gone for and didn't get. He said he appreciated my directness and the nerve it likely took to write the letter, much less send it. He said it earned me his respect. He said that, if nothing else, he now knew I was a straight-shooter who wasn't easily afraid—a job requirement for the fast-paced world of TV—and he wanted to give me a shot.

As anyone well versed in the art of chutzpah knows, you can say almost anything if you say it the right way. You don't have to tell people what they want to hear. You just have to tell it to them in a way they'll be willing to hear it: with respect, humor, and sincerity.

In 1978, I was still at WGBH and assigned to work temporarily with Russ Morash, one of the fathers of how-to programming—he helped introduce the world to Julia Child. He was already a legend by the time I met him. I was tasked with helping him edit a TV pilot featuring an interior design columnist for the *Boston Globe*. The show's premise was simple enough: The columnist would tour stately homes in the Boston area and talk to the owners who'd restored them.

But while watching the raw footage from the pilot episode, shot inside a Victorian Italianate house in Newton, I felt that something was askew. The *Globe* writer was okay as a host. But the real star, I said to Russ, was the Cuban American homeowner (with great facial hair) who'd done the renovation and given her the house tour. He's the one who had *amazing* on-screen presence. And he's the one who should have his own show.

Russ had not asked for my opinion (though perhaps he would have come to the same conclusion himself). And by most people's estimations, I probably had no right to give it. I was twenty-eight and had been working on that pilot for just a few weeks; to date, kids were the only audience I had experience programming for.

It was chutzpah that prompted me to share my perspective anyway. It could have gotten me in trouble for speaking out of turn, or simply laughed off the job. But I delivered my opinion respectfully and humbly—stating it as *my* opinion, and not as a universal fact—and it was taken sincerely. That house tour pilot never aired, and instead the show evolved into a home improvement series called *This Old House* that is still on the air today. I was hired as an associate producer. And the host we went with? None other than the owner of that Victorian Italianate house, Bob Vila.

Tied into the misconceptions people have about chutzpah is the belief that it's taboo—offensive, even—to voice a differing viewpoint. Or they're afraid of conflict and think a conversation that isn't totally compatible will lead to chaos. As a result, respectful disagreement, or just respectfully piping up, has become a dying art. But most people appreciate being pushed to consider something they hadn't already thought of. Staying quiet when we have something real to communicate, something we really feel or believe, serves no one.

And chutzpah serves us—in more ways than one. If we always wait for opportunities to come to us or wait to be asked our opinion before sharing it, we can languish. We don't feel empowered to act or speak up because we haven't experienced it making a difference . . . which makes us less likely to do it in the future.

As I rose in my career, I never lost my chutzpah. Twenty-plus years after I told Russ Morash that his host wasn't right, I had a similar conversation about the actress who had been cast as the lead for a new Sci-Fi Channel miniseries—only this time, my conversation was with *the* Steven Spielberg. (Let me let you in on a little industry secret. No matter how important you get, he will always be *the* Steven Spielberg.)

Against all conventional wisdom (and many industry naysayers), the network I was running had decided to spend a whopping $40 million on a limited-run, ten-episode show called *Taken*—a brainchild of the legendary movie director and producer who rarely dabbled in television. Before shooting began, I ruffled feathers by insisting the writing wasn't strong enough and the script needed punching up. But that was small potatoes compared to what I said *after* watching a cut of the first episode: The lead actress in the alien abduction series wasn't strong enough, either. Saying that when millions of dollars have already been spent on filming is audacious. Saying that to Steven Spielberg—well, that's chutzpah.

But I made my case, he listened, and eventually he agreed to swap out our lead for the actress I recommended instead: a ten-year-old named Dakota Fanning. To this day, she's one of the most prodigious on-screen talents I've ever worked with, requiring far fewer takes to nail a scene—and knock it out of the park—than the older, more experienced actors around her. On the strength of her performance in *Taken*, the Sci-Fi Channel spent two straight weeks as the top cable network and took home our first major Emmy.

I've seen what chutzpah can do (and has done) in my own life—which is probably why I gravitate to it so strongly in others, and why I've seized the opportunity to work with go-getters. I don't just encourage my team to use their voices; with brainstorming sessions, planning meetings, and a collaborative culture in which everyone is expected to contribute, I demand it. And I have very little tolerance for even the smartest wallflowers who wait and watch as others act.

The way I see it, chutzpah is the ability—and desire—to find a way forward where others may see roadblocks or even make a U-turn. It's the willingness to speak up when staying quiet might be easier. It's the fearlessness and confidence that made me an asset to the teams I've been part of, and that I've sought out above all else for every team I've ever built.

## The Time Chutzpah Worked on Me

Dawn Olmstead used chutzpah on me and won. When I started UCP, a cable production studio where we could create and produce our own original programming in-house, Dawn was a very successful long-time show producer, but she had no studio experience. She talked her way into me hiring her. Her pitch was: "I don't know if I want to do this job, but let's talk about it." Then, she proceeded to ask questions that made me curious and want her more. She was also ballsy enough to say, "Look, why don't we try it? If in eighteen months, I don't work out, I'm gone, no issues there. Or if I decide that I don't want to be here, then I have the option to leave as well . . . But I think this could be a marriage made in heaven." It was, and she (and her home-grown chutzpah) stayed to successfully run the studio, ultimately becoming the president of UCP.

## NAIL IT

Not everyone is born with chutzpah, and that's okay. The attribute can be developed and cultivated, even in those to whom it doesn't come naturally. If the Chinese philosopher Lao-Tzu was right when he supposedly said that our words become our actions, and our actions become our habits, and our habits become our character—and I believe he was—then the first step to having more chutzpah is to start acting with more chutzpah. While there isn't much academic literature explaining exactly what that looks like, there *is* a whole lot of life to draw from (and a fun mnemonic to reference, too).

So . . .

### Count Yourself In

Too many people live life following an operating principle they aren't even aware of: When in doubt, they count themselves out. Unsure if they can achieve something, they don't go for it. Unsure if someone will say yes, they don't ask. Unsure if their opinions will be well-received, they don't share them.

So the first step to cultivating chutzpah requires a mindset shift: Count yourself in, even if you might not win. Notice when you're holding yourself back—when you're being agreeable for the sake of being agreeable, when you're sugarcoating your views and censoring your thoughts, when you're not going for something that you desperately want—and ask yourself why. Is it because you're truly out of line? Or, scared of crossing a line or unwilling to put yourself forward, are you just counting yourself out? Then stop thinking about all the reasons that things might not work, and instead focus on how your life, career, even your day might change for the better if they do. Look at the upside of every situation, and remember: Worst case, you get a no in response—a bummer to hear but hardly the end of the world.

## Humble Yourself

People who associate chutzpah with hubris have a fundamental misunderstanding of it. For chutzpah to be effective, the "supreme self-confidence" should be found in *what* we're saying or asking for— but never *how*. Chutzpah is the courage, as an intern, to respectfully share your opinion on a new product with the CEO in the elevator; it is *not* demanding time on the CEO's calendar and then stating your opinion as fact.

Chutzpah is the audacity to ask for an early promotion when you feel you deserve it (and then being prepared to back up that ask with supporting evidence and examples); it is *not* insisting you're better than your peers and that the company would go under without you. Hubris destroys chutzpah. Humility, on the other hand, will make you friends and win you fans. So humble yourself.

## Use Your Power (to Empower)

Chutzpah is an incredibly powerful tool. But it's also a soft power. Some people think it's combative. But the truth is that chutzpah is only effective when used to influence or persuade people and get them on your side: to say yes, to agree with you, to give you what you want. It's not about overpowering anyone through shame, force, or coercion. It's about *empowering* them to help you out through charisma, charm, smarts, and empathy. So put yourself in their shoes: What would you need to see, hear, or understand to come around? What would make you change your mind? What would make you want to do whatever you're asking of or suggesting to them? And what would hold you back?

**A Verbal Slice of Humble Pie: How to Make Your Chutzpah Feel Like Anything But**

- "I wonder if . . ."
- "Thinking about this from a slightly different perspective . . ."
- "Is it possible that . . . ?" OR "Would it be possible to . . . ?"
- "I'm sure this isn't the only way, but have you considered . . . ?"
- "I may not be the best person to ask, but in my experience . . ."
- "Forgive me if I'm speaking out of turn . . ."
- "Would you be willing to consider . . . ?"
- "I figure there's no harm in asking . . ."
- "I've been thinking about XYZ . . . What's your view?"
- "I know I'm asking for an exception to the rule . . ."
- "This is what I might do, but how would you approach ABC?"

Your odds may seem long, and your ask may be audacious. But your chutzpah can still bear fruit if you understand what's in it for the other person, align your interests with theirs, and make them feel good about saying yes to you.

## Take One for the Team

Even when used humbly and respectfully, chutzpah can be considered a self-interested (if not selfish) pursuit. But it's often even more effective—and respected—when it's done on behalf of someone (or some *ones*) else, when you take the risk for the team. If your division has logged long hours working late nights and weekends for the past year, be the one who fights for bonuses on their behalf, even if that means having an uncomfortable conversation with the boss to lay out the argument and explain why it's deserved. If you feel an employee has been overlooked for a promotion, be the one who advocates for them to the powers that be—especially if you're in a position of power yourself. If your boss is continuously losing their temper at your coworkers, be the one who steps up, asks what's going on, and lets the boss know the consequences their actions are having on office morale. Take the risk for the team; eventually, the chutzpah you have on behalf of others may even lead you to be seen as the team leader.

### When in Doubt, Answer It Out

Chutzpah is like riding a bike: You get better at it with time, until it becomes intuitive. But until then, there are training wheels available in the form of questions you can ask yourself while deciding whether to say or go for something. Don't wait it out—answer it out:

- Who does this benefit? Is it just me, or does it help others?
- Am I doing or saying this because I want to receive credit?
- What am I contributing? Is it additive? If I'm shooting something down, is there something I'm proposing in its place?
- What's the worst that can happen?

## Zero In on Your Goal

If there's one thing people with chutzpah have in common, it's that they are direct. They're clear about what they're saying, asking for, and trying to accomplish. So before you say or ask for something, make sure you've determined what it is you actually want . . . or simply want to accomplish. Are you speaking up or speaking out because you want something to change? Are you trying to prevent something from happening in the future? Are you doing it on your own behalf, or on behalf of someone (or something) else? Which solution would make you happiest, and what could you still live with? Are you armed with the necessary details? Are you talking to the right person about the issue? Do your homework. Zero in on your goal. Be crisp, clear, and ready, so you don't waste time blathering because you're unprepared. Then, and only then, go for it.

## Provide Backup Options

The best way to get a yes is to give someone more than one thing to say yes to. That doesn't mean being unsure or unsteady about what you're trying to achieve—remember, there should be a goal you've zeroed in on. It does, however, mean doing the legwork yourself to give someone additional ways to help you achieve that goal, if the exact thing you're asking for in the exact way you're asking for it doesn't work. Say your company typically promotes people from associate to director after four years. Don't be afraid to ask for an early promotion two or three years in if you feel you deserve it; that's chutzpah. But be sure to come with backups in case your primary request is rejected. That could be a raise. It could be a commitment to revisit the conversation in six months. It could be additional opportunities to prove yourself—another client, an extra project, an agreement to sit in on additional meetings and get exposure to other departments. It could even just be a concrete checklist of what's needed to move up to the next level.

When people feel backed into a corner, they're less inclined to want to help . . . even if they can. But if you provide alternatives and show you're flexible, they're more likely to be receptive to what you're saying.

## Appeal Personally

When it comes to chutzpah, personal appeal means two things, and it works in two ways. The first is straightforward: You need to be an appealing person, which is determined by your presence inside and out—how you interact with people, how you carry yourself, and even how you dress. But to master chutzpah, not only do you need to *have* personal appeal—you also need to *make* personal appeals. That is, you need to appeal specifically to the person you're engaging or attempting to win over.

There's no one-size-fits-all approach to chutzpah; you have to tailor what you say and how you act to the situation. Make every effort to understand your audience and who they are. At the very minimum, figure out how your request impacts them. Look at the situation from their point of view. Understand the consequences for them—or at least what's at stake. After all, it's a lot easier to ask for something unexpected—or say something uncomfortable—if you can do it in a way that makes the other person feel seen and heard and respected. And you're more likely to get them on board eventually if you get what's potentially in it for them first.

## THE FINAL WORD

### H is for HURRY UP

Life isn't like our favorite streaming show. There's no pause button. We can't stop time. Even if we stay put, it keeps going. If we don't make decisions, they're made for us. If we don't act, our default becomes passivity. If we don't speak up, our silence still speaks volumes. That doesn't mean we should do things impulsively that we may come to regret. It does, however, mean doing *everything* to make sure we don't squander opportunities.

That's chutzpah: It's understanding that good things come to those who *don't* wait. It's understanding that the only control we have over time is how we spend it. It's understanding that if we want something to happen, it's on us to stop dragging our feet because of obstacles that may not even exist—or using those obstacles as excuses—and then get moving to make it happen.

# 10. There's Nowhere To Go But Up / Success Has Multiple Directions

**What We're Told:** *"There's nowhere to go but up."*

This refrain has its roots at rock bottom. It's something we hear when things are at their worst. It's what we tell each other (or ourselves) to inspire a belief that things will get better. But in the workplace, it describes the mindset that many people have when it comes to the ideal career trajectory. To get ahead and grow on the job, the thinking goes, we have to move up vertically. We have to pick a single path—and once we do, we have to stay the course. Doing otherwise, we're told, is a distraction that will keep us from reaching the top of whatever mountain we're climbing.

**The Truth:** *"Success has multiple directions."*

Although many of us may have first encountered the "zigzag" as a roadside warning sign in driver's ed, zigzagging is in fact an excellent way to plot a career.

Unfortunately, many people are convinced that the only way forward at work is up. It's not surprising why. Almost all the language we use to describe professional progress is vertical. We get raises and promotions for a job well done. If we need more training to do our work (or to do it better), that's called upskilling. We ask if a company or industry offers upward mobility. Perhaps most importantly, we grow up believing that our careers will—and should—resemble a ladder: We begin our lives on the bottom rung, and if all goes according to plan, we follow a vertical, linear trajectory until we reach the top of our department, our company, even our industry. We rise, we ascend, we move up.

As a result, ambitious professionals are obsessed with increasing responsibilities, seniority, and pay while climbing step by sequential step and succeeding rung by rung. We seek out a specialty and then stick to it, hopeful we'll be rewarded for staying the course.

In corporate lingo, the phrase for this trajectory and mindset is *vertical growth*.

But there are some real pitfalls involved with this approach to professional progress. What if the role we've spent our entire career mastering gets automated one day? What if the company we've dedicated our entire career to suddenly goes bankrupt or gets bought? What if the industry to which we've dedicated our entire career becomes obsolete? What if we get to the top of the ladder and realize we don't like it, but we have nothing to fall back on?

Horizontal growth, on the other hand, describes the less traditional, less well-trodden career moves we're less inclined to make and often resist—the ones that bring us neither a more prestigious title nor a better salary. Instead, they bring us to a new department, division, company, or even industry *without* an accompanying promotion or obvious value proposition.

By most tangible metrics, horizontal growth often doesn't feel like growth at all, especially not in the moment. In my experience, though, lateral career moves can also serve as a step up. When approached and executed the right way, horizontal growth can become what I call *diagonal* growth—and enable us to progress professionally further, faster, and in a much more secure manner than a vertical upward path ever could.

That's because, with a career that zigzags, we're adding breadth and not just height. The goal isn't to move up, necessarily, at least not exclusively or immediately. It's to gain vast experience, learn new and varied skills, and get exposed to a variety of people inside and outside our organization—people we might not have encountered, connected with, or learned from had we marched straight up to the top.

By zigzagging, we're not climbing a ladder—we're spinning a career web, one that can extend infinitely in any direction, with many options for development and progress. It isn't just more exciting and interesting than the alternative. It also opens us up to a world of possibilities that might have otherwise remained impossibly out of reach. By the way: It's way less roundabout and indirect than it may seem.

While I believe the start of our careers is all about following the opportunities to figure out what it is we love and want to do with our lives, I believe the rest of our careers should be about expanding the possibilities we have and maximizing our potential. We can only do that by zigzagging and crisscrossing, rather than walking in a straight and narrow line.

What it looks like is different for everyone. But generally, zigzagging means remaining a generalist—at least for a little while—and fighting the urge to find a niche too early. As David Epstein, author of *Range: Why Generalists Triumph in a Specialized World*, argues, limiting our expertise and experience to a single subject or skill set can end up constructing an artificial ceiling on our growth and hold us down.

It may seem like specialists, who identify and start working toward a goal quickly, have a leg up. But according to Epstein, they tend to plateau earlier. Generalists—who experience a "sampling period" in their professional lives that helps them recognize and continue to refine their interests and abilities—tend to surpass them. By remaining open to other possibilities and getting a variety of preparation, training, and experience, generalists gain an advantage. In short: The skill that serves people most in the workplace is, as Epstein's title puts it, range.

And we get that range by zigzagging. By familiarizing ourselves with topics that aren't in our purview, learning skills that aren't in our job description, and seeking out (or simply saying yes to) unexpected responsibilities in a role we already hold—and unexpected roles relative to our interests.

Occasionally, that requires us to leave our jobs entirely. It's a sad and sorry fact that women are less likely than men to become CEOs by moving up internally in an organization.[1] More often, we end up leading when we come in from the outside. So if leading is our goal, we have to leave where we are to get where we want to be.

But even if our ambition isn't to become chief executive or join the C-suite, there are reasons to depart a comfortable position rather than stay. As every good zigzagger knows, our jobs shouldn't be measured by how long we've worked somewhere but by what we've learned and accomplished . . . and how much is left for us to keep learning and keep accomplishing. Once there isn't much left—or once it becomes clear that there's more potential for challenge, fulfillment, and growth elsewhere—it's time to go. If we're bored, we're getting stale. If we're coasting, we're not staying sharp. And disinterest and disengagement don't go unnoticed, at least not for long.

Hopping from one role, one company, even one industry to the next may still feel risky. But in many ways, zigzagging *is* the modern career path. With technology evolving at the speed of light, entire sectors of business rising and falling with the click of a button, and jobs that took years to train for disappearing or morphing into something else entirely, the best way to survive and make ourselves more valued and valuable is to be a zigzagger—to expand our options, pursue every possibility, and stay open to the potential of our destination changing—all while truly being made better by our journey.

The world of work has always been ever-changing; only the rate of change feels faster these days. The way to keep up has always been to stay one step ahead by having more than one skill set, interest, and area of expertise.

In doing so, we avoid putting all our eggs in one basket. We also harden our shells and make ourselves less vulnerable to drops, cracks, and any other external pressures.

Of course, making it to the top of a career ladder, or the apex of some metaphorical corporate mountain, can be our goal. It's good to have goals! Maybe we end up at the top of the mountain. Maybe we end up on another mountain entirely. But we don't have to climb straight up. Whatever our final destination, we can and should get there by zigzagging.

## MY TAKE

Even after I decided the TV industry was my passion and my calling, my trajectory was anything but straight-up, defined, or predetermined. That's largely because I started working in cable around the same time that cable came into existence. It was the Wild West back then, and we were the pioneers and the cowboys, with no real rules to adhere to or role models to aspire to—and certainly no clear path to follow. As a result, my career has been marked by a series of zigs and zags—governing everything from where I lived to what I did to what I worked on to whom I worked for and with—that led me to where I am today.

When I was hired to be vice president of original programming at the USA Network, I'd worked for five different companies and had almost fifteen jobs—at least—in the time since I finished graduate school less than fifteen years before. Millennials and Gen Z get a bad rap for bouncing around from role to role, but I'm right there with them. I zigged, and I zagged. Even when I thought I was settled into my role at USA, my journey continued to be anything but vertical, hierarchical, or even, to most people, sensical.

Sometimes willingly and sometimes under pressure, I took on new roles and responsibilities that others would have considered de-motions, or at the very least detours. Agreeing to try and revitalize WWE, the wrestling conglomerate, was one of them. Deciding to go run the Sci-Fi Channel was another.

In 1992, three years after I started working at USA, the network launched the Sci-Fi Channel. It was USA's little sister of sorts, a place to air zanier and more genre-specific science fiction series and films. (As I once put it, the channel was created to be a home for "any-thing outside of what we know to be true.") In our little "family" of channels, the prestige was with USA, which is saying a lot, because for much of the history of television, cable itself was considered the "stepchild" of the broadcast networks—less established, less main-stream, way less watched—with little prestige in comparison.

So, a few years after the Sci-Fi Channel launched, when I was working as the VP of original programming at USA and given a choice—leave to lead Sci-Fi, a small start-up of sorts, or stay on at

USA, the more established institution—my decision should have been obvious: Stick with USA, which had more respect and viewers, made more money, and seemed like it had more opportunities for growth (or at least a clearer path to a cushy executive job) to both insiders and outside observers. That's where the eyeballs and dollars were. Instead, I said sayonara.

Fortunately for me, I was curious, and I didn't know exactly where I wanted to end up; I just believed I would learn a lot more, grow a lot faster, and open myself up to more possibilities while leading an organization versus following someone else's lead. At Sci-Fi, I'd be responsible for everything that went into creating a successful network: the marketing, branding, press, schedule, budget, advertising, and affiliate sales . . . and, of course, content.

Given that Sci-Fi was an underdog that was already underestimated, I knew my team and I would be able to operate under the radar, with more freedom to experiment. If we failed, we wouldn't be blamed—Sci-Fi hadn't had much success yet anyway, and being only six years old, it had no long legacy we could tarnish. But if we succeeded, we would probably get the credit. Plus, I had already mastered the rules of the USA road. I didn't feel the need to keep doing what I already knew I could do, especially when I had the opportunity to try something I'd never done before.

I didn't worry that I was removing myself from the rungs of a ladder I had already begun to climb. If anything, by joining the Sci-Fi Channel, I'd have my footing on *two* ladders, with the potential to reach many more.

That's exactly what happened. In hindsight, I even sidestepped a career rut. In six years, we doubled Sci-Fi's audience, and as a result of that success, I was made president of the USA Network, too. In essence, I reached the top of a ladder I hadn't focused on climbing. In truth, I probably only reached the top *because* I wasn't concerned with doing so, and because I didn't let it determine my actions.

Zigzagging helped me land some great jobs in some direct ways. Still, I'd argue that it has been even more critical to my career for how it's contributed to my success *indirectly*—with everything I learned while zigging and zagging that I was able to apply later on.

In the three and a half decades since I first joined USA, the company went through a whopping seven corporate takeovers—seven changes in ownership of the networks and divisions that I worked for or led. To explain each of these upheavals in detail would essentially recount nearly the entire history of television. At one point, USA Network was owned by each of the following: Paramount, MCA, Time Inc., Viacom, Seagram (yes, the beverages), my friend and mentor Barry Diller, a French media company called Vivendi, General Electric (yes, the home appliances), and now Comcast, the cable conglomerate.

It was a confusing and complicated few decades—especially for those of us who were working inside it and experiencing it firsthand. For many, the instability wasn't just unnerving—it was unmanageable. Each time we got used to the way things were, they changed. A new owner took over, new leadership was installed, and new rules had to be learned. Each regime had different priorities, different evaluation metrics, even different definitions of "business casual." If you were certain of the path you wanted to follow and the destination you wanted to reach, you were likely sorely disappointed time and time again. Paths that seemed ripe with limitless potential turned into dead ends overnight, while others that seemed like needlessly windy detours became shortcuts to senior roles. There was no real way to ever know for sure.

But if you were willing to embrace the chaos, disregard the doom-sayers, go where you were needed, *and* make yourself useful there, the possibilities were limitless.

That's what zigzagging prepared me for. It taught me how to feel comfortable not knowing, because I was always having to learn new skills in each new job. And it prepared me to pivot, to channel the skills I already had to new ventures, while giving me a keen under-standing that flexibility was one of my greatest assets. By taking the job across the hall rather than up the elevator, literally and meta-phorically, I ended up working, befriending, collaborating, and net-working with all types of people outside of my prescribed domain.

Hell—I had no prescribed domain.

I often say that I made it through the mayhem and many, many different bosses because I know how to read a room: to understand a specific culture, determine what I can offer, quickly learn what I need to, figure out the group dynamics, get to know as many people as possible, and prove that I'm a team player. And I know how to read rooms with such fluency for one simple reason: I have been in oh so many.

That, I think, is the secret to success. For me, it was my willingness to open the door and walk into a room in the first place, when so many people prefer to stay put. Or maybe it's my knack for seeing a door at all, where so many others simply see a wall. Either way, by constantly finding (and putting) myself in different and unexpected situations earlier in my career, I figured out how to effectively sell my story in almost every possible context. Getting comfortable with discomfort and making the foreign feel familiar became my standard mode of operating—so by the time I was forced to navigate a sea change that I *didn't* choose, it was intuitive.

More than that, it was exciting. Rather than view myself as a victim of change, I saw myself as fortunate to be experiencing whatever shakeup was occurring and asked myself what possibilities existed. And I *always* asked myself how I could capitalize on them—even and especially when it meant diverging from the path I was on or extending the role I was in.

That's how I zigzagged across the industry from the creative side of TV to the business side, and then to multiple positions in which I oversaw both. I was often hired to fill roles that didn't exist before, and I developed a reputation for saying yes to those opportunities, which opened new doors. While most of the people around me were gunning for the top of the mountain, I approached my journey like a slalom course. I swerved around obstacles, picked up speed on my turns, bounced around moguls (so to speak), and tried to enjoy the view from wherever I was.

Truly great careers zigzag. They crisscross. They go sideways and get turned upside down. They include breaks to refuel and reevaluate. But if we can manage to forgo a fixed destination, we can cover a lot more ground and have a whole lot more fun.

## NAIL IT

It's a fallacy to believe there's nowhere to go in our careers but up, and no professional moves worth making but the vertical ones that lift us up a rung on the corporate ladder. There's almost always another, sometimes better, way to move. Often, there are many. So rather than work rigidly on our rise to a predetermined top, we should adjust our stance, consider looking in other directions, and expand our definition of growth and success. If we do all that, the sky—and not just the top of a ladder—is the limit.

So . . .

## First, Look Down

Before making any big decisions—personal or professional, forward, backward, upward, sideways, or any which way—you have to shore up your foundation. That means looking *down* and figuring out the principles, values, and priorities that ground you. Long before I had any concrete career goals, here's what I knew I wanted: to have a career and not just a job; to wake up in the morning and enjoy my day, rather than feel like I was barely eking out a life; to not travel *too* much; to work in a culture and environment that encouraged collaboration and growth, and to be surrounded by other people; and—at the start of my career, believe it or not—to be able to bring my dog into the office or on set with me. (I even got my way, until the CEO stepped in another dog's shit, and all dogs were banned.) When I considered any sort of job or career move, I didn't look up and measure it by how it would get me to the top of a mythical lad-

### Watch What Happened . . . to Andy Cohen

Many people know the welcoming, funny, and whip-smart Andy Cohen as the host of Bravo's *Watch What Happens Live* and the unflappable mediator of many a reality-TV reunion catfight. (You also might recognize him as the cohost of CNN's annual New Year's Eve celebration from New York City's Times Square.) On air, Andy's a voice of reason and humor. What many people don't know, though, is that Andy started his career far away from the bright lights and the cameras, as a behind-the-scenes producer and then development executive. For ten years, he launched scripted and unscripted Bravo shows, including the reality franchises he's now part of on-screen. He zigzagged.

der. Instead, I looked "down" at what grounded me and measured it against that.

If you analyze opportunities according to your principles, values, and priorities—if you allow yourself to consider the upside of every job and role that fits this bill—you'll be establishing a floor for your professional possibilities that includes more potential for lateral movement. Best of all, you'll be leaving the ceiling wide open.

## Stretch Yourself (and Your Assignments)

At its simplest, diagonal growth occurs when we elevate ourselves or improve our prospects by doing something other than whatever it is we're already doing. In corporate America, "stretch assignments" are those that give employees additional responsibilities beyond what's found in their job description—expanding their purview, increasing their skill set, and unleashing potential that might not have been uncovered yet. It's how we grow on the job without ever leaving our jobs.

In many ways, my time spent working alongside the macho men and women of WWE was a stretch assignment. It increased my skill set, but not my salary. So was my first exposure to editing a TV show, when I was working at a children's show in Boston and was sent to LA to do my boss's job because we were behind schedule. But that experience eventually led to my first job as a postproduction supervisor, which led to all my other jobs as a producer. Time and again, these stretch assignments transformed my trajectory and supercharged my career.

So, if you are looking to elevate your career, seek out stretch assignments. Perhaps these are short-term contract positions, temporary assignments, extra projects, or mentorship or management opportunities for junior employees. Often, they're calculated risks that take you outside your comfort zone. But if you're open to them, and you do them right, they can increase your comfort level and expand the possibilities in store for you. And they might also be fun.

## How to Stretch

- Raise your hand and be the yes person, even when what you're volunteering for or being asked to do is far outside your job description.
- Ask to observe. If someone's doing something, presenting something, even having a conversation with someone and you think you can learn, ask to (silently) sit in.
- Offer to review people's presentations and decks after they've made them.
- Become management's go-to person for your willingness to take on extra assignments and any odd jobs.

## Adjust for Size

In conversations with employees of all levels, I've identified two seemingly opposite issues that are really two sides of the same coin—and in response, I've offered seemingly opposite solutions that are really rooted in the same idea. The first issue: People working at smaller organizations occasionally feel like they've reached the limits of what work can offer them; they're no longer learning, no longer meeting new people, and they have nowhere to go . . . not sideways, and not up. The second issue: People working at larger organizations occasionally feel like they're lost or drowning in a sea of others who are just like them, not getting the exposure or opportunities they desire because the competition is so fierce and the employee roster is so crowded. For both issues, I have the same solution: Adjust for size.

Going from a smaller organization to a bigger one—even in a lateral role with the same pay and, on paper, the same responsibilities—can end up being a promotion of sorts, because any job at a larger organization will, almost by default, be more complicated, require you to meet more people, and open you up to new opportunities. Meanwhile, going from a bigger organization to a smaller one can advance your career, too—giving you access to more opportunities (because there's less competition), granting you more autonomy (because there are fewer layers of supervision), and getting you more recognition (because you'll be more visible in a smaller crowd, and sometimes all it takes to become more senior is to be seen more).

Either way, these career moves aren't a one-way street. If you zigged from one company, you can always zag back. With new experience under your belt, you're likely to return at a higher level than you could have reached had you stayed in place. Just look at how I ended up leading USA after leaving the network for the Sci-Fi Channel.

## Caveat: Loyalty Is Great Until It Isn't

Loyalty is a necessary and wonderful trait, but if you pledge allegiance to any one company (or boss) and view linear growth there as your best trajectory, you're risking doing it wrong. I say this as someone who, in hindsight, may have done it wrong at times.

I haven't been a perfect zigzagger: As much as I bobbed and weaved, I stayed loyal to one industry, and mostly to one company within that larger industry. What I should have done—what more women should be doing—is pledge allegiance to myself. Women are still less likely to be promoted than our male counterparts, even though we're less likely to quit. In fact, men get promoted—and rewarded—more often *because* they're more willing to walk when they don't feel valued. Women need to do the same. When I felt screwed over by my bosses or passed over for a promotion that I knew I deserved, I stayed the course. I was a loyal soldier. You could argue it got me where I am now; on most days, that's exactly what I would argue. And luckily for me, my company—with its size and its seven changes of corporate ownership and culture—laid some zigzags on my path, even if I didn't ask for them.

And yet: Had I been willing to pack up my desk and venture elsewhere when I had the opportunity, had I been willing to zig and zag even more, who knows where I would be today?

## Be Flexible

When it comes to our professional journeys, people are, for the most part, more rigid than we believe ourselves to be. But when there's a breakdown in our lives or our careers—big or small, in or out of our control, whether it affects only us or a whole group of others—being rigid can often cause us to break . . . To set ourselves up for success, then, we have to be flexible instead.

That's easy to say and harder to do. We can't exactly change our modus operandi overnight. But there's a shortcut for flexibility that can act as a safeguard in turbulent times and prevent you from breaking (or making a big career mistake): patience. When disruption shows up on your porch, wait a minute before you slam the door in its face or sneak out the back door. Instead, take time to get to know what's going on—figure out who's running the show, talk to people who are in the same boat as you (or who've been there before), follow the news, and find the facts. Maybe your distrust is warranted, in which case the two weeks you spent stalling before making a decision won't matter in the long run. But maybe you have nothing to fear and everything to gain. If that's the case, then patience in the face of disruption can end up saving your career.

### Shift Your Perspective Before Your Location

Sometimes, an unfulfilling job really is worth quitting, and an unstable company really is worth leaving. If that's where you are, get up and go. But occasionally, what we need to shift isn't our location— it's our perspective. That doesn't mean looking on the bright side if there isn't one, but it does mean doing basic due diligence and looking *for* a bright side to begin with. Even if you feel like a role has nothing to do with what you want to be doing, see if you can frame the experience in a way that sets you apart from others who are pursuing the same path. Maybe you've learned a transferable skill that will come in handy. Maybe you've made a connection that will serve you down the line.

Ask yourself if your outlook has been clouded by the judgments of others. It's okay to make a decision that feels risky and take (or leave) a job based on instinct. But if you make moves after your instinct has been influenced by the negativity of others, you'll likely come to regret it. Again, you have to know your own values.

## THE FINAL WORD

In yoga, long a part of my routine, the trick to balance is simple: You can look up or down to orient yourself, but your eyes should ultimately stay fixed on the horizon. You have to be able to see what's in front of you—not just what you want to see, not just what you hope to avoid, but all of it. That's the secret to great careers, too. If you blindly follow a predetermined path, if you always look up instead of ahead or around, there's a good chance you will fall or fail. But if you can keep your eyes (and yourself) open to everything on the horizon, you'll realize there's more than one route to wherever it is you want to end up. As my yoga instructor Vicky likes to say: "Look where you're going, and you'll get there."

part three

# STEPPING UP

## HOW TO LEAD AT EVERY STAGE

- Double-check your gut

- Sweat the small stuff

- Learn how (and why) to lose

- Strike the right balance between work and play

- Fix "it" before it's too late

# 11. Trust Your Gut /
## Check Your Gut

**What We're Told:** *"Trust your gut."*

It's comforting to believe there are easy answers to tough questions. It's even more comforting to believe those answers live somewhere deep inside us. No wonder people like to refer to the gut as a second brain or a sixth sense. No wonder we're reminded time and again to rely on it. In an age of overthinking and overanalyzing, trusting our gut can seem like a worthy counterpunch. And acknowledging the sometimes unexplainable pull we feel toward certain people, places, and ideas can help us cut through the noise and come to a decision.

**The Truth:** *"Check your gut."*

That pit at the bottom of your stomach? It isn't a member of Mensa. And trusting it isn't always a genius idea.

To those who know me, those sentences might sound heretical. After all, I've spent my career extolling the virtues of going with one's gut. To family, friends, and especially colleagues, I've asked the question "What is your gut telling you to do?" more times than I can recall. I've also read more books (and listened to more audiobooks) than I can count on the importance of intuition in leadership.

And yet, as I watch people stumble at work and in their personal lives—and use their gut instincts or reactions as the fall guy or gal—I need to clarify: The gut is a real (and really important) factor to consider in decision-making. But by itself, it's unreliable.

What do I mean by real? Well, the sensations that sway us in one direction or another aren't irrational. The butterflies and nausea in our stomachs, the tension in our muscles, the tightness in our chests, the clammy hands, the increased heart rate—the bodily reactions that make us feel certain of right and wrong—also aren't in our heads; they often come straight from our gut. It's known as our second or unconscious brain for good reason: It's the only organ (other than the brain) with its own nervous system, able to act independently and influence our behavior. It really does have a mind of its own, responsible for around 95 percent of the serotonin and 50 percent of the dopamine our bodies produce.[1] So when we have a feeling we can't shake but also can't explain, it's probably related to the five hundred million neurons firing in our guts.[2] When a sense of anxiety or calm feels as physical as it is mental—that's because it is.

All of that makes our guts incredibly smart organs. And yet, they're also incredibly fallible for two big reasons.

The first is simple: Our guts are *our* guts. The reactions they trigger within us are rooted in *our* life experiences, *our* previously held assumptions, and, yes, *our* biases—especially the unconscious ones we don't acknowledge we have. So going with our gut alone, by default, leads us to undervalue the perspectives of others, often at our peril. At work, that can leave us with blind spots. We might approve an advertising campaign even if someone voices concerns, without adequately considering how it offends a certain population we're not part of. We might forge ahead with a business development strategy we've used in the past if it worked well enough then, without taking sufficient time to learn about newer strategies that might work better.

The second reason our guts fail us: They aren't just biased toward us and our perspectives. They're biased toward the past and present, too—and against the future. We often hear that change and growth are uncomfortable; well, our guts are a big contributing factor. As humans, we're creatures of habit. That's why subconsciously, at the gut level, we're drawn to conclusions and solutions that perpetuate the status quo rather than disrupt it. It's our conscious mind that pushes us to try new things, whether that means trying a new food, moving to a new city, starting a new job, or opening up to a new romantic partner. Nine times out of ten, our gut would rather we stick with what we already know.

While our gut can provide a great snapshot of our feelings at a certain moment, it doesn't have a great long-range lens—which means it isn't adept at considering how we might feel down the line. If we're dissatisfied at work, our gut instinct might be to barge into our boss's office and quit. If we're out at a party and meet someone cute, we might feel butterflies so intense that they convince us we have a deeper connection with this stranger than we do with the partner who's sitting at home waiting for us. If we act on that gut instinct and make decisions with longer-term implications based on it, the consequences can be devastating, and the damage can be irreparable.

The truth is that the best decisions are made when we consider our gut *and* whatever other information that we have available to us. Research even shows that intuition, when paired with analytical thinking, leads to better, faster, and more accurate decision-making, and more confidence in our decisions once we've made them.

It's not an either-or. It's a both-and. We need to balance our gut instincts with gut checks. After all, the gut really is our second brain. Sometimes, we just have a feeling we can't shake. Sometimes, our bodies know what our brains haven't yet processed. We just can't forget to also use our first brain. It really is a sixth sense. But we shouldn't completely ignore the other five along the way.

## MY TAKE

Back in 2011, the *Hollywood Reporter* said I had "the best gut in the business." A year later, that gut came back to haunt and taunt me. And I learned the hard way that no one's instincts are infallible—especially not my own.

Like most big stories in my life, this one involves a TV show. But if you've never heard of *Political Animals*, well, that's exactly my point.

By most measures, the show should have become a smashing success. It premiered on the USA Network in July 2012 with plenty of well-executed and well-earned fanfare. Sigourney Weaver, a three-time Oscar nominee, starred in the lead role, playing a former first lady now serving as secretary of state with a failed presidential bid under her belt and future presidential ambitions on the horizon. (I'll let you decide which real-life politician may or may not have inspired her character.) And she was backed by an all-star supporting cast that included Ellen Burstyn, one of only fifteen women in history to have won the "Triple Crown of Acting": an Oscar, Emmy, and Tony.

Then there were the behind-the-scenes reasons why I believed *Political Animals* should have been an all-around hit. The show was created by the award-winning Greg Berlanti and staffed with a stable of thoroughbred writers and directors. The costs, though high, paid off in the form of some incredible production value: the sets, costumes, and lighting all looked terrific. But after just six episodes and the lowest numbers of any original show on the USA Network in fifteen years, *Political Animals* faded from the screen and everyone's radar.

What went wrong? While lots of factors contributed to the show's failure, in hindsight, all of them boiled down to this: Not only did my team and I trust our gut, we also treated it as the final word. We were so convinced *Political Animals* would be a hit that we didn't bother doing our homework.

Like a show horse, a TV show has to jump through hoops before it's greenlit for the viewing public. Traditionally, before production even begins, the network conducts research, checks the cast's Q scores—the industry standard to measure a person's popularity—and considers already-existent public sentiment on the context and themes. If the show passes muster on all those fronts, the network greenlights a pilot episode. Once it's completed, the process repeats itself, this time with focus groups assembled to collect feedback on everything from the title to the characters to the dialogue and the use of humor and profanity, providing even more perspectives to consider. Only afterward, if the pilot is approved, does shooting of the rest of the season go forward. Even afterward, research can still influence the promotion and marketing of a show and help determine when it should air.

None of that happened with *Political Animals*. Not only did we abandon the industry-standard process for testing TV shows—we abandoned our own process for developing them. At USA, we had churned out an unparalleled string of hits, and very few misses, precisely because we had implemented our own safeguards against the "golden gut" decision-making that's so popular in Hollywood. No matter how much we liked a character or the writing of a show, my team would deliberate and then vote on it in as objective as possible a way. We used charts, scoreboards, and checklists that helped us see beyond our own feelings so we could try to accurately predict our viewers' reactions.

But we were so confident in *Political Animals* that we skipped over all of that. Instead of making a pilot, we went straight to making a six-episode limited series. Forget about conducting any original research—we refused to even consider some key insights and data we already had on USA's audiences and other USA shows, and the many ways they were telling us to slam the brakes on what we thought was a small-screen blockbuster.

After all, I knew good TV. My team knew good TV. And *Political Animals*—with Sigourney Weaver *and* Ellen Burstyn, with a sexy storyline *and* smart dialogue, with juicy historical *and* present-day parallels—was good TV. Many critics even agreed. But our audiences emphatically didn't.

When *Political Animals* was rejected, my team and I were stunned. In an email I sent to my boss, Steve, I called the ratings "shockingly low" and described my team's reaction as "totally shell-shocked." In hindsight, we shouldn't have been. The red flags that became obvious in our postmortem were there all along, and they should have stopped us before we ever gave the show the green light—or at least forced us to change course.

For starters, the show was much darker than USA viewers, comfortable with the signature "blue-skies" programming that defined our brand—lighthearted and escapist dramedies often shot outside under the sun to brighten the mood—were accustomed to. The marital problems, struggles with sexuality, drugs, deception, and death in

*Political Animals* might have appeared elsewhere on the network, but the dollop of humor that balanced out those subjects on our other shows was missing from this one. While we accurately predicted that TV audiences generally were trending toward edgier content, we were wrong about the speed at which *our* audiences were willing to go there.

Then there was the subject of our series: a strong-willed, independent-minded Democratic female politician. At the time, USA was basically a "red states network." And red states like their programming traditional, which on TV has traditionally meant male-centric. If our viewers were going to relate to a female protagonist at all, it probably wouldn't have been the one we gave them. While we never poll-tested our main character's likability, there *were* plenty of polls on the likability of the real-life character that ours was based on, and they didn't paint a pretty picture.

The show's subject matter should have also given us pause. Across the country, people were growing sick of politics. Approval ratings of elected officials in both parties were at all-time lows. Even in my own social circles, friends who once watched *The West Wing* with fervor and may have sympathized with our protagonist wanted an escape. How did we respond? By putting "political" in the show's title. Big mistake.

We were so blinded by the lights, camera, and action of a show we loved that we couldn't picture anyone feeling differently. We couldn't see the writing on the wall. With our eyes closed, we learned the truth the hard way: by crashing into it headfirst.

Compare (or, more accurately, contrast) that with the story behind another USA show you probably *have* heard of, *Burn Notice*, a spy drama that became one of the most successful series in the network's history. In the early 2000s, a writer came to us with an idea for a darkly written detective series set in the bowels of New Jersey. My team and I loved the idea and the writing. But our data and experience told us our audience wouldn't—at least not as the show was currently conceived. When we scored it, the script didn't pass muster. We knew the programming that did best was character-centric (check), with likable but flawed characters (check), shot under blue skies (minus), with dramatic dialogue and storylines made light with humor, snark, and wit (minus).

So rather than rely only on our instincts, we used all the information we had—our conflicting feelings and facts—to arrive at a different decision: challenge the writer to relocate the show from Newark to Miami and add in a dollop of USA humor. At first, he thought we were crazy. His gut was telling him the show should be more serious and mysterious. But eventually, he delivered a script that had the same intrigue, smarts, and heart with a lighter, brighter beat. (The show's first line perfectly captures what I mean: "Covert intelligence involves a lot of waiting around. Know what it's like being a spy? It's like sitting at your dentist's reception area twenty-four hours a day. You read magazines, sip coffee, and every so often, someone tries to kill you.")

That version of *Burn Notice*, created only because we trusted *more* than just our guts, ran for eight seasons and made a ton of money for USA and Fox Studios. For a time, it was even one of the most watched scripted series on cable . . . second only to another USA show, *Royal Pains.*

Were my team and I surprised by how well *Burn Notice* did? Perhaps. But were we surprised *that* the show did well? No, not really. After all, we knew our audience. We knew what they wanted. And we gave it to them with a show that played it safer and tempered our gut instincts with more reliable metrics for success.

In a choice between how I felt then and how I felt when *Political Animals* belly-flopped, there's no choice at all. Who doesn't prefer winning to losing? Yet I continued taking risks with the series I chose to greenlight, the characters I chose to champion, and the territory I chose to push my networks and their viewers toward. At times, I still went (and still go) with my instincts and intuition over everything else. What changed after *Political Animals* was this: I no longer trust my gut blindly.

A third TV show—or rather, the story behind a show—illustrates what I mean. The year was 2014, not long after the *Political Animals* misfire, and I was sent a script from my development team unlike anything USA had ever aired. Nothing about it fit our checklist. There were zero blue skies. The protagonist was unreliable and pretty unlikeable. There was barely any humor. My team and I understood this, but up and down the network, from executives to assistants, we also felt we had a hit on our hands.

We went back and forth ad nauseam, discussing and debating every possible option and outcome. We could ignore our communal gut, go with what we knew, and pass on the show entirely. To us, that wasn't an option at all. We could do what we'd done with *Burn Notice* and ask the writer to edit the script, so it better catered to our viewers. But we knew he would almost certainly reject our offer and bring it to another network instead, which was a risk we all agreed we weren't willing to take. We also agreed that even if the writer were willing to USA-ify the script, it would do the eventual show a real disservice.

Or we could trust our guts even though we had a valid reason not to and commit to the script and the show as they were. We knew we might be wrong, and it could flop spectacularly, wasting time, money, and talent along the way that we would never get back. But we decided we could live with that potential for failure—because there was also the potential for astronomical success. If we were right, if audiences loved the show as much as we did, we knew it would take USA to a whole new level.

With eyes wide open, we said yes.

The risk was big but totally calculated. We weighed the potential of the show meeting our expectations against the decent likelihood it wouldn't, something we'd never even accounted for with *Political Animals*, and decided the upside was better than the downside was bad. Only then did we jump. While we couldn't anticipate how the show would be received, we did what research we could—shooting a pilot first and running focus groups for feedback—not to change it but to try and market it to a more expansive audience that might be more receptive.

After decades in television, I knew there was more to success than only meeting viewers where they were and making shows that tested well. I knew gut wasn't everything—but it also counted for more than nothing. Four seasons, forty-eight episodes, wide critical acclaim, with a 94 percent rating on Rotten Tomatoes, and multiple Emmy, Golden Globe, Screen Actors Guild, and Critics Choice Awards nominations and wins later, *Mr. Robot* had proved us right.

The show—a brainchild of the incomparable Sam Esmail—tells the story of a brilliant hacker with social anxiety, dissociative identity disorder, and a medley of other mental illnesses, who's recruited by a group of anarchists on a mission to cancel all consumer debt. It helped launch Rami Malek, a generational acting talent and all-around great person, and features one of the best performances by Christian Slater that I've ever seen (and I think I've seen all of them).

At USA, I was fairly used to audiences loving our series while critics overlooked them, but *Mr. Robot* was the rare show that checked both boxes. It was a risk, but it came at the right time—launching in a moment of political upheaval and speaking directly to our millennial audiences' concerns about the world in a way that USA's blue-skies programming, which mainly targeted Gen X and boomers, never even attempted. In the process, we transformed the perception of our network from pedestrian to prestige.

My gut was finally vindicated.

## NAIL IT

I often say that good decision-making is more an art than a science. There's no one answer to figuring out the right answer, no single way to forge forward. Looked at another way, though, decision-making is also a language with its own alphabet. Some people are fluent in it. Some stay foreigners their entire lives. Most of us, though, are somewhere in the middle—still learning. But too many people, me included, are guilty of skipping through our ABCs to get to G—Gut. The decisions we make as a result are often confusing, chaotic, even inconsistent. At best, they fail to communicate (or get us) what we actually want.

So . . .

### Practice Your Decision-Making ABC(DEF)s

#### A Is for Analyzing

We are all guilty of sometimes acting on impulse. We make decisions in the heat of the moment, before we have enough information. Before we understand their implications for us and their impact on others. Before we even understand the situation itself.

We might quit a job because we feel underpaid, before learning our salary is above the industry average (and by the way, a recession is looming). In today's swipe-right-swipe-left times, we might nix a suitor with soulmate potential based on a single photo of him with a somewhat receding hairline. Left unchecked, our unconscious biases might prompt us to mistake a female executive for an assistant— and then say something unintentionally offensive.

But we *can* control our gut *reactions*, even if we can't control our gut instincts . . . by simply waiting to react. Take a deep breath. Take a beat. Take time to analyze whatever situation you're in before you make assumptions. Remember how deeply connected your gut—the unconscious brain—is to your unconscious biases. Question how they might be influencing your thoughts before you say them out loud and knee-jerk your way into trouble. Inquire about whatever you're uncertain of before going with your impulse. Above all, consider what you know, what you don't, and what might make a difference in your thinking. The first thought you have—the one your gut is pushing you toward—isn't always right.

### Meditate on It

Making big decisions without analyzing them is shortsighted. But even the best attempts at analysis can fall flat if they're rife with distraction. It can be hard to hear what your gut is actually saying— much less whether or not you should listen—amid the constant hum of phones, friends, and relatives. To find out, you need to drown out the noise. Give yourself permission to meditate. You don't have to go to India for three months. You don't even have to sit down. (I "meditate" on morning jogs.) Just turn off your devices. Find somewhere you can be alone. Quiet your brain. Focus. See where your unconscious mind takes you.

## B Is for Brainstorming

When it comes to decision-making, there's no such thing as too many opinions, because it never hurts to entertain alternatives. If you're faced with a choice—even if you already know what you want to do, but especially when you don't—don't storm into a room with your gut. Instead, brainstorm with others (using the other brain, in your head).

Talk through each possible option, even the unrealistic or un-

---

### Make Room for Brainstorming

Whenever I've led brainstorming sessions for my teams—something I've done with every team I've ever led—I set ground rules to guide our conversations:

1. What happens in the room stays in the room.
2. The more variety (and varied opinions) in the room, the better.
3. If someone can't disagree with you, the room's too small.
4. In this room, we speak up.
5. In this room, we listen closely.
6. In this room, we don't judge each other.
7. In this room, we don't take things personally.
8. In this room, cursing (for f*cking sure) is acceptable.
9. In this room, the quantity of new ideas should challenge the quality of established ideas.
10. In this room, we don't forget the snacks. (After 3:00 p.m., we may add in wine and beer . . . Sorry, HR.)

comfortable ones, with people who have varying viewpoints. Take each of them to their logical (or illogical) conclusion, like my team and I did with *Mr. Robot*. Make a list of pros and cons. Be clear that nothing is off-limits. (Maybe none of the options in front of you is right.) After all, at least in theory, no idea is a bad idea—and testing, rehearsing, and arguing through a decision with all its potential negative consequences can save you from mistakenly making it. In the face of uncertainty, a good back-and-forth can bring clarity to an otherwise complicated situation. It might even convince you that an option you've barely considered is the only one truly worth your consideration.

## C Is for Comparing

If you're confused about what you should do, what you *should* do is draw comparisons.

For the most part, when we were considering a potential new show, the first thing we'd do was compare what was in front of us to what had already been on any of our networks. We'd ask ourselves: Have we had characters like this before? Have we tackled this controversial subject or premise? And then we'd look at other shows on other networks and compare them to whatever form of entertainment we were considering. If they had never done something similar, we'd ask ourselves why. If they had, we'd ask ourselves what worked, what didn't, and what we would have done differently. We'd also ask ourselves if the idea was overdone, if our potential show was too late, or if it would oversaturate the market. This helped us learn from previous mistakes so we could avoid them, learn from previous successes so we could try and repeat them, and avoid the disasters that come from not knowing what else is out there.

But comparisons aren't just for TV shows. Why do you think

every new bride is advised to try on multiple wedding dresses, even if she falls in love with the first? It's not because her gut is wrong, necessarily. It might just be overwhelmed or confused. She's probably in love with love and at least somewhat into the idea of a wedding. Of course, the first dress is exciting. The way to feel even more certain, then, is to test it against alternatives: another fit, another price, another sleeve length, another designer. If dress number one is still her favorite after changing out of dress number seven, her gut was right.

## D Is for Devil's Advocate

While no one loves the devil's advocate, they serve a purpose: By poking holes in your argument, they test its strength. And when it comes to making decisions, you should be wary of the ones that can't withstand scrutiny. So seek out the devil's advocates in your life and challenge them to challenge you. If your argument collapses midway through a conversation with them, or you're struggling to even articulate it, you probably have your answer. If your argument is still standing tall by the end of it, you've probably made the right decision. And if your argument and thinking change over the course of it to incorporate and account for counterpoints, lucky you. Your decision will be better as a result.

When needed, you can always assign someone to play the role. But, when possible, you should do as Adam Grant, the organizational psychologist (who possesses one of my favorite smart brains), instructs and unearth a real devil's advocate—someone who truly and sincerely disagrees with you. After all, the dissent and debate that come from actually dissenting and debating aren't easy to replicate. The way to be sure your decision can withstand its harshest criticism is to find its harshest critics.

## The Big Idea

In his landmark TED Talk on original thinkers, psychologist Adam Grant explains that there's a difference between doubting ourselves and doubting our ideas. "Self-doubt is paralyzing; it leads you to freeze," he says. "But idea doubt is energizing; it motivates you to test, to experiment, to refine." When it comes to your gut, try aiming your doubt squarely at the ideas or solutions it's pushing you toward—and not at the intelligence or creativity or thoughtfulness of the person who came up with them. It's great to second-guess your decisions, but second-guessing yourself will stop you from making any decisions in the first place. And that's often even worse than making the wrong one.

## E Is for Expertise

You're not going to be the best at everything you do. Hell, you probably won't be the best at most things. The good news, though, is that being the best has almost nothing to do with success.

I always say a big reason I've made it in this business is that I've never had the desire to be the smartest in the room. (As the kid sister of a child prodigy, I never had the option growing up.) On the job, I've wanted the opposite: to be surrounded by people who knew more than I did, had more relevant experience than I had, and were more skilled and adept at whatever it was we spent our days doing. I learned early on that there was no shame in asking for help and learning from others. It didn't make me look bad—it made me better, period. (Ten times out of ten, humility will get you further in life than hubris.) And when I've been torn over what to do in a certain situation, turning to someone with more expertise and asking their advice made my eventual decision better, too.

So approach the experts before acting on your gut. If you're distraught over your relationship, seek out a therapist before breaking up. (Friends and family who know you both well can serve as experts, too.) If you're convinced that you're in the wrong field, find a mentor or professional coach before quitting. Experts come in all shapes and sizes, and utilizing them is a sign of strength, not weakness. Some of them cost money but many are free—and it pays to find out what the experts think about your gut before going with it.

## F Is for Facts

The fact of the matter is that when it comes to making big and small decisions, the facts matter. While your gut lives in you, the data, numbers, and evidence surrounding a situation live in reality. Yes, they can be less objective than they claim to be. Yes, they can contain biases, too. They may tell only part of the story or paint only half the picture—but they're a piece of the puzzle, nonetheless. While you don't have to believe them, refusing to look at them is setting yourself up for failure.

So when you're tasked with making a decision, act like a United Nations envoy and go on a fact-finding mission of sorts. Look for any relevant research, statistics, polling, or even scientific studies that might help (or hurt) your cause. Do the math to confirm that there's at least a possibility that the decision you're making will add up to the outcome you're hoping for. Most importantly, don't do what we did with *Political Animals*. If your gut is telling you to act, don't ignore reality—face the facts. And if the odds are still against you, put in the work like we did with *Mr. Robot* to defy them.

## THE FINAL WORD

### G Is for Gut

Some of us trust our guts too much, to the point of excluding everything else. But some of us are plagued by the opposite problem: We depend too heavily on facts and figures, anecdotes and experts, or comparable situations and critical analyses instead. We ignore the voice in our head—er, stomach—at our peril. There's a reason we call that type of decision-making gutless.

What we need to aim for is balance. We need to tap into all six senses. We need to use the brain in our head *and* the brain in our stomach. We need to practice our ABCs, up to and including G. Doing that, after all—looking outward *and* inward when making a decision—is what makes us, well, gutsy.

# 12. Don't Sweat The Small Stuff / Sweat All Stuff

**What We're Told:** *"Don't sweat the small stuff."*

On the clock or off, there are only so many hours in a day—and only so much we can care about and take care of before we reach our limit. We can't be everywhere and do everything all at once, and we'll burn out if we try. Our time and energy are finite resources. We're taught to spend and expend them wisely, to focus on the big picture, the big problems, the big deals, the big moments, and milestones. The rest? Don't sweat it. The small stuff? Don't worry, it's no biggie.

**The Truth:** *"Sweat all stuff."*

Back in 1997, a psychotherapist named Richard Carlson published a book titled *Don't Sweat the Small Stuff . . . And It's All Small Stuff.* That phrase became part of our lexicon, and it's easy to see why. The basic premise behind it—that fixating on the little things in life holds us back from happiness and success—is compelling. To this day, people cite it as a permission slip to do and care *less.* They think it's proof that focusing only on the big-picture perspective, and not getting mired in the minutiae, is how we get ahead.

Unfortunately, the phrase doesn't live up to its promise. While our culture claims to idealize the thirty-thousand-foot view, we don't practice what we preach. We don't respect the people who focus only on broad strokes and blow the rest off. We don't celebrate the people who believe minor details and decisions are beneath them.

On the contrary, the people our culture elevates—the people who end up leading, succeeding, and inspiring us—are the ones who make time even for the small stuff *and* take it seriously. Put another way, we prioritize people who seem to treat everything and everyone as a priority. That's why my own personal philosophy might as well be called *Sweat the Small Stuff . . . Because It's Not Small Stuff.*

In a way, diamonds teach us this lesson. Their quality is not necessarily found on the surface; it's determined by the details. Often undetectable to the naked eye, these specs, more than raw size and weight, decide a stone's value and worth. If you're a jeweler, you sweat the small stuff.

If you're a restaurateur, a chef, or a maître d', you sweat the small stuff, too. You know it's not just the entrées that matter. An appetizer or aperitif can make or break a meal. (So can restaurant lighting or the music playing in the background.) Anyone with experience in the service industry knows it's the little things that make a big impact—and make for much bigger tips. A genuine smile while serving, a complimentary dessert, a booster seat strapped to a toddler's chair before the parent has to ask, getting the other waiters and waitresses to sing "Happy Birthday" in unison . . . that small stuff, more than good versus great food, can make the difference between five extra bucks and fifty. It can also send new customers your way.

This applies to every profession—even and especially when there's more at stake than a good steak. If you're a lawyer, then considering every potential suspect, piece of evidence, witness, and alibi can make or break your case. If you're a doctor, being thorough and meticulous can lead to faster diagnoses and better treatment plans for your patients (and, yes, it can be a matter of life or death). For surgeons, the margin of error is often less than a millimeter; sometimes, it doesn't exist, so they better sweat each cut.

And it isn't just surgeons for whom not sweating the details has a cost. A contractor who reads or writes blueprints sloppily might get an angle off by a degree or two, and only realize later that they've accidentally built the leaning tower of Pittsburgh. If they don't do necessary soil tests before beginning construction on a suburban lot, they might find themselves (and the house they're working on) in deep shit—figuratively and literally—once it rains and the septic system malfunctions. Missing numbers from a Form S-1 can tank a private company's attempt to issue an IPO and go public. Seemingly mundane mistakes, like a CEO's poorly worded tweet, can tank a public company's stock.

And that's just at work.

Rush through a recipe, and two tablespoons of salt instead of two teaspoons might turn your split pea soup into the Dead Sea. Grab the first two black patent pumps in your closet and your outfit might lose its balance—literally—with two different heel heights. And who among us hasn't accidentally set a PM alarm and overslept for an important meeting or flight?

Little details make a big difference. But so do the small gestures that too many people carelessly overlook and speed through, if they follow through on them at all. It's remembering not just big milestones but little moments in people's lives and sending a bottle of red wine to help them celebrate (or a pint of Graeter's Mocha Chip, shipped straight from Cincinnati, to help them commiserate). It's a thoughtful thank-you note after a job interview, a timely "I'm thinking of you" text after hearing someone's bad news. It's taking a few moments out of our day to personalize the card or message, rather than relying on the generic option . . . or our assistants.

At work and in life, not being careless is the bare minimum, the baseline. If we really want to get ahead, we have to actually be care*ful*—by which I mean we have to put care into all our work, all our interactions, and all our ideas, even the stuff that other people may think is too minuscule to matter. The small stuff we focus on, the minor decisions we make, and the casual relationships we maintain might seem insignificant in the moment. But they can end up making a bigger difference than any of us can imagine.

It's no coincidence, after all, that both God and the devil are found in the details.

## MY TAKE

I like to think of my attention to and appreciation of the small stuff as a family heirloom.

It was passed down to me by my mother; she received it from *her* mother, an immigrant who worked as a tailor in Odesa (then part of Russia, now part of Ukraine) and later Brooklyn, ten minutes away from the two-family home in East Flatbush where I grew up. My grandmother was meticulous. She'd search the entire borough for a matching button. Her hemlines were notorious. If something looked off, even if a client wouldn't have noticed, she refused to go home for the night until she figured out—and fixed—the problem. Bad tailoring, my grandmother used to say, sends a message about a person that has nothing to do with money. "If you don't care about the little things, why should anyone trust you with the big things?"

Even though I was just six when my grandmother passed away, her words—which my mother repeated constantly—have never left me.

Throughout my life, I've been focused on tiny details. It's why my clothes are organized by color, category, and utility. My ear gravitates toward alliteration and assonance. Poor contrast and saturation on a screen make me squeamish. So does a lack of symmetry. I have a master calendar to keep track of important dates in the lives of people who are important to me; I add to it at least weekly. I'll spend hours going back and forth with a writer until we come up with the perfect turn of phrase—and then spend the next day picking out the perfect bottle of rosé champagne to thank them for putting up with me. The words "it's no big deal" aren't in my vocabulary.

Sweating the small stuff is just who I am. As my husband, kids, and the many people who've worked with and for me over the years will all corroborate, it can be annoying as hell. But I keep at it because I've learned time and time again that the small stuff is just as likely as anything else to make or break a friendship, a relationship, or even a membership to your preferred gym. It can also make or break a show, a network, even a career.

As a TV executive, I was a bit of an anomaly among my peers, known for both big-picture thinking and tiny-detail analyzing. While most people would reach a certain level and begin to delegate the less important decisions, I liked to have my hand in almost everything. (Sorry, team.) I was just as likely to ax a potential series from our lineup because the pilot didn't fit our network's brand as I was to provide feedback on the formatting of an opening scene's credits (or color or copy) because they weren't perfectly aligned. I would even tear out photos from fashion magazines and send them to producers to illustrate how I wanted each cast member to be dressed.

My thinking was simple: If something was appearing on my network, it was implied that I had signed off on it. So I better actually sign off on it.

My team learned this when we shot the promotional materials for a new USA original series called *Starter Wife*. The show, starring Debra Messing, looked great. But one glance at the photos and I knew something was off. I encountered many eye rolls when I insisted that we change up Debra's wardrobe digitally, swapping her out of a red dress she loved but that washed out her fiery hair for a purple one that added some pop and contrast. That choice was ultimately plastered on billboards in Los Angeles, Chicago, and New York, and it helped make our ratings pop just like the color. To this day, I don't think anyone has ever rocked a purple dress better.

I will fixate on wardrobe minutiae. On set, if I noticed an actor was dressed in more expensive clothes than their character could hypothetically afford, I'd make them put on something else. I'd do the same thing if the fit of a suit was off, or the color of a shirt was too gloomy.

When I ran the Sci-Fi Channel, I made a simple and what some might call superficial and substance-less decision to rename it SYFY. The change was just two letters (or three, depending on how you want to count). But I believed it was significant. We couldn't own the entirety of science fiction as a genre, and yet, calling ourselves Sci-Fi made it seem like that was our goal. The name was limiting our scope, causing shows that weren't perceived as strictly science fiction to feel out of place. We also couldn't trademark it or, even more importantly, secure the website domain.

I wanted a brand we could own that would allow us to live in the world of science fiction and explore beyond it. I knew the name change would confuse some people if they noticed at all. I had skeptics in every direction, telling me the rebrand was a waste of time, money, and publicity that should be channeled toward the actual shows on the channel instead. But Adam, who headed the network's global marketing at the time, and I believed that it would eventually transform how general audiences perceived us—and help our content evolve from hardcore science fiction to broader storytelling. Spoiler: With new shows developed for SYFY about space, techno-fantasies, underwater myths, paranormal activity, supernatural characters, superheroes, magic, apocalypses, dystopias, and utopias—many of which pulled in strong ratings—we were right.

As much as the on-screen details have mattered in my life, though, the off-screen "small stuff" has arguably mattered more. Paying attention to the little things—taking them seriously, handling them with care, and remembering them—may be the most important key to my success. At the very least, it's responsible for the keys to my house . . . and the house itself, as well as my job.

Around the same time that we were rebranding SYFY and putting Debra Messing in purple, my husband and I renovated our home. We fully funded it with some vested stock I'd received as a standard part of my compensation. When the work was done, I reached out to say thank you to my former boss Barry Diller, with a funny email about how we'd turned a dark, leaky, well-worn, full-of-"character" stone colonial from the 1930s into something way more livable. I attached some photos as proof. My subject line and first sentence: "This is the house that YOU built."

The email took me just a few minutes to compose and send, and I didn't think about it afterward. But apparently Barry found my gratitude refreshing and my note, well, notable. A short while later, when Comcast bought NBCUniversal, he forwarded it to my new boss as a testament to my character with a note of his own: "She's a keeper," he wrote. "The real talent to protect." As a result of a heartfelt email that I could have easily never sent, I survived a merger that cut short the careers of several of my peers.

A thank-you note saved my job—not a formal application or an official interview.

## NAIL IT

If you sweat the small stuff instinctually, welcome to the party. If you don't, then becoming someone who focuses on the nitty-gritty and cares about the nuts and bolts can almost feel like becoming someone else. As compelling as the evidence may be, sweating the small stuff can feel like too big of an ask, too big an adjustment to the way you live your life. But even if it's hard to change your big-picture perspective overnight, there's some small stuff you can do that makes a big difference.

So . . .

### Sweat, Don't Stress

Most experts recommend sweating a little every day, and for good reason. It helps us stay calm, cool, and collected. By increasing blood flow to the muscles, it even reduces our recovery time from injuries. And I believe that, metaphorically, sweating the small stuff has the same effect. Sure, putting a little extra effort—or any effort at all—into everyday tasks that could be done mindlessly (or skipped over entirely) might feel arduous, in the same way that working out when we could be lounging on the couch might. But both literal *and* figurative sweat on the front end keeps us in shape, builds up our stamina, helps us move confidently through life, and saves us time and suffering on the back end. The point isn't to pointlessly overexert ourselves; it's to take pointed and thorough action early on, even if the issue at hand seems like no big deal, so we *don't* have to overexert ourselves later.

## The Parable of the Dishwasher

When it comes to the dishwasher, my husband and I are polar opposites. (I often joke that every relationship has a Bonnie and a Dale, and not just when it comes to the dishwasher.) I'm intentional about the way I load it. Everything has its place—the serving spoons, the salad plates, the soup bowls. Dale sometimes teases me about the extra minute and two extra brain cells it takes me to do what he does haphazardly, putting anything and everything wherever there's space, even if it doesn't fit. But I get the last laugh, because it takes Dale two loads to wash what I'm able to fit in one—and ten minutes to unload and sort the dishes and utensils when it takes me mere seconds. I put in a little sweat on the front end. But his carefree dishwasher tendencies make him sweat way more in the end. (Unless I can't help myself and rearrange what he's already done.)

## Mark Your Calendars

Behind every small-stuff-sweater is a master calendar full of reminders and can't-forget dates (and, perhaps, an assistant who knows to keep it current). Take a page from our playbook and keep one of your own. The important events and occasions in your own life should, of course, be in there so you don't miss a deadline or dentist appointment. But the way to really distinguish yourself is to keep track of key moments in the lives of *others*.

Start small, with birthdays. Everybody has one, and the date stays the same year to year. When you encounter one in the wild—say your boss's husband sends her birthday flowers—take note. When Facebook notifies you that a childhood pal turned fifty, add it in. When your brother-in-law mentions a new piece of tech he wants to try,

## Master the Master Calendar

My approach to the calendar is "when in doubt, write it out." Even when I don't act on its information, I'd rather know what's happening in someone's life than forget and feel bad later. Here is a not-at-all-exhaustive list of things I've immortalized in my calendar:

- All the birthdays
- All the anniversaries (marital, professional, divorce-aries, death)
- The due dates of pregnant friends (and, more recently, their kids)
- The premiere dates of many TV series' launches
- The dates of loved ones' upcoming medical procedures
- The day Jesse and Elizabeth adopted their new dog
- The day a colleague was going engagement ring shopping
- The day a colleague's partner left for two months of work travel
- The day a friend was getting back the results of a biopsy
- The day a star employee was interviewing for a new job
- The day a soon-to-be-former star employee was starting a new job
- The week a friend's less-than-easy parents stayed at her house
- The names of friends I had to text if the Rams won the Super Bowl versus the ones I had to text if the Bengals pulled ahead
- My grandkids' favorite colors
- Christmas and Hanukkah gift ideas that came to me in July
- A note to text single friends something funny on Valentine's Day
- The name of a hotel my colleague is staying at (and the dates they'll be there) to send a surprise bottle of champagne
- Any event I want to remember; any thought I don't want to forget

add that as well, so you're not scrambling for gift ideas. Do the same thing when you go out to dinner with a friend and observe their choice of wine. Once you get it going, the calendar is really a matter of maintenance. Simply update it whenever you remember or learn of a noteworthy day in the life of a family member, friend, or close colleague, and indicate (on your digital device of choice) whether it's recurring or one-time-only. The more fleshed out your calendar is, the more time, energy, and headaches you'll find yourself saving or avoiding. Eventually, you may even find that a quick calendar glance each morning makes you a better family member, friend, and colleague.

## Act on Afterthoughts

All of us are bound to experience at least a few would've-should've-could've moments, to have thoughts—after the fact—about something we wish we'd done (or done differently). When that happens, whether it's an hour, a day, or a month later, it's tempting to let it go. Instead, turn your "it's too late" into "I won't wait any longer," and act on your afterthoughts. Send that happy birthday card or text, even belatedly. Send your friend a podcast or restaurant recommendation that made you think of them, even if that thought came a few days ago. Apologize for not proofreading before you pressed send. Certainly, acknowledge if you dropped the ball ("I wish I'd done this sooner," "I know I'm late to this," "I've been thinking about this a lot," etc.). But then pick it back up. Cliché as it may be, better late than never.

## Look (and Listen) Again

I know a middle-school English teacher who used to say to his students, "The first reading is just a greeting." He was right. The best way to be sure we pick up on details and review something thoroughly is to give ourselves more than one chance. That goes for our own work, of course, but also for someone else's. That's how I treated scripts and pilot episodes. While my gut opinion was often formed after the first reading or viewing—sometimes within the first minute—I'd still always flip back to page one or rewind to the opening credits and do the whole thing over again. If I was going to reject something, I wanted to be sure there wasn't some redeeming aspect I'd missed that could be salvaged. If I was going to greenlight something, I wanted to be sure that liking it hadn't blinded me to properly weighing the pros and cons. If I was going to criticize or express concern over something, I wanted to be sure I hadn't missed something significant or even subtle.

## List It Out

The definition of the word *listless* is "lacking energy or enthusiasm." If that's the case, then I might be the most energetic and enthusiastic person alive. Meanwhile, the definition of *listful* is "attentive." That fits better—and, fittingly enough, I'm full of lists. I use multiple to-do lists to keep my days on track. I keep packing lists for every possible vacation or trip; pick the weather, destination, and length of stay—there's probably a list I can lend you. I don't do the grocery shopping in my family (that's what husbands are for, right?), but if I did, I'd probably be just like one of my employee's mothers, who organizes her shopping lists by aisle so she's in and out of the store most efficiently. I have a bucket list that *might* end up being responsible for me running (or, realistically, walking) a marathon in my seventies. I almost never make a decision before writing out a list of pros and cons. (Even this book started out as nothing more than a list of mantras, maxims, and cliché catchphrases I believed to be misguided.)

Sometimes, I go one step further and make lists of lists—to remind myself of the itemized lists I might otherwise forget.

I rely on lists for everything. If you want to sweat the small stuff, you should, too. For starters, list-making helps turn the insurmountable-seeming big stuff into tackle-able small stuff—for example, by breaking down a busy day into individual tasks. Lists also help us *remember* the small stuff: the email we have to send, the oat milk we have to buy, the dress we have to get dry-cleaned by a certain date, the bill we have to pay before it's too late. They bring order and structure to chaos and disarray, which can relieve stress. They keep us on schedule and keep us from procrastinating. They can keep us motivated until we reach the end—something all lists have. So make a list. Check it twice. And then make another.

## Stay Grounded

Obviously, the most powerful and esteemed among us don't have a monopoly on good ideas, insight, and feedback. But some people forget that basic truth. Just like they think it's a waste of time to sweat the small stuff, they think it's unnecessary to make time for and take seriously the "little guys"—people who are less established than they are, or who occupy lower levels of a company hierarchy. That's bad leadership, and at work, it's a big mistake. If you want a well-rounded view of what's going on at your organization, you have to stay grounded and welcome feedback from every direction. After all, some of the most profound wisdom in life comes from the mouths of babes—not bigwigs.

## Thank Fully

Expressing gratitude when it's owed is no small deal. It's a requisite. But a generic or pro forma thank-you is sometimes worse than

### A Formula for Thank You . . . And a Few Examples

While no two thank-you notes should ever look alike, there *is* a formula that you can follow to make yours memorable:

**Author Detail + Recipient Detail + Acknowledgment of Gift (or Deed) + Humor + Joint Memory + Hope for Future (Immediate or Long-Term) = A Good Show of Gratitude**

In the thick of the pandemic, an editor I really liked working with let me know that she had taken a new job—and that our first project together would likely (and sadly) also be our last. Fast-forward to today. She's had two other jobs since, but we kept in contact, and we keep bouncing ideas off each other—this book included. She recently told me that the note I sent in response to her departure, a note I barely remember writing, was her reason why:

My dear Jord,

Oh no . . .
Though I'm thrilled for you, I'm so so so sad for me.
I LOVED working with you—so fun, so easy, so thoughtful. You "got" my voice quickly. And you brilliantly added your own voice and intellect seamlessly.
Let's definitely stay in touch.
I suspect we WILL find a way to work AND play together again.
And, of course, coffee OR better yet wine or tequila, in the flesh, in the new normal . . . whenever that may be.
Enjoy Brooklyn, my birth town.
Send me your new address and all pertinent info.

Hugs,
Best of luck,
Bonnie

none at all. Notes that are obviously written by an assistant or an AI bot aren't much better. Even with the best of intentions, they can leave recipients feeling neglected, not worth the few extra minutes it would take to put in a little extra effort. So give thanks like you mean it by giving meaningful thanks. Let your personality shine through—the shinier, the better. (Even in a note thanking a hiring manager for taking the time to interview you, humor is your friend.) Personalize it to the recipient. Acknowledge the gift given or deed done, and then explain why it was meaningful to and appreciated by you.

And remember: The thank-you notes that sometimes get you furthest (and almost always get remembered) are the ones people didn't expect to receive. Maybe it comes from a lifetime of watching TV credits roll, but my modus operandi is to always acknowledge when people play a role—even if it's behind the scenes. Life is hard, but saying thank you is easy. Doing it well doesn't cost, but it certainly pays off.

## Use Your Team

We don't have to step on someone's toes to have a hand in what they're doing. What we can and should do is find people we trust, teach them, and then delegate deliberately.

If you're a manager, don't expect the people who work under you to be mind readers; show them how you like things done. Surround yourself with people who think like you—who share your strengths and priorities—and people who think differently and see your blind spots. When hiring, assess a candidate's potential for growth as much as their current capabilities. You don't have to believe they could do your job on day one, but you should believe they could do your job one day. After all, the higher you climb in your career, the less time you'll probably have for the "small stuff." But if you manage well, hire right, and delegate deliberately, you'll rest (and rise) easier knowing that someone you trust is sweating it for you.

## Follow Closely (and Follow Up)

A company-wide, all-caps "I QUIT" email (any resignation, really) is often the final sign of employee dissatisfaction. Almost certainly, it's rarely the first. But an employer who doesn't sweat the small stuff probably won't notice those signs if they weren't hollered in their face or inbox. Even if they do, they might dismiss them as no big deal. But by the time the problem becomes unignorable, it's often too late to address or fix.

So follow the small stuff closely. Keep your eyes peeled for minor red flags (what I call "pink flags")—slight changes in behavior, almost unnoticeable drops in work quality, more unexplained absences than usual—and take note of them. Have conversations about what's going on and whether you can help. Best case scenario, you're able to nip the issue in the bud, when there's still time to prevent it from snowballing and ensure that the small stuff doesn't become big stuff. Worst case scenario, at least that "I QUIT" email doesn't take you by surprise.

## Follow Through

It's not possible to carry the entire weight of the world on your shoulders, and you'll collapse if you try. "Sweat the small stuff" doesn't mean doing everything thoroughly. But it does mean being thorough about the things you choose to do and care about. It means looking at situations comprehensively and realizing that the big tasks and small tasks required of you are equally important. It means avoiding a typo in an email to a hiring manager because you understand that it might impact your chances, even marginally, of landing the job. It means not cutting corners. It means picking your battles—but then actually fighting them to win. It means doing it, doing it precisely, and doing it right. It means following through.

## THE FINAL WORD

More than a decade before Richard Carlson told people not to sweat the small stuff, a writer named Robert Brault gave some different advice: "Enjoy the little things, for one day you may look back and realize they were the big things." The small stuff makes a big difference. When it comes to making changes to our mindsets, our approaches, and our daily habits, the small stuff *is* the big stuff. And who we are in the grand scheme of things is determined by all the little things we do. It all adds up.

# 13. The Winner Takes All / Winning Isn't Everything

**What We're Told:** *"The winner takes all."*

We see it all the time: in the lottery, in our elections, even in most sports. When we come up short, what matters doesn't seem to be how we lost—it's *that* we lost. In a winner-takes-all world, the winners . . . they take all. To the victors go the spoils. And to the rest of us losers? In real life, there are no participation trophies. In real life, when we walk away from failure, we often walk away empty-handed.

**The Truth:** *"Winning isn't everything."*

What do Theodor Seuss Geisel, Michael Jordan, Jerry Seinfeld, and Abraham Lincoln have in common? They all struck out before they struck gold.

The most popular children's book author in history, also known as Dr. Seuss? His first manuscript was rejected by twenty-seven different publishers.

The "greatest basketball player of all time," according to the NBA itself? He didn't even make his high school's varsity team.

The richest comedian in the world? He was so nervous at his first open mic night that he forgot all his jokes and was heckled off the stage.

The president widely considered to be the best in American history? He lost nine different races for seven different roles in government before finally getting to the White House. He also had a nervous breakdown that left him bedridden for six months. And he once borrowed money from a friend to start a business that went bankrupt within a year . . . forcing him to spend the next *seventeen* paying it back.

These men were all losers before they were winners, and they're just a few in a huge club. The list of leaders and luminaries who failed before they succeeded in every industry and from every generation is so long and so comprehensive, it can't be a coincidence. When it comes to success, prior failure appears to be not just a pattern but a prerequisite.

Something else these men all have in common: They're all, well, men. That's no coincidence either. Of course, women have also fallen flat on our faces before eventually finding our stride. But high-profile female failures-into-successes are a lot less common.

What's going on? Is it that women fear failure more from the outset, so we take fewer risks to begin with? Is it that we take failure more personally once it happens, so we're less inclined to get back up and try again?

The answer, in my experience, is both. But contrary to what culture tells us, this aversion to failure isn't innate. Instead, from an early age, girls are treated differently from boys by their parents. A comprehensive 2015 study in the journal *Developmental Psychology* found that baby boys are more likely to be bounced on laps and thrown up in the air and tickled. Baby girls, meanwhile, are more likely to be caressed and spoken to in soft voices.[1] By early childhood, a gender disparity starts to emerge. According to Reshma Saujani, the author and founder of Girls Who Code, a nonprofit working to close the gender gap in technology and computer science, it has to do less with strict biology and more with socialization.

In her TED Talk, "Brave, Not Perfect," and her subsequent book of the same name, Reshma explains how boys are encouraged to go big or else go home . . . even when it leads to big busts and dramatic drops, in which case they're encouraged to get back up and try again. That isn't an anecdotal observation, by the way: Studies have shown that boys receive more freedom during playtime, especially outdoors, with less supervision from parents and babysitters.[2] They swing for the fences—or at least the monkey bars—and know that if they fall and end up with a scrape or a bruise, it won't last forever. (And they're taught that scars and battle wounds are cool: something to show off to friends at recess.) In class, they call out the answers, get disciplined, go to detention, and do it all over again. In short, men are raised to be bold and resilient.

Women, on the other hand, are more often raised to be timid and play it safe. Of course, that isn't the intent—the intent is to protect us. In one study from New York University in 2000, mothers of eleven-month-old babies were shown an adjustable sloped walkway and asked to predict the steepness that their child could successfully climb, as well as the steepness their child would willingly *attempt* to climb—successful or not.[3] Consistently, the mothers underestimated the girls—in both ability and willingness to attempt—and overestimated the boys.

Parents and cultural norms continue to protect girls throughout childhood. On playgrounds and at sleepovers, little girls are more supervised than boys, discouraged from getting hurt, and given more direction and assistance when things get hard, even in the class-room.[4] For birthdays and holidays, we're gifted dolls, dream houses, and art supplies where there's no *wrong* way to play—it's all creative and imaginative. Our male counterparts, meanwhile, are given building blocks that can topple over or be knocked down and basketball hoops that require lots of practice. We're less likely to engage in competitive sports where there's a winner and a loser, and more likely to engage in activities like dance, where everyone gets to participate in the recital.

Thank goodness things have changed since I was younger, and little girls today have more options—especially in sports, in large part thanks to Title IX. Still, a lot of the socialization is quite similar. Boys are developing grit. We . . . aren't.

In our younger years, we find more success in the classroom.[5] But even the positive reinforcement we receive there can impact us negatively later. It rewires our psyches to view praise as fuel, and to avoid situations where it might not be received. It's a form of counterproductive coddling. By the time we get to college, as a Harvard study has shown, women are twice as likely to drop a major if we get a B in a single class.[6] At work, of course, that tendency—often labeled "perfectionism"—to only pursue all-but-certain success and avoid anything less can be devastating. Why? Because failure is unavoidable.

Messing up, screwing up, fucking up, *and* coming up short. Getting rejected and feeling dejected. Losing. Sometimes, it's our fault and a consequence of our own actions. Other times, it just happens to us and is out of our control. Either way, these setbacks happen to *all of us*. But too often, women are less prepared to recover. Resilience is a muscle—and, like all muscles in our bodies, it must be exercised and regularly used to get strong. But we haven't done enough to build ours up.

It's time to start. It's time to stop being afraid of losing. It's also time to kill our limited conception of "failure" entirely. It's toxic and untruthful. Failure implies finality, when more often than not, it's a temporary setback. Failures are not the end; they're part of an ongoing, never-ending process of trial and error that is key to our development.

We live in a world of trial and error, of falling down and getting back up, of striking out until we strike gold . . . *not* a world where the winner always takes all. Success isn't finite. There's always another route to take, another race to run. The world's most successful people know that. We have to follow their lead, to err and fall and strike out over and over again, because they're onto something. With each loss they suffer, "losers" are forced to innovate, to improve, to improvise, to investigate other options and ideas and techniques. They become more resilient in the process. As Michael Jordan once put it: "I've failed over and over again in my life. And that is why I succeed."

Persistence is what differentiates those who win after losing from those who stay losers. So does perspective. If we can transform our view of failure, we can transform how we approach it. If we can understand what went wrong and commit to doing better, it becomes *something* we can learn from and move past—not *someone* we are.

And far from being a barrier, it's often the key we need to open the door and get where we want to go next.

## MY TAKE

If success after setback were impossible, then my career would have been, too. I've been passed over, rejected, and I've screwed up more times than I can count. But I've been able to pick myself up by my ankle-bootie straps, dust off my leather pants, and fight (or at least roll out of bed) another day for one reason: To me, getting knocked down is just a good time to reset, reevaluate, reassess, and figure out my next move.

Back in 2004, just two years before *Borat* made "mockumentary" everyone's favorite movie genre, I greenlit one that could have cost me my career.

At the time, I was president of Sci-Fi and I'd just been promoted to president of the USA Network, too, when both channels were bought by General Electric and became part of the NBC universe. Until then, Sci-Fi (and I, and my team) had been operating without much oversight. In the world of cable, we were still a relatively young upstart channel and a zany and weird one at that—which meant less was expected *of* us and invested *in* us. That was especially true when it came to our marketing and our marketing budget; if we wanted to make a splash, we had to strip down and jump into the pool ourselves.

In lieu of expensive, flashy billboards on Sunset Boulevard, we engaged in lots of publicity stunts and guerilla marketing— unconventional tactics that were meant to make headlines. Our goal was always to get more people talking about our shows and programming, while we spent less money. That forced us to think outside the box and embrace controversy. Given that our genre toed the line between fact and fiction (what I like to call "friction"), it seemed reasonable that our approach to marketing and publicity would do the same.

In advance of the premiere of a show called *The Chronicle*—about a young journalist who learns that various monsters, aliens, mutants, and other supernatural and paranormal subjects of his tabloid's articles are, in fact, real and living in the sewers—we deployed teams of "fumigators" throughout New York City to spray the word "quarantine" on manhole covers. This was in 2001, not Covid-era 2020, but our channel was issued significant fines for tampering with public property. In 2003, I enlisted former Bill Clinton chief of staff John Podesta to help Sci-Fi sue the federal government to declassify files on UFO sightings so they could be scrutinized by the general public to, as I said at the time, "take away the blur between fact and fiction." And to herald the release of the now cult classic *The Blair Witch Project*, we made a mockumentary that went "behind the scenes" to unveil the truth—with complementary missing person leaflets of the actors, mock police photos, and chat room plants who spread the idea that there was more to the movie than met the eye—and also saddled us with concerned phone calls and even police inquiries. But it also set all kinds of records and helped spawn an entire new genre of horror movie.

The risks usually paid off—until one day, they didn't.

Leading up to the release of famed director M. Night Shyamalan's anticipated film *The Village*, the Sci-Fi marketing team decided to have some fun. We made a "documentary" about the director's "buried secret": a suspicious, mysterious drowning in a lake near Shyamalan's childhood home that we said first fueled his interest in the supernatural.

I assumed it was obvious that the drowning never happened. The story we told about the documentary's origins, that Shyamalan had agreed to participate but then soured on it, and that Sci-Fi was releasing it without his authorization under threat of legal action, was outlandish. I also thought it was obvious that the director was in on it from the start, all the way through the end. My team and I wholly committed to the stunt. We put out faux press releases written by faux employees (with fake phone numbers and email addresses) about the mockumentary, gave on-the-record interviews about the legal grounds we had to air it, and claimed Shyamalan had attempted to shut down production.

It wasn't all that different from previous guerilla marketing campaigns we'd engaged in—though we maybe took it a bit too far. What *was* different though was that now we were part of a much stricter corporate culture at GE and NBC. They had a far lower threshold for stunts, especially ones like this that misled reporters (which makes sense, given that the organization was renowned for its news division). I was playing the same game I'd always played, but the rules had changed. I should have anticipated that when we greenlit our unconventional marketing ploy. Because I didn't, my actions had created a serious scandal, or at least a PR nightmare, for the new brass at 30 Rock.

I swung, I missed, and then the bat flew and hit my new bosses in the nose. If I had wanted to make a good first impression, I had just done the opposite. If a head had to roll, if a body had to fall on the sword, it would have—and should have—been mine. I felt like crap. I was not only shocked but humiliated. I'd lost the company a ton of money. I knew there was a chance I'd get fired. But I was never going to just call it quits. Instead, I went on an unofficial apology tour, starting with my brand-new boss, Jeff Zucker. I called up his assistant, asked for a meeting the next morning, and marched into his office with my tail between my legs. I was transparent about what had happened and took full accountability, saying, "I should have thought about how this stunt would reflect on NBC before I greenlit it, and next time I will." Then I explained the guardrails I'd be putting in place to ensure that the powers that be wouldn't ever be surprised in this way again.

Just my luck, not even a week after the scandal was an annual meeting where the heads of the big networks presented new shows to the Television Critics Association. Before I could talk about everything exciting on our upcoming schedule, I had to apologize, in front of the industry's biggest critics, journalists, and all my peers, for what we'd just done. It was a difficult and uncomfortable hour, and part of me wished I could disappear.

That failure was entirely my fault. As someone who believes first impressions are everything, I had made a lousy one. I had come into a new culture and acted without first assessing the landscape—a mistake I never made again. Going forward, I ran all my teams' crazier ideas and decisions by legal. I thought through the negative ramifications of our actions alongside the positive ones. And I also *really* learned to read a room: its culture, people, agendas, sensitivities, pressure points, rules, and red lines. Knowing how to read a room is a big part of why I was able to survive the corporate takeovers that followed.

I've been trying desperately to avoid using the term fail forward—the idea that we use our setbacks as stepping stones to success—because it's overused. But I took a very public flop, and I flipped it by owning it but not dwelling on it, and also by looking to the future.

I did the same in the aftermath of setbacks that were objectively *not* my own doing—the blows dealt *to* me that I was forced to deal with anyway.

The year was 2007, and my boss at the time had all but promised me the job of president of the entertainment division of NBC's signature broadcast channel, the company's golden child, where we all watched *The Office, Law and Order,* and *Saturday Night Live.* The promotion would have been a big step up and was considered as such among my peers and in the industry. I didn't ask for the opportunity, but the job was dangled in front of me. Then I watched it go to a guy twenty years younger with a quarter of my experience.

I was livid, dejected, and frankly embarrassed. I eventually found out why I was passed over: not because of something I'd done poorly but because of what I was doing so successfully. My team was making GE/NBCU a *lot* of money. USA was the number one cable channel at the time—and we were raking in more than double the earnings of the more prestigious broadcast channel. My USA Network and Sci-Fi Channel were the company's sacred cash cow, and they wanted to keep milking it as long as they could.

That didn't blunt the sting of losing the top job, not then or now. If anything, it made me feel worse. I'll never know if sexism also contributed, or if they just wanted a company outsider to come in and shake things up. What I do know is that I felt like I was being punished when my networks' performances should have notched me a top prize.

But even though I didn't land the powerful job I wanted, I knew that I still had power. If what the top brass at the company was saying was true—and I believed it was—then they really didn't want to lose me. They quite literally couldn't afford it. So when my contract came up for renewal, I took my time signing—almost half a year—until my salary was nearly doubled. And I used my leverage to ask for what I really wanted now: the go-ahead to create a cable production studio, Universal Cable Productions (UCP), out of nothing.

Many people assume that a channel or network gets in on the ground floor of a TV show's development—that they're the ones who read through scripts, hire writers, build the set, find the cast, and on and on and on. But that's often not the case. The entity responsible for all that is a studio, and often, the network comes into the process only after the show has been greenlit (sometimes, after it's been filmed entirely). Networks are basically shopping for content that fits; they're not necessarily in the factory making it. Even then, once the network decides to "buy" the show and air it, they're really only renting. Most of the time, the studio retains the rights, and the show eventually returns as its property.

Until then, USA, SYFY, and all of NBC's other cable channels had no in-house studio producing scripted content. If we had an idea for a series, the best we could hope for was that another studio was making something similar, or that they'd like our idea enough to want to work with us on it. So I asked for a studio. If I had to stay in cable, I wanted to be involved in the process from inception to completion. If I had to stay in cable, I needed my networks to have more agency and to develop and own the shows we'd end up airing; after all, we knew our brand better than the outside studios ever would. If I had to stay in cable, I was going to make the best shows, period . . . and make my business even more profitable in the process.

I only came up with that request after coming up short elsewhere. But it ended up being one of my very best ideas—one that brought me, my team, and my company a *lot* of prestige and money. UCP gained a reputation in the industry as a go-to studio for talent on the rise.

And staying in cable because I didn't get the job in broadcast ended up being one of the greatest things that could have happened to me. I sometimes shudder to think what would have happened had I gotten that top broadcast job. The upside: It was a powerful figurehead position with a deep legacy, and exceptionally high-profile as a result. The downside: Having more eyes on me would have prevented me from being as creative and innovative as I wanted and was used to. The reality, too, is that at the time, cable was on the rise with no real ceiling. Broadcast, meanwhile, was still dominant but in decline—but neither I nor others realized it quite yet. Had I switched from the former to the latter, the likelihood that my career could have survived, much less thrived, is slim.

Under my leadership, cable ended up being hugely profitable for NBCUniversal—by far the company's most profitable division at the time. As a result, a few years later, I ultimately joined the C-suite as cable entertainment chairman. In that role, I oversaw twelve different channels (including USA, SYFY, Bravo, E!, Oxygen, G4, Esquire, Sprout, Style, and Universal Kids) while running two cable studios—a dream job I could have never dreamed up myself.

And that guy who got the broadcast job over me? He was out in barely two years.

While these two "failures"—one that I caused by approving a controversial marketing campaign and one that happened to me when I failed to get a job I wanted—may seem to have little in common, they're united by a critical shared thread: In both situations, I was forced to accept a reality I did not like, and would not have chosen, and had to turn it into something better. In doing so, I was able to realize that failure is just an event—but it never has to be the main event, and it *definitely* doesn't have to become my identity.

In a recent leadership training, I learned about a framework called "What? So what? Now what?" only to realize I've been employing it for much of my career. Whenever something's gone wrong, whether it's been in my control or not, I've accepted *what* happened. I've figured out *what* the implications were and what the loss or mistake meant to me—no sugarcoating allowed. Then I've asked myself *what* the hell I do next, and where the hell I go from here.

Because there's *always* a way forward.

## NAIL IT

The secret to success isn't to avoid setbacks. It's to accept that they're inevitable—and that if we haven't yet experienced one, we're probably not taking enough risks. So lean into opportunities where failure is a possibility. Swing from the monkey bars on the playground and the rafters at work. Get comfortable falling. And when you do? Don't look at it as a loss. After all, there's always a chance for a redo. Far from being the end, your setbacks can and should become a chance to reinvent, retry, redirect, and reset.

So . . .

## Reframe "Failure"

Failure gets a terrible rap. I'd argue it's the worst "F word" out there. It implies an end, a "game over," but unless you're dead, there's always another beginning (though some believe you get another beginning then, too). Your failures may be setbacks or slipups or strikeouts or slowdowns, but they're only the final leg of a journey if you let them be. If you don't, they're actually good for you and great for your growth. They can even be fuel that propels you forward.

Change the way you frame the mistakes you make, the mess-ups you're responsible for, and the rejections you receive. They're not a reflection of you—they're just something you did (or didn't do). Change the way you think and talk about them—to yourself; your family; your employees, employers, and coworkers; and your friends. That, more than anything else, sets the tone for everything else that follows.

## Review What Happened

When something goes really wrong—or really right—it's important to honestly assess what happened. That's the only way to be sure it won't (or will) happen again. So be truthful about the situation, even the ugly parts. Be willing to see the ways you messed up, even if you didn't mean to—or the ways you could have predicted what

**Say This, Not That**

It's time to swap out our losing language for winning words:

- "I failed." → "I learned something new."
- "This was a waste of time." → "This was a valuable experience."
- "I'll never be good at this." → "I need more practice."
- "This is too hard." → "This is a worthy challenge."
- "I made a mistake." → "I discovered a way that doesn't work."
- "I can't do this." → "I can't do this *yet.*"
- "I'm a loser." → "I can try again."
- "I'll never achieve my goals." → "I'm still working on my goals."
- "I messed up again." → "I need to try a different approach."
- "I'll just give up." → "I'll find a way to keep going."

was coming, even if you couldn't have stopped it. Figure out what, if anything, could have made a difference. Seek the perspective of others who were involved; they might be able to see what you're missing.

## Respond Quickly

When you've messed up, time is *really* of the essence. That goes for the professional mishaps you cause and the personal mayhem you wreak. The sooner you apologize, take accountability and ownership, make amends, and begin moving forward, the less time you leave someone to ruminate over everything you've done wrong—and the more time you give them to focus instead on all the ways you're already beginning to make things right. The longer you wait, the deeper a hole you dig. So rather than throw yourself a pity party and drag out the despair, move quickly so you can move on, and then celebrate the start of something new.

## Refrain from Pointing Fingers

The blame game is never a winning strategy. But at work, it's also a telltale sign of insecure leaders, unstable teams, and nonexistent loyalty. So instead of coming up with a litany of reasons you aren't at fault, step up to the plate and take ownership—even if that means you take one for the team. It's a sign of great leadership, wisdom, trust, confidence, and a healthy workplace culture.

## Reconsider How You Do Things

If things go south, for whatever reason, your instinct might be to quit. Not so fast. But you should reflect on the way you do things—and consider whether you need to change your approach. Maybe that involves a change in how you manage a team or communicate with your boss. Maybe you implement a new process, like having legal sign off on all your marketing stunts. Maybe you fight the urge to indulge your knee-jerk reactions and take more time to come to the table with a counteroffer instead. Maybe you start sharing your instincts with a peer you trust to see if they raise any caution flags. If nothing else, failures are good reminders that you aren't infallible. Neither are your instincts, ideas, and approaches.

While second-guessing yourself might be humbling and require admitting you were wrong, it doesn't make you weak. In the aftermath of some failed attempt, self-doubt might serve you well—and increase your odds of achieving an outcome that feels like winning to you. Plus, that humility will work overtime to impress others around you, too.

## Read the Room

The most important rule governing winning and losing is that there are almost no consistent rules. What works in one situation won't work in another, and what works in a third may not work in the first. If something's gone wrong or simply hasn't gone your way, the reason might be as simple as the room you're in. The publicity stunt might be genius; the corporate environment or culture you are part of might have no tolerance for it. So take a look around, notice who and what is in there, and learn how to read it all.

## Revise the Attempt

Rather than simply try again, why not try something different? Return to an old problem with a fresh perspective. Approach a dilemma from a new angle. Seek out additional sources of advice. Switch up your materials. Make backup plans. If you've already lost one round of negotiations, emphasize something else that you bring to the table in the next round—or find something else to ask for entirely. Find another door. And if the doors won't budge, crack open a window or break down a wall.

## Realize What You Still Have

The truth is that you won't always get what you want or have it your way. That doesn't mean you're left with nothing. No one can take away your foundation—even if it ends up being the groundwork for a different building. When you feel like you've lost something great, or like you'll never come back from a grave mistake, realize what you still have. Write out a list of the experiences, accomplishments, connections, and skills you've acquired over the course of your career. That doesn't go away, even if an opportunity you'd been hoping for does. Then try to figure out what assets you still hold: an unparalleled track record, a client relationship you've cultivated, a tool you've mastered, a team that's unfailingly loyal to you, even another offer or a willingness to walk. You don't have to use them—especially not right away—but realizing those assets exist can empower you to get back up and give something another go.

## Redefine Winning

The winner *doesn't* take all—not even close. There's always more than one path to victory and more than one definition of success. It's just a matter of perspective and priorities. If you don't get what you thought you wanted originally, challenge yourself to come up with three other solutions that will make you happy and try to go for those instead. Most of the people who've taken a setback and used it to fuel success—a successful venture, product, creative endeavor, company, or career—ended up taking home a prize they never even knew was an option originally. Think big, think outside the box, and think positively. (And know that sometimes, winning is as simple as refusing to let up or give in.)

## THE FINAL WORD

Winning isn't everything. But knowing how to lose is. Whether it's our personal or professional life, whether it's our mistake or something entirely unexpected, there is always an opportunity to turn things around, to use our setbacks to set ourselves up for success, to leverage our short- or medium-term losses into long-term gains. Figuring out how to do that might not make us overnight success stories. But it will make us more interesting, resilient people. That's what gets us closer to the finish lines in life—and that's what really matters once we're there.

# 14. Don't Mix Work With Play / All Work And No Play Makes Everyone Dull

**What We're Told:** *"Don't mix work with play."*

Despite the valiant efforts of HR departments across the country, there's still no objective, all-encompassing list of workplace dos and don'ts. There probably never will be. It's impossible, after all, to predict every possible professional scenario and make a hard-and-fast rule to govern it. Instead, we're taught to use our best judgment and err on the side of caution. And one way we're taught to do that is to keep our personal and professional lives separate, to avoid mixing work with play. If we don't want to cross lines, why blur them in the first place?

**The Truth:** *"All work and no play makes everyone dull."*

Today, "mixing work and play" is often a euphemism for something sinister: the misbehavior and misconduct that result when people treat the workplace like a personal playground. From sexual and romantic relationships between colleagues or between superiors and underlings, to unwanted, unreciprocated, and uncomfortable advances, to excessive drinking and partying at after-work gatherings, this "play" is sometimes rated PG-13, sometimes rated R.

Let me state plainly and clearly for the record that none of *that* belongs anywhere near the office . . . physical, digital, or otherwise. That type of "pleasure" has no place in business. It makes for a toxic work culture.

But enjoying what we do, forming and maintaining friendships, and having genuine fun is precisely the type of play that *should* belong in our workplaces and *should* be mixed with business. It's essential to a healthy work culture.

The average person spends almost one-third of their time each week on the job—ninety thousand hours over a lifetime, according to Bob Nelson in the *Harvard Business Review*—and 56 percent of Americans spend more time with their "work families" than their actual families.[1] Enjoying being around our colleagues is good for employees, and it's good for employers. Aristotle spewed a lot of wisdom back in his day, but perhaps nothing as wise as this: "Pleasure on the job puts perfection in the work." The data agrees.

To start, fun places to work are—statistically—great places to work. Each year, *Fortune* magazine publishes a "100 Best Places to Work" list. Year after year, around 80 percent of employees at companies that make the list describe their office environments as "fun," compared to just 60 percent of employees at companies that didn't make the list. Those fun workplaces, meanwhile, lead to less stress, more optimism, and increased engagement and creativity.

Similarly, having friends on the job helps us enjoy our jobs. Multiple studies have shown that workplace friendships improve our well-being, foster a sense of purpose within us, and make us feel happier, more satisfied, and more fulfilled. There's an assumption that these friendships will serve as a distraction—but that's actually not true. Gallup researchers have found that, in fact, they make us more engaged *and* more motivated to succeed.[2]

Company-wide camaraderie has been proven to increase trust and inclusion, which boosts employee retention numbers, innovation, and organizational performance. The reason, according to two psychology researchers? Compared to acquaintances, friends are more committed to each other, collaborate and cooperate more, are quick to encourage one another, communicate better, and don't hesitate to deliver critical feedback.[3] That makes it easier to get work done—and to do it right and feel good about it.

The inverse is true, too. People who report lower levels of connection at work perform more poorly on the job; when they feel disengaged and disconnected, they're also more likely to look elsewhere for employment and eventually quit. Perhaps less predictably, they even miss more work than their better-acquainted counterparts; they're twice as likely to stay home due to an illness and five times more likely to stay home due to stress. Meanwhile, as researchers in Australia and Singapore have documented, workplace boredom causes people to feel both overexerted and underutilized, all while making them more anxious, distracted, and disillusioned.[4]

This loneliness and disengagement costs the American economy up to $550 billion a year.[5] Meanwhile, motivated and engaged employees—those who feel fulfilled, find enjoyment, and have friends on the job—can increase a company's profits by almost 50 percent.[6] What does that mean? It means that blurring the lines between work and play helps the bottom line.

Fun in the professional sphere is more than the sum of its parts. It makes people happy and eager to show up in the morning and not race out in the evening. It makes people proud of the work they're doing and keeps them motivated to continue doing it. It leads people to collaborate with each other rather than compete against one another. It helps people feel seen and understood. Critically, it fosters deep trust and loyalty, which encourages people to tell the truth even when it's hard, take feedback even when it hurts, and try new things even when there's a risk of failure. That makes it the cornerstone of great teams and the keystone of every great corporate culture.

In work-speak, "culture" is a catch-all term we use to describe the values, views, and practices that unite an organization. It's *how* an organization does what it does. In biology, culture is slightly different: It's a verb, not just a noun, to describe the process of cultivating living material in suitable conditions for growth. But in a way, that's what the best workplace cultures do, too. They help us grow.

Sometimes, that growth happens when we take our professional relationships outside the office and see where they lead us. Sometimes, it's the refusal to stick strictly to business that improves our business.

Men have a lot of experience with this. Historically, mixing work and play has been their domain. It's men who made a religion out of golfing with coworkers and clients alike, who see nothing unprofessional about setting up office-wide Fantasy Football leagues. It's men who've kept bottles of whiskey (or perhaps, today, tequila) in decanters on their desks à la *Mad Men*. It's men who rub shoulders and pat backs—public displays of what they consider platonic affection—without thinking twice.

For most of history, women haven't had the same privilege. When we entered the workforce, first during World War II but even in the sixties and seventies, we weren't invited to play golf with clients or join colleagues for after-work drinks. Even when we were, it was only as a courtesy—one we almost always had to decline to race home and prepare dinner for our spouse and kid.

Still today, women are pulled in two directions. Though we may want to, we're often unwilling to let our guard (or even our hair) down because we're worried about being perceived as unserious. And yet we know we're at a disadvantage when we don't.

Anyone who tells you they go to the Aspen Ideas Festival or the World Economic Forum in Davos, where men outnumber women three or four to one, purely for work is lying. Even if the goal is to close a deal or open a line of communication with someone, "play"— the happy hours, the interesting panels and talks, the networking opportunities—is a critical means to that end.

So we should be equalizing the playing field (or the putting green). Corporate cultures full of good clean fun and good close friendships should be ubiquitous—and fostering them *for everyone* should be a no-brainer. We should *all* be getting to know each other outside of work, learning to see our colleagues as people and not just worker bees, pursuing ways to find enjoyment and fulfillment on the clock rather than waiting until it strikes 6:00 p.m. so we can leave as fast as possible.

But just the opposite is taking hold. Instead of seeing more work-place friendships, we're seeing fewer. More than 20 percent of Americans say they don't have friends at work. Almost half say they don't have a "true friend." *Over* half don't look forward to work because of their coworkers, a third don't trust them, and many feel no sense of connection to the people they spend their days with. It's no surprise then that rates of employee engagement, satisfaction, and happiness are all at record lows.[7]

What's going on? For one thing, people don't stay in jobs as long as they used to. That lowers their incentive to want to form durable, personal connections at work, and drives them to look elsewhere for companionship and enjoyment.

Then the Me Too movement rocked nearly every industry and the world. It triggered both a cultural awakening *and* a shift in corporate culture. It wasn't just the bad guys (and yes, they were overwhelmingly guys) who needed to be brought down. The entire system that enabled and empowered them had to be dismantled. Almost overnight, the rules governing professional conduct and relationships were rewritten, with the intention of making the workplace work for everyone in it.

In a lot of ways, these aims were achieved. Thank goodness. Today, the consequences of certain types of conduct are explicit, reporting harassment and abuse is less taboo, and gender-based misconduct does feel less frequent.

And yet, by focusing so squarely on what *isn't* allowed and *won't* be tolerated, we forgot to talk about how people *can* and *should* interact. As important as they are, the new employee handbooks ignore the majority of people at work, who have good intentions and want to do good work—and who know implicitly that strong relationships with coworkers are critical to doing it. With no positive vision to follow and no happy medium to seek, many of them feel their only option is to build a wall between the personal and the professional, even when human resources departments don't explicitly demand it.

The result? In some industries, the dominant corporate culture is now all work, no play; all professional, no personal. The environment is one of fear and distrust. Comradery, warmth, and joy are seen as risky. So are vulnerability and openness. Instead of breaking down the barriers separating them from their colleagues, people are erecting obstacles. In an effort to keep their jobs, people are keeping their distance and keeping things curt and even cold.

Covid only made this phenomenon more acute. If the takeaway from 2017 was that mixing business with play is unacceptable, then perhaps the takeaway from 2020 was that it's simply unnecessary. Isolated from the office and absent any potential for spontaneous interaction, it was easy for employees to view jobs as purely transactional and forget the value that comes from putting more of ourselves into them. Who needs workplace friendships or workplace fun when work is a verb and no longer a place?

The answer, of course, is that we all need connection and joy at work. Our lives and jobs and relationships and passions are better when they're allowed to exist in harmony. When we have friends and fun at work, we want to keep working. When we mix business with the right kind of pleasure, doing business *becomes* a pleasure.

## MY TAKE

During my time running the Cable Entertainment Group at NBC-Universal, there was a running joke at 30 Rock that cable was a cult. We would sit together at corporate meetings, travel together, grab dinner together after work, and celebrate (or commiserate) over drinks after long presentations. What other explanation existed for how loyal we were to each other, how devoted to our jobs, how happy we always seemed to be, and how much all of us wanted to stay and none of us wanted to leave?

Here's how I put it to another executive: "I love the theory, but it's off by three letters. The secret to our success isn't a cult. It's our cul-*ture*." And the secret to that culture? Mixing business with play—lots of it. We worked hard. We played hard. We made the professional feel personal.

When I became president of USA, I began a process of transforming our network. But I firmly believe that what made all the difference in that transformation was the team *behind* our work and our culture at USA— one that prized and prioritized collaboration, communication, and, critically, the satisfaction of a job well done, and the good times that came along with it. What set USA apart and up for success on-screen also set us (as a team) apart and up for success off-screen and away from the set or studio, whether the cameras were rolling or not.

Just like our shows, we were character-centric. On our team, competence and expertise were a necessity. But no one was expected to be perfect. Quite the opposite, in fact. Everyone at the network was expected to be—and respected for being—a real human being, with warts and worries and all. Many of us spent more time together than we did at home (a consequence of our industry), which amounted to too many hours, in too close quarters, to put on an insincere act in the office. So we were open and honest with each other about the professional and the personal—from a kid graduating kindergarten to a spouse going in for surgery. We brought our whole selves to work.

That transparency fostered a deep sense of trust, which was fundamental to everything we did. As a leader, I am completely averse to silos. At USA, I made sure to break them down. If we were deciding whether to develop or greenlight a show, every one of my top lieutenants—from marketing to programming to ad sales—would have to review the scripts and discuss casting, even if it was completely out of their wheelhouse.

That collaboration was critical to eliminating most of our blind spots and largely error-proofing our predictions of what would resonate with our audiences. But it only worked because we knew each other (and our respective strengths and vulnerabilities) well, which allowed us to understand where people were coming from . . . and which helped us assume the best intentions, even during disagreements.

And there were many disagreements. In the high-pressure world of network television, it's hardly kumbaya. We argued about everything from the color scheme of a billboard sign to what time a show should air. But we could do it over a bottle of wine (or two) late into the night and come back to work the next morning with a smile on our faces—feeling like we had accomplished a lot in the process, without resenting the process itself. And when it mattered, we were always on the same side. In public or to the press, we presented a united front and never aired another person's dirty laundry. (Doing so was, in my book, a fireable offense.)

Just like the characters written for our shows, I think we were all pretty likable—by which I mean, well, we all really liked each other. We saw one another as people first and coworkers second. We celebrated birthdays and weddings. We rooted for each other's successes, just like our audiences rooted for the protagonists they watched on-screen each week. We opened up and confided in one another when we were having issues, not just at work but at home. That allowed us to take feedback to heart constructively, rather than defensively; we knew it was for our own good, and we received it the way we would have if a friend delivered it—because that's exactly what our team was: friends.

Meanwhile, much like our shows, our default mode was "drama" with a couple of extra dollops of humor. We were passionate about every project we pursued. We each took ownership over it as if it were our own and the fate of our careers hung in the balance—because each project was, and it did. That meant we took our jobs seriously. But we didn't take *ourselves* too seriously. In the weeks leading up to the end of the year, I'd carve out time on my morning and evening commutes to write a personal limerick that was equal parts roast and toast about each of my direct reports (and sometimes their direct reports, too). Then I'd perform the limericks live at the annual holiday dinner I hosted—and allow everyone to roast my delivery.

Was it silly? Of course. So was the choice a few colleagues and I made to don football helmets for a meeting with NBCUniversal's

CEO to request a big budget increase for our network, which we brainstormed at an unofficial happy hour the night before. (We knew we'd be on the defensive and had to protect ourselves, and our ideas, from being tackled to the ground.) But silly was exactly the point.

While we couldn't predict where the conversation would go, we *could* ensure that it started with a chuckle. Humor can make people drop their walls, and it worked. We got the money (and a lot of smiles).

Countless studies have shown that laughter has a host of benefits, particularly in the workplace—spurring productivity, collaboration, and creativity on the job. Some researchers in Japan and Norway even believe that laughing makes a person live longer.[8] If they're right, someone from my team at USA might end up setting the Guinness World Record for old age.

Then there was our ethos of perpetual blue skies—also a signature of USA's scripted series, which we literally filmed outdoors, in the sun, whenever possible. Coast to coast, the USA office culture was positive and supportive, and the outlook was upbeat and optimistic. Our optimism also extended to the cloudy days and tough-to-weather storms, of which there were many. When we suffered a setback—when a show flopped, when our budget was cut, when we blew a deal—we didn't sugarcoat it. But we didn't dwell on it either. After all, failure is less daunting when it's shared. And in our hyper-collaborative culture, every failure (along with every success) was shared—which meant there were no big, paralyzing doomsday events.

Instead of heading home alone afterward, we'd head to the Top of the Rock (or a dedicated conference room on the twenty-first floor) for a drink. We'd make toasts like, "Cheers to our try!" or "I guess we tempted fate with that attempt!" Only after downing some spirits would we then go our separate ways—always in higher spirits than we would have been otherwise.

Because we respected and cared about each other outside of work, no one decision could define a person—no less a team—even if it was a really bad one. Instead, without pointing fingers, we were able to ask ourselves what we learned and what we could do better next time. We were able to face anything head-on because we faced everything together.

Ours was a culture in which getting along and having fun—in other words, play and pleasure—were considered critical to doing business. The payoff came in loyalty not just from viewers but from my team: During my entire tenure at USA, there were very few departures of senior employees, even when the going got tough. Why? It turns out that people who form genuine connections with the people where they work end up feeling more connected to their work. And when they're empowered to find joy while they're on the job, they actually enjoy their jobs.

So when my portfolio eventually expanded to include all of NBC-Universal's Cable Entertainment Group, I brought the work-meets-play culture along. By then, I was overseeing USA Network as well as SYFY, E!, Bravo, Oxygen, Esquire, Sprout, and a bunch of other smaller channels, along with two production studios. My inner circle had expanded, and my team had grown much bigger. But we still worked hard together, traveled together, laughed together, cried together, applauded individual successes, and supported each other when things didn't go as well.

While I couldn't possibly get to know every member of my two-thousand-plus-person division, I made sure they had ample opportunity to get to know each other through group-wide off-sites, holiday parties, and social events on the ice-skating rink at Rockefeller Center. I even initiated something called "Hammer Games," an employee summer Olympics, with sporting events, relay races, and trivia, which were played both on an LA beach and in New York's Central Park.

Far from discouraging workplace friendships that transcended the workplace, I continued to hope for them and help them along. Far from getting more serious as we got more seniority, I made sure we still had lots of fun. Every part of me believed—and I knew—there were only upsides.

Sure enough, just as USA became the crown jewel of the cable world, cable ended up becoming the crown jewel of NBCUniversal. In one exemplary year, we delivered almost $3 billion in pure profit—by far the biggest contributor to the company's bottom line—while 129 million Americans tuned in to watch one of our cable channels each week.

How's that for good business?

## NAIL IT

It's clear why most corporate cultures these days discourage mixing work and play: People don't understand what the ingredients in that mix even are. They may have rules and regulations that govern on-the-job behavior and misconduct—but most of the time, those only dictate what can't and shouldn't be done.

What people need more than ever is a positive set of guidelines—of what we *can* and *should* do—that will stand the test of time and tackle the toughest questions of culture. Here are my Ten Commandments of Corporate Culture.

So . . .

### 1. Thou Shalt Lead by Example

You don't have to be a leader in the traditional sense to lead by example and impact your workplace culture. At any level of an organization, in any role, you can help usher in a change simply by starting to embody it yourself. If you value open communication, communicate openly and straightforwardly. If you value vulnerability, reach out to coworkers when there's something you're struggling with and ask for help. If you want a culture of accountability and honesty, own your mistakes—early. If you value collaboration (and you should), find ways to work with people in different divisions; ask colleagues for feedback on a proposal you've labored over, and offer to serve as a second set of eyes on something of theirs. If you want to work somewhere joyful, be a source of joy: Crack a joke, eat lunch with people in the cafeteria (or a conference room you book for the occasion) and not your desk, surprise your cubicle buddy with a birthday cupcake.

Whether you're an executive or an executive assistant, what you do reflects what you believe—and it can set the tone for others to follow. So practice what you preach, preach what you practice, and lead by example.

### Bosses Make or Break the Culture

Too many executives peruse the pages of *Harvard Business Review* or read the results of their latest employee survey only to miss something critical: As the highest profile and most visible workers at an organization, they are responsible for shaping its work culture. And their actions speak louder than words. My old boss Jeff Zucker used to take the time to sign personalized birthday cards for everyone who worked under him for this very reason.

### 2. Thou Shalt Know Thyself

Take it from someone who knows: You're going to enjoy work a whole lot more if you have similar values to the people you

## Values to Value

While no two organizations will have the exact same values, there is usually at least *some* overlap among successful organizations—because certain values make for good business and a great culture:

- Accountability
- Adaptability
- Calculated risk-taking
- Collaboration
- Communication
- Cooperation
- Creativity
- Curiosity
- Flexibility
- Fun
- Growth

- Honesty
- Humility
- Humor
- Leadership
- Learning
- Openness
- Optimism
- Teamwork
- Transparency
- Trust
- Vulnerability

work with. While you can't meet them all before you accept a job, you *can* do a little research into your potential employer. Do they prioritize independence and self-starters, or teamwork and learning? Are people out of the office by 5:00 p.m., or do they like to hang around? Is there a culture of staff retreats, holiday parties, and off-sites? Try to glean if their professed values align with your own. If they don't, then don't be surprised if you end up being a cultural misfit in the company environment. If they do, there's a decent chance you'll find some like-minded colleagues who can turn into friends . . . which will make the work experience more rewarding.

Once you accept a role, make sure you learn what's expected, what's allowed, and what's off-limits. Mistakes, misfires, and miscommunication on the job are often the result of some cultural misunderstanding; if you know who you work for, you're less likely to mess up.

## Why You Should Value Values

If the first step to solving a problem is recognizing you have one, then the first rule of improving corporate culture is *ensuring* you have one. And not everyone does. There's a misconception that culture is found in (or simply synonymous with) an organization's mission, purpose, or goal. In fact, it's found in your values—or the way your values are put into practice by the organization's people. So, before you do anything else, establish those values. Then communicate them clearly across your organization. Make sure they live somewhere—online, on a bulletin board in the office kitchen—so everyone is aware of them, and no one can ever use "I didn't know" as an excuse. And be consistent. You can't expect people to live up to your organization's values if they don't know what's expected of them in the first place.

## 3. Thou Shalt Know Thy People

I've made many of my dearest friends on the job. Even once I left, or they did, we stayed in touch because we cared about each other— and we cared about each other because we had gotten to know each other personally, not just professionally. That made work more enjoyable and meaningful, both on a day-to-day basis and when I look back on the memories. So make friends with your coworkers. Learn their hobbies, their birthdays and anniversaries, their favorite sports teams. Ask them out for coffee—and then about their families, their backgrounds, and their goals. Congratulate them on their kids' graduations and, if you're invited, attend their kids' celebrations. Share the same about yourself, even if it makes you feel vulnerable. Don't be afraid to open up . . . and *definitely* don't fall for the falsehood that work friends and life friends can't be one and the same. In my experience, some of the best ones always are.

## Really Know Your Team

The most fundamental part of being a boss is knowing your team. After all, you can't set them up for success if you don't know their strengths and weaknesses, personalities and priorities, wants and needs, and hopes and fears; if they're not set up for success, you're not either. Your team also needs to know you back—because you can't lead people who don't trust you, and it's not easy for a stranger to earn people's trust.

So get off your high horse and get to know the people who work with and for you—because there's no better way to both see what's going on at your organization *and* make the people at your organization feel seen. Spend a day in the cubicles. Shadow them on the job. Join them for lunch. Seek out their advice. An always-open-door policy might be unrealistic, but try setting up office hours to see who shows up and what you learn. Regularly gauge how they're feeling about work. The more senior you are, the more un-seamless (and maybe, at first, unwelcome) your efforts will be. But the more effort you make—even through proxies, like people who report to you— the more welcome you'll eventually be. If you want employees to treat their jobs as more than a nine-to-five, you need to treat them as more than a name in an employee directory.

## 4. Thou Shalt Acknowledge and Appreciate Freely

When it comes to work, a little recognition can go a long way. On a fundamental level, it just makes people's days a lot more pleasurable, and plants the seeds of positive workplace relationships that can blossom into something great. So start acknowledging and appreciating colleagues, both formally and informally. When someone reaches a career milestone, celebrate it. When someone does a great job in a client meeting—even if that something is part of their job description—tell them. Let them know you noticed. Stop them in the hallway. Send them an email. Sing their praises to their supervisor, and if that supervisor is you, sing their praises to *your* supervisor. While I was writing this book, my former head of research at USA reached out to share a note I'd written to her after she knocked a presentation out of the park. I didn't remember it; she told me it was the highlight of her 2015.

### Three Key Rs: Recognize, Reward, Retain

This isn't just a feel-good tactic. It's also good for business. Companies where good performance is regularly recognized and rewarded—those with a "recognition-rich culture"—have much lower turnover rates than companies where such acknowledgment isn't the norm. People leave when they don't feel appreciated, but they work harder if they believe their contributions will be recognized. Who *isn't* more likely to want to hang around work—and the people they work with—when they're made to feel good, seen, and appreciated there?

### Bosses: Host Your Version of Breakfasts with Bonnie

When I was running the NBCUniversal cable division, I hosted monthly breakfasts, each with around twenty people from across my division and every department. Not invited? My direct reports, or theirs; we spent enough time together, so I already knew all of them. My goal, over coffee and croissants, was to get to know the people I didn't yet—and get them to know me. From assistants to vice presidents, a long conference table would fill up as I laid out my one and only rule: The room was Vegas, and whatever people said there stayed there. I would introduce myself, tell them a bit about my own story—always peppered with one of my many imperfections—and share the latest happenings and goings-on from across the networks, channels, and studios, which they might not yet be aware of.

But then I'd get down to the real purpose of the breakfast: getting to know them and asking for their perspectives. I'd always inquire, "What are you hearing about the business and what are you afraid to tell me?" And eventually, some brave soul always spoke up and broke the ice for everyone else. Because I earned their trust, I learned who was a great but underutilized manager (and who was floundering at leading), which workplace initiatives were considered overrated, what was making people happy and what was making them bored, whether or not they had clear and defined goals, if they felt supported and part of a team, how something that was going well could be made even better, and, of course, what their new favorite show was.

## 5. Thou Shalt Do Better than Pizza and Ping-Pong

It's almost a parody by now. In an effort to make work more fun and engaging, companies and their relevant human resources operations jump to the lowest common denominator of socializing and entertaining. They throw a pizza party or bring a Ping-Pong table into the lounge and think they've solved the problem. Not even close. Short-term fixes like this, the futurist and author Jacob Morgan explains, are more like an adrenaline shot—temporarily boosting morale and then quickly wearing off.

So if you work for an organization where pizza parties *are* the only "culture" to speak of? Don't rely on them. You can do better. Invite a new hire out for coffee in their first month and get to know their stories. Organize a happy hour for your team to celebrate meeting a big deadline or coming in under budget on a project—and invite everyone to bring their partner or a friend if they'd like; by default, the presence of people from your lives outside of work will help you begin to see colleagues in a different light and break down those work life–home life walls. Start a book club, and then invite people to join from across divisions and departments. If you know a colleague loves to hike, and you're traveling together for work, plan one. If the person two desks down has a picture of their dog taped to their computer monitor, ask them about their good boy—and then share a picture of yours.

It's easy to blame a lack of real work culture on the higher-ups who are ostensibly most responsible for fostering it, but you aren't helpless even when you're entry-level. If you want to work somewhere that values office friendships (and you should)—if you want to be able to say, five or fifteen years from now, "I met this lifelong friend at work"—then step up and put in the work to make it happen. It may seem like you're doing your company's job for them, and maybe you are, but you'll be helping yourself most of all.

## Don't Pin Your Plans on Pizza

If you have a poor workplace culture, no amount of free pizza is going to fix it. Pizza parties only last an hour, maybe two. Company culture, on the other hand, is how people spend the rest of the day, week, and even year. While no one hates free pizza (if it's actually free pizza and not a replacement for a raise), social events, extracurricular activities, and perks at work are merely additive to the underlying environment.

When done right, those social events, extracurricular activities, and perks can add a lot. They can complement a culture that's already established—and make the values that undergird it seem deeply consistent, rather than shallow and insincere. For example: If a workplace that shows no regard for employee well-being places a nice basket of toiletries in each bathroom, the gesture might seem ironic, insensitive, and even insulting. But in a workplace where the mental, physical, and emotional health of every employee is consistently prioritized, that same toiletry basket serves to positively reinforce a culture of caring. One quick rule for events though: Unless it's an off-site or a fun holiday party at night, do it on the company dime and company time. And make it optional because forced fun for all is no fun at all.

## 6. Thou Shalt Mind Each Other's Business

Bringing people into processes outside their wheelhouse reinforces the team aspect of your culture—making everyone feel valued for their viewpoints and invested in the entire puzzle, rather than just one piece of it. (It also makes solving that puzzle a lot more enjoyable!) And it shows that you see someone for everything they can bring to the table, that they're not just some professional automaton to you who's good at one thing and one thing only.

So break down the silos within your team, your department, and even your organization. View no one as competition and everyone as a potential collaborator. When brainstorming, open your mind and the room up to others. When trying to solve a problem, ask yourself who would be the last person you'd turn to for help—and then turn to them. Don't be so arrogant as to think you know best—or to even think you know who knows best. More than anything, forget about minding your own business. Remember: It's *good* business to let people into yours.

### Build a Bigger Kitchen

Contrary to popular belief, there's no such thing as too many cooks in the kitchen. In my view, the more the merrier. The best proposals, scripts, research, PR campaigns, and even schedules are the result of a range of stakeholders sharing their perspectives and expertise. That kind of collaboration also makes for more open, seamless, and ego-free communication, which will help your employees catch mistakes *before* they make them and quickly address any issues that do arise. Encourage it.

### 7. Thou Shalt Be Up-Front

While trust is foundational to any great relationship, it's critical for turning professional ones into personal ones. And trust is earned through transparency in good times and, *especially*, bad times. So speak your mind and speak the truth. When someone asks for your feedback, give it honestly (while always respectfully). When you're frustrated about something, initiate a conversation to hash it out before it spirals or snowballs into something else; *don't* be passive-aggressive and expect things to pass. Welcome productive conflict; don't be afraid of it.

And when something has gone wrong—whether you yourself have made a mistake, or you've just heard bad news and you're unsure whether to pass it along—be up-front. Don't wait to share what's going on. Whether there's an industry-wide issue or a company-specific concern, be open early on and invite people to come up with solutions. Best-case scenario, they help solve the problem (or at least stop the bleeding). Even if they don't, they'll appreciate that the impending storm wasn't kept a secret from them—and all of you will be better prepared to weather whatever it brings together.

## 8. Thou Shalt Welcome Collisions

Anyone who's worked in an office before—and I'm aware that isn't everyone these days—knows the feeling. You're huddled by the water cooler, your desk, or the office of a colleague. You're talking with them about something personal. It wasn't planned, but you're getting *into it.* And then someone (often more senior) walks by, prompting you both to quickly scurry back to work as if you were doing something wrong. But what if I told you that you were doing something right? What if I told you that what we've so long viewed as a distraction from work is in fact good for work?

I'm telling you now. These interactions are called "collisions," and they're fundamental for building personal relationships between colleagues, which are, in turn, fundamental for business. Yes, they often start out as small talk—which has an undeservedly bad

### How to Connect in a Remote World

So your job is fully remote. Now what? More like so what. There are still plenty of ways to connect with your colleagues and mix business with pleasure—even if you're doing it via URL instead of IRL:

- Join your Zoom/Teams/Webex meetings and calls a few minutes early and then stay on a few minutes late; it's a great opportunity for spontaneous conversation, the closest thing you might get to a run-in by the water cooler.
- Start a virtual book club (or recipe club). Read something (or cook something) the same week as your colleagues, then gather on a video call to discuss.
- Invite a colleague to take a coffee break over video. Better yet, share a glass of wine when it's five o'clock for at least one of you.
- If *anyone* from your company, at whatever level, lives in the same city, try to see them in person! Get coffee. Go on a walk during your lunch break.
- If your environment is hybrid, connect with one or more colleagues to go to the office on the same day and make a plan to meet in person for lunch.
- Talk to your company's HR team about organizing an ice cream social or bagel morning.

rap. (According to Nicholas Epley, a psychologist at the University of Chicago, more frequent small talk makes people happier . . . and it even has that effect on introverts.) But over time, that small talk can organically evolve into deeper conversations, leading to genuine relationships. So make like a crash-test dummy and go for the collisions.

## 9. Thou Shalt Initiate Intermissions

No matter how much you love your job, you're going to end up hating it if you don't take a break. You're going to burn out eventually if it's all work, no play. But the idea that you can't temporarily escape work unless you also escape your coworkers is laughable; it also reinforces the idea that a separation is needed between our professional and personal lives—a separation that only hurts you in the long run. So initiate intermissions *with* people. Step out for lunch or coffee with someone on your floor. Take a SoulCycle class together to rejuvenate. Go for a walk around a park in tandem—even if you do it largely in silence. Trust me that your return to work will be more palatable with the reminder that you have someone you can turn to on the inside.

And if a coworker seems extra stressed or underwater, and looks like they could use a break? Never hesitate to invite them to take an "intermission" with you.

## 10. Thou Shalt Assume the Best

Optimism should be just as common at work as a desk. There are so many positives to positive thinking, and so many upsides to looking at the bright side. Not only does it make us happier, healthier, and more productive but it can also lead to better problem-solving by helping us see the big picture and gravitate toward a workable solution. This isn't about being Pollyannaish—it's about common sense. If we think a certain ideal outcome is within reach, we're more likely to devote the time and resources necessary to achieve it. That's especially true compared to pessimists who, according to psychologist

Michael Scheier, as quoted in a 2012 *Atlantic* magazine interview, "tend to deny, avoid, and distort the problems they confront." In that regard, assuming the worst sets you up to do worse. When in doubt, assume the best-case scenario, and then work toward it, instead of constantly catastrophizing.

When it comes to other people's words and actions, assume the best once again. In great workplaces, trust is baked in from the start and implicit at every subsequent step. But even when it isn't a given, the benefit of the doubt should always be your first instinct. You'll work better and more collaboratively—and probably even grow on the job—if you look at even negative feedback in the best light and believe it's coming from a good place to make you your best self. And you'll sleep better at night believing you have friends in your corner rather than opponents working against you.

If a journey of one thousand miles begins with a single step, then the journey toward a better workplace culture can begin with a single smile. As the physician and Yale sociologist Nicholas Christakis argues, optimism is a "collective phenomenon"—it really is contagious.

## THE FINAL WORD

In today's "new normal," mixing work and play is increasingly considered nefarious. That's because the phrase has been co-opted by bad actors, and, as a result, people with good intentions aren't acting on them. That's bad news for everyone. The good news, though, is that there are ways to reclaim a version of what's been lost—a healthier, more positive version that helps everyone thrive. And if we strike the right balance, if we mix work with play the right way, we'll be making ourselves a pleasure to do business with along the way.

# 15. If It Ain't Broke, Don't Fix It / If It Could Be Better, It Might Be Broken

**What We're Told:** *"If it ain't broke, don't fix it."*

*Don't let perfect be the enemy of good . . . If it works, it works . . . Never trouble trouble 'til trouble troubles you . . .* In case it isn't yet obvious, the English language boasts a multitude of phrases (and tongue twisters) directing us to leave well enough alone. They're all rooted in the same operating principle: As long as it's sufficient, the status quo is often all that's necessary. And attempts to improve upon it can backfire, expending precious resources on what ends up being nothing but a waste of time and resources.

**The Truth:** *"If it could be better, it might be broken."*

As a wise and anonymized Reddit user once put it, we would still be living in the Stone Age if our ancient ancestors had only fixed what was already broken. We owe our heated homes and hybrid cars and handheld devices to those who came before us—who saw lightning strike a tree, discovered fire, and thought: "Raw meat is fine, but maybe this flame will make it taste better."

We owe it to the first people who said: "Maybe good enough *isn't* good enough." After all, innovation often comes not from fixing broken things but from testing and trying out *new* things. Small evolutions and big revolutions alike have resulted not from accepting the status quo but from challenging it.

That's true if we look at the course of human history. It's also true if we look at the course of a day in our own lives. Drive a car to work? That's because of people like Henry Ford, who developed the moving assembly line to mass-produce his Model Ts and kickstarted the modern automobile industry—all while disregarding those who insisted carriages were a perfectly adequate mode of transportation. In Ford's famous words, "If I had asked people what they wanted, they would have said faster horses." Step out for coffee with just your smartphone, which also functions as your wallet, your computer, your camera and photo library, your alarm clock, your calendar, your weatherman, your calculator, your GPS, your album collection, and even your TV remote? That's because of everyone who thought a pocket-sized phone wasn't enough.

Literally and figuratively, history has often been made by people who refused to leave well enough alone—who disrupted our way of doing things, and the world, and left them forever transformed.

Defined in business terms as "radical change to a market or industry due to technological innovation," disruption has technically been around forever. Those unwilling or simply unable to meet the moment have often lost out or been left behind. Charles Darwin was onto something when he said that the ability to adapt to a changing environment matters more to a species' survival than pure strength or intelligence. It's a point we should all take to work—especially today, as the pace of disruption is picking up.

Large or small, disruption is now the rule, not the exception.

The only thing faster than the speed at which jobs, companies, and entire sectors are becoming outdated—and getting obliterated—is the speed at which the jobs, companies, and entire industries that replace them are being created.

Seemingly overnight, while most people weren't paying attention, artificial intelligence went from the stuff of science fiction to reality. As artificial intelligence only gets more intelligent by the day, and our interconnected world grows even more intertwined, no job, company, or industry will be immune to the disruptions that are coming our way. If it's not as sweeping as AI, or even a pandemic, it will be something else—a change in management, a rival company, a merger, a shutdown, an acquisition. It always is. But we're not helpless. If we choose to prepare for disruption and embrace it when it comes, this ever-evolving world can be ours for the taking.

That's easier said than done, and understandably so. For too many people, being passive is our standard mode. That isn't a knock—it's a fact. So when change is headed our way, it makes sense that many of us head for the hills. We may find it easier to live in denial than to internalize the warning signs that something's seriously awry. Especially when issues don't seem existential, we may not deem them worth addressing.

Yet in the blink of an eye, a distraction we've tried to ignore, dismiss, or wait out can become a disruption. If we are unprepared, that disruption can become destructive. But it doesn't have to be. If our eyes are open to it, disruption can also become something else: a time of introduction, instruction, production, and construction. We can meet someone new. We can learn something new. We can make something new. We can build something new. Ultimately, we can even *become* someone new.

As the world around us shifts, we don't have to stay the same. Most of the time, that's the worst of all options. With every adjustment to the industries that we work in, the relationships we cultivate, and the places we call our professional and personal homes, there are new challenges we'll certainly face. But there are also boundless opportunities available if we know where (and how) to look.

## MY TAKE

Back in 2004, shortly before George Bush was reelected as president of the U.S.A., I became president of USA . . . Network. My staff was smaller than his, my budget was sparser, and my job didn't come with a private plane or personal chef, but I, too, entered the office with a "Day One Agenda." At the top of my list was a plan to shake up the very entity I'd just been entrusted to lead.

In the twenty-four years since the network was first launched in 1980 at the dawn of cable programming (and having been through what felt like twenty-four owners), USA had become a grab bag of shows—from U.S. Open tennis matches to old broadcast shows like *Miami Vice* in reruns, WWF wrestling, old movies, the Westminster Dog Show, and occasionally, a new, scripted series like *La Femme Nikita*.

Although USA had something for everyone, it didn't have any one thing that it stood for or was recognized for. Yet, at the same time, USA had strong viewership; in the industry, it was doing *just fine*. It surely wasn't broken.

Still, I knew it could be doing better. Focus groups had taught us that people saw the network like an old loafer: basic, comfortable, and familiar. Meanwhile, the "patriotism" of the American flag in our logo, combined with the domineering, all-capital U-S-A letters, felt off-putting to some—more fitting for a televised political rally.

What appealed to our viewers most about the United States was the American people—the characters. And our target demographic of eighteen- to forty-nine-year-olds was optimistic and looking for hope.

So I decided to fix what wasn't necessarily broken. My goal sounded simple: Create a brand for USA that people could emotionally connect with so it wasn't just another channel but a destination, with characters to whom they could relate. But executing it would be complex: We had to figure out an intrinsic identity for the network—not just a superficial slogan—that could unite our diverse content *and* guide every decision we made about what to air in the future. It also had to incorporate what we knew about the people we wanted to reach.

In a way, we had the opposite problem of most other cable channels at the time. They appealed to niche audiences—think MTV and music fans, Nickelodeon and kids, Discovery and nature buffs—but wanted to expand and attract a more general audience. We were hoping to do the reverse. We wanted to take a huge network and make it feel personal, almost like a private club.

One could argue that this approach had been tried by a few other "general interest" cable networks and channels. TBS had rebranded itself using the slogan "Very Funny," trying to become the go-to destination for comedy. TNT went with "We Know Drama." But neither had really transformed their business, outside of a great new tagline.

We were going to try.

Others were skeptical. Many didn't believe we needed a rebrand, much less a reinvention; after all, USA was reliable and predictable, like meat and potatoes. But I thought we needed to add a little sushi and salsa to the mix—to update and spice up our offerings. If we were an old loafer, I wanted us to be a Louboutin pump. Then there were those who believed this change was impossible. How, they wondered, do you brand something as broad as "USA"?

My team analyzed a USA original hit, *Monk*, to get some ideas. The show, a police drama, starred Tony Shalhoub as a grief-stricken, obsessive-compulsive detective named Adrian Monk—more recently, he's been a star and Emmy winner on Amazon's *The Marvelous Mrs. Maisel.* Critics and audiences loved *Monk.* (Proving his enduring appeal, he recently returned in a movie streaming on Peacock.) *Monk* "worked" because it was character-centric, with a lovable, quirky, undoubtedly flawed protagonist and a relatable cast of characters. It was a lighthearted drama that used great writing and sharp, witty dialogue to tackle serious issues. It was upbeat and aspirational rather than downtrodden and depressing.

That became the essence of our brand filter: Going forward, we decided we would only greenlight shows featuring the right kind of leading characters, written with the right mix of drama and humor, set in the right (bright and sunny) locations. And we'd extend that character-centric, blue-skies approach to our on-air promos, our billboards, our print ads—impacting not just the new stuff but also how we packaged and promoted our tennis stars and show dogs and wrestlers, too.

For our rebranding at USA, we made the USA logo less stilted and more playful, removing the flag and swapping out the uppercase letters for lowercase ones. And then we adopted a slogan that encapsulated the brand *and* extended a hand to viewers tuning in: "Characters Welcome."

Those two words, more than anything else, were the common thread that tied together *Monk's* Tony Shalhoub, WWE's Stone Cold Steve Austin, *Law and Order's* Dick Wolf, and a beautiful Westminster Dog Show golden retriever who, in our promos, was seen strutting next to women's tennis legend Billie Jean King. It was also an invitation to viewers: Like what you like and be curious about what you're curious about; if you're an interesting person, there's probably something that will interest you on our network. If you yourself are a character, well, characters welcome.

"Characters welcome" might be the two most defining words of my entire career.

USA would go on to become the most watched cable entertainment channel for a record-setting fourteen years straight. It would also become the single most profitable network at NBCUniversal, raking in billions. That success positioned me to eventually lead the company's entire cable entertainment portfolio. And when I did, USA and all the characters we welcomed led cable to become the most profitable division in the NBCUniversal universe—at the time, more profitable than our news and broadcast channels, our theme parks, even our film and studio groups.

When people ask me how we did it, I talk about the collaborative spirit of our team. We were always on the same page—clear about what we were doing and why we were doing it. But I also talk about the rebrand. We understood what our audiences wanted, even when they weren't directly asking for it. We garnered their loyalty and trust for consistently delivering it, with a brand filter and development process that couldn't guarantee hits but did eliminate a lot of misses.

From the moment I stepped into USA's offices, I had noticed the metaphorical ground wasn't as sturdy as it could be. Rather than ignore the foundation simply because it hadn't yet buckled, my incredible team and I reinforced what felt flimsy and then renovated what looked outdated. Like a great house, the bones were already there—our task was to bring out its character, no pun intended, and make it last.

It was a risk. The rebrand took time, money, and energy—resources that we could have spent elsewhere. And transforming something people were comfortable with into something new and improved could have backfired, losing us the viewers we already had without garnering us new ones. USA was known as a channel of mostly reruns, and we were trying to make it *the* channel for original programming.

In hindsight, I credit part of our willingness to try fixing something that wasn't broken with the culture at USA and cable generally back then. We were an upstart industry that functioned a lot like a start-up—we moved fast and broke things, made up the rules as we went, and abided by no status quo whatsoever since there *was* no status quo whatsoever. We didn't have prestige or fancy network names to rely on for viewers, and we didn't have big budgets to blow on every show, so we had to come up with a different formula from broadcast if we wanted to make hits.

In a way, our vantage point on the "fringes" of the industry gave us an outsider's perspective that allowed us to see what others might miss. Without the pressure that comes from carrying on an entrenched legacy, we were more willing to shake things up and try doing them differently. If a broadcast show failed, it would get a ton of bad press. If a cable show did the same, it could fly under the radar, get no press at all, and simply fade away. So we could take more risks, like engaging in guerilla marketing stunts, or swapping out characters mid-season, or coming up with an entirely new identity.

Upstart or start-up, there's a reason disruption often comes from the less established and less esteemed corners of corporate America. They spot the holes and shortcomings in the status quo. That's what we did at USA—and in the process, we transformed our business and disrupted what people expected from a television network: cable, broadcast, or otherwise.

Entrenched institutions, on the other hand, are often comfortable with the status quo; clearly, whatever's going on is working for them. It's harder to find flaws in a system responsible for your success—

much less want to change that system entirely when your success relies on it staying exactly as is.

But here's the thing: The status quo is always at risk of being disturbed or disrupted entirely. Even if we don't rock the boat, the boat eventually gets rocked. If we're unprepared, we might capsize. At minimum, we get really, really wet. Most likely, we get lost at sea, at least for a little while.

That's what happened initially with NBCUniversal and streaming, and we had to reorient ourselves.

At the start of the 2010s, NBCUniversal had some of the most popular networks and channels on air. There was NBC Broadcast along with USA and SYFY, but also Bravo and E!, plus a whole host of other top-tier programming, including MSNBC, CNBC, and sports channels. Our film and TV studios were winners, too. All our metrics said we were doing great. The past and present told us they'd keep leading into the future. Linear television, the kind you watch on a TV in real time (not on your own time), was still dominant. Netflix was still niche and mailing DVDs. Hulu was more of a "huh?"

Inside our company, there was chatter about streaming, of course, and discussion over whether we should funnel resources into making a platform of our own. But there was even more pushback from smart and savvy business minds who insisted we not mess with a good thing. To them, any minute or dollar spent on anything not linear was a waste—time and money that could and should be used to maintain our dominance in the dominant arena we were already dominating.

More than that, NBCUniversal is and was owned by Comcast—one of the largest cable companies in the country. Its profit model had principally relied on bundling and distributing channels to subscribers. Or, in plain English: Comcast made money from selling those once ubiquitous but increasingly rare pieces of technology we call cable boxes. Even unintentionally, an NBCUniversal streaming platform might end up playing for the other side and encouraging people to cut the cord and cancel their Comcast cable TV service. It didn't make sense, many argued, to invest in something most people didn't yet understand—especially when that success might work against our own bottom line. At the very least, it had the potential to disrupt Comcast's primary business model.

It wasn't that we didn't see what was coming. No one was asleep at the wheel. No one's eyes were closed. No one was oblivious to the fact that streaming services were being developed by all types of entities. But Comcast and NBCUniversal weighed present certainties against an unpredictable and ever-changing future. And we chose to stick with what we knew. Despite my and several other senior executives' efforts during long-term planning meetings and annual reviews, the company held off on creating our own streaming platform.

Instead, we licensed our NBC Network and cable channel content to other streaming platforms. And we had lots of content, from the shows on our networks to the movies from our studios, all under our massive umbrella. As a result, countless young people today associate *The Office* with Netflix and not NBC, where it originally aired. They associate *Suits* with Netflix, too, and *Covert Affairs* and *Mr. Robot* with Amazon, and not USA. Countless people subscribed to Netflix and Amazon—and Hulu, and Apple, and more—because they loved, or fell in love with, a series or film that *we* created. Sure, we made a profit in the process, because we'd sold the streaming rights to those platforms. But our subscribers and audience members followed our creative content to the streamers—and left us.

By the time our NBCUniversal platform, Peacock, finally launched in March of 2020—thirteen years after Netflix launched its streaming service—we weren't just late to the game. We'd been lapped by Netflix, Hulu, Apple, and Amazon. Even Disney, another legacy media institution weighing some similar pros and cons, got out of the gate before us. (For them, the question might have been "If we make a streaming service and put our movies on there, will people stop going to theaters?")

We had started out with an objective advantage: decades of original content we already owned. But we gave that advantage away—or, rather, we sold it to companies who disrupted our industry while we sat in endless meetings, going back and forth about whether we would have to adapt.

In the years since, we've made up for lost time and recovered a good deal of lost ground. We surveyed the landscape and made the wise choice to straddle the old and the new. We offered an old-school version that was free, but included advertising, like a traditional TV network experience, as well as a paid-subscription version, where viewers could bypass ads. Here, we were the leaders, and other services eventually followed our model.

But past success is no guarantee of future dominance, and the entire streaming world remains ripe for disruption. I say this as the person who was tasked with developing and launching the platform when it was finally given the go-ahead—creating the brand, giving it a name, and recruiting the initial team to bring Peacock to life. It was no small task. We had to work to get our original shows and movies back, and then create originals to help define the new platform, before we could get Peacock off the ground and make it worth anything.

As a company, we too often debated the future instead of tackling it head-on. We prioritized security and profit margins over the risk of new investment and the potential reward that could have followed.

Does that mean we should have taken a wrecking ball to what was then our golden goose: linear television? Of course not. But we should have tried to do two things at once: maintain our dominance in the comfortable TV world and be curious enough to enter the new world of streaming services. We didn't need a Magic 8 Ball to tell us what everyone with eyes and ears recognized: Streaming wasn't just coming; it was already here. Viewers' viewing habits were changing and we weren't changing with them fast enough. While we didn't have to lead the way, we could have at least been a bit more prepared . . . and a bit more competitive.

I'm confident television and entertainment will continue to radically change. If streaming is the new TiVo, and TiVo was the new cable, and cable was the new colorized TV . . . Well, who knows what the next decade or two will bring?

Perhaps the big bet that Comcast and NBCUniversal didn't make until very late will end up paying off. It's clear that today's viewers are getting over-saturated with streaming services. We've gone from a common, shared calendar of high-quality content options to an uncharted world where the content providers are expanding exponentially, and quantity often matters more than quality. Audiences and critics alike have taken note. Perhaps our company's insistence that our primary identity is being a creator of good movies and TV series, and not just a platform to air any-and-all third-party creations, will end up proving prescient and working to our advantage; so, too, might our decision to diversify our product line and continue selling our home-grown shows to other streamers. Perhaps the "cable box" concept will make a comeback, bundling streaming services with linear channels, as people crave simplicity . . . and a single subscription. Perhaps legacy institutions will reclaim their perch atop the industry.

But perhaps not. Having weathered overlapping strikes by both writers and actors in 2023, which upended the entertainment world and were largely due to disruptions from streaming, the entire film, streaming, and television entertainment industry is now also confronting a potentially massive external disruption from the future use of AI. No one knows what the media landscape will look like in two years, let alone five or ten. No one. All that we know is that there will be one, because people crave the fundamental joy of being entertained.

While disruption is uncomfortable, if we approach it the right way it's not something to fear. It's an exciting opportunity to change our lives, our industries, and maybe even the world. It might even disrupt them all, too.

## NAIL IT

Almost by definition, disruption is unpredictable. But we don't have to wait until it's already taken a sledgehammer to our lives to act. If we know where (and how) to look, we can anticipate when, where, and why it might be coming, and what impact it will have. And we can act appropriately once it arrives—so that even the twists and turns we never saw coming become opportunities we never could have dreamt up, instead of nightmares we wish we could have slept through.

So . . .

### Look Ahead

When things are going well at work, it's easy to get comfortable, complacent, and dare I say careless. When we're not on edge, we sometimes lose our edge. Our strengths can blind us to our weaknesses, and our success can make us forget how close all of us are—always—to falling behind. Even when you're at the front of the pack, keep looking ahead at the big picture. Understand all the possibilities, all the options open to you, and all the paths you may be able to take.

## Look Back

No matter how much we think we know, history is still our greatest teacher. That's especially true when it comes to disruption. While it's tempting (and understandable) to focus squarely on the future and dismiss the past as outdated, the reality is that—at least some of the time—the answer to what lies ahead of us actually lies behind us. As Mark Twain aptly put it, "History never repeats itself, but it often rhymes." If we want to know how to stay ahead of the curve, we have to look back and understand where we've already been.

## Look Around

As young children, we're taught to not worry about what others are doing, and to focus on ourselves. It's good advice . . . but only up to a point. If you think about it, paying attention to ourselves and ourselves alone is quite literally the definition of narcissism—and in a world (especially a professional one) that requires us to interact, collaborate, and compete with others, it's also a surefire way to lose touch and fall behind whatever curve exists in our industry. While ignorance may be bliss, it isn't a business strategy. Looking around at what others are doing, and studying the latest innovations, approaches, and technologies used by friends and foes alike, is key. Listen to industry chatter. Follow the news (and the trends). Note differences in interactions with or preferences from customers, clients, and audiences. Don't ever let your worldview become so myopic that your only view is of your own world.

## Look Inside

If we want to survive and thrive during times of disruption—and these days, those times are all the time—there's something even more important than taking in the world: looking at, and really seeing, ourselves. If something radical or transformative is headed your way, and you find that you're closed off to it, do the work to figure out why. Take a triple-A approach to self-reflection: Ask. Answer. Address.

First, ask yourself what scares you about what's coming and what's holding you back from embracing it. Have you always been a creature of consistency? Do you feel unprepared for or underinformed about a new system or technology? Are you nervous that your skills might become irrelevant, that your role might become obsolete, that your job might be eliminated? Ask these questions about yourself—and ask them about your team, your company, and your industry. Then answer them honestly. If you can't do that alone, open up your circle. And finally, address the answers. If you fear being laid off, have a conversation with your boss. If you lack a transferrable skill set, start learning something new that you can bring to another industry (or whatever table eventually exists). If you're worried about income, start budgeting and figure out where you can make up the difference.

No matter how we feel about the disruption headed our way, fighting it is often futile. Ignoring or minimizing it can be even worse. What we can do, though, is fight *through* whatever's holding us back from making the most of it. Only once we do that can we eventually move forward.

## Look Beyond

You don't have to endlessly surf the disruption wave in your industry; you can go to another beach. Soon after Barry Diller sold USA Network, he called me cold, something that never happened even when I worked for him. He had a job offer: Would I want to move to a new location and become the head of one of his other ventures,

Match.com? I had just signed my new TV contract, I didn't know anything about online dating, and I had kids in school. Would my skills translate? Would moving be too disruptive to my family? Would I survive another round with Barry as my boss? (The first one had been pretty tough.) I thought about the offer for a few days, but not nearly as seriously as I should have, and then I let it go. Had I said yes, I might have fallen flat on my face. But I also might have succeeded in ways I couldn't imagine—after all, isn't online dating trying to tell our best, most impactful story, and a lot like what I was doing in television? I'd likely have made tens of millions of dollars—that's what Match.com stock did for its execs—and I could have written my own

## Sometimes You Need a Push in a New Direction

After thirty years in television, NBCUniversal's talented head of research began to reevaluate her career choice. (She is the woman whom I mentored to become more approachable in meetings, after which her career took off. She became not only enormously valued professionally for her work but also very much appreciated personally for who she was.) But watching students, including her own daughter, struggle in some aspects of school, she realized that she had an underlying passion for psychology and social work. She told me that she was considering returning to school for an advanced degree, even though it would be a tremendous change and a unique challenge after such a successful corporate career. My advice to her was simple: Pursue your passion now. "This is your decade," I told her. "If you are going to try something new, do it." And she has. She's embarked on a whole new career. I can't wait to see how her next chapter unfolds.

story after that. Sometimes, when faced with change, the opportunities we regret are the left-field ones we didn't take.

## Look on the Bright Side

I've preached optimism throughout this book because it's that important: While it's good to always prepare for the worst, it's immensely beneficial—to our emotional well-being *and* to our professional prospects—to consistently assume the best. Few people realize how helpful positive thinking is to our survival during times of transition, especially at work. When sudden changes occur, people gravitate toward those who manage not to catastrophize, and who instead point out all the potential positives. So be that person, whether you're the boss or an employee.

You don't have to sugarcoat the parts of disruption that will be harder to swallow—and those exist, I won't lie. But just like there are two sides to every story, there are two (at least) to every shift and change in life, even the unexpected ones. If you can look on the bright side, you'll find the upside that exists on the other side of disruption. It always does.

## THE FINAL WORD

Disruption may feel scary when it strikes—but it's the air we breathe. It's a critical part of life, and we need to learn to live with it to survive. Embracing disruption won't suffocate or choke us; holding our breath and fighting it will. So allow yourself to inhale and then exhale. Open your eyes to what may lie ahead and open your mind to what may feel uneasy. Get comfortable being uncomfortable. It may not seem like it in the moment, but in the end, it's the only thing that keeps us going.

# 16. The Only Constant In Life Is Change

**One Big Truth:** *"The only constant in life is change."*

I've spent my life fighting back against the destructive lies that live inside everyday clichés and catchphrases. (I've spent the past fifteen chapters doing it, too.) But there's one aphorism I haven't yet mentioned—that I can't dismiss or dismantle—because it's undoubtedly true: Change really *is* the only constant.

Resisting change anywhere in life, but especially on the job, is an exercise in futility. Eventually, it comes for all of us—no matter your stage, your age, or your wage. It's a question of *when*, not *if*.

My own career is proof. In so many ways, the world of television—what we watch, where we watch, how we watch, even whether we pay to watch (and if we do, whom we pay)—bears little resemblance today to the TV industry I first started working in. Back then, a stream was just a small body of water. And in the last three decades, I've lasted through six corporate takeovers and served under eight different bosses (most of them named Jeff or Steve). With every change in ownership and leadership, I wasn't just assigned new roles and responsibilities, I was also forced to navigate entirely new waters with entirely new rules. As soon as I hit my comfort zone, it happened again. Each instance was sink or swim.

While I was writing this final chapter—fittingly enough—it hap-

pened once more. The CEO of NBCUniversal, a man I'd been working with for eleven years, was fired abruptly on a Sunday morning,
part of a twenty-four-hour news cycle dubbed the "most shocking day
in TV history": three media moguls were let go by three different
media conglomerates, leaving three massive messes behind. Again, I
found myself treading water, swept up in a current of absolute chaos
I never could have predicted. Fortunately, I have a lifetime of running *with* change—and not from it—to use as experience. I embrace
whatever new reality I'm faced with as *my* new reality, and I do it
quickly. I don't dwell on would've-should've-could'ves.

But there's a third option: We can also run *toward* change. We
don't have to wait until it has knocked down our door and disrupted
our lives to act, and we don't have to act out of fear.

Earlier in the book, I wrote about the importance of following opportunities. Well—if we run toward change, we can create them for
ourselves. I believe it's no coincidence that if you view change from a
slightly different angle, if you squint your eyes and shift your perspective, it can look a lot like chance. With the right outlook, that's what
change is: a chance to do better, do different, do more.

Today, as one of the most senior (in two ways) women at NBCUniversal, I am grappling with change again. I often joke that our society
isn't ageist so much as *sageist*, prejudiced against the wisdom that is
acquired from years of experience. But that wisdom is why I'm here
today. It's pushing me to keep going toward the next great opportunity, the next unpredictable adventure—and I intend to stay in the
driver's seat. If I spend my time looking nostalgically back at the past,
all I gain is a bad neck. Instead, I'm looking at all the opportunities
and possibilities that are still in front of me.

As I explore what the next leg of my ride might look like, I find
myself returning to the same advice that's served me at other mo-

ments of change in my career and life. It's my advice for how to prepare for and grow from the twists and turns thrown our way. In short, it's the advice of this book. Like life, each chapter is key to the journey—we better embrace them all.

So . . .

Get to know yourself—your strengths, weaknesses, and what makes you tick. No matter where you want to go, that should be your starting point.

Keep learning and caring about others and about the world. Curiosity makes your journey rich.

Stay open to the unpredictable opportunities that might come your way. You never know when lightning—the good kind—will strike.

Understand that professional worth fluctuates, but you can always put in the work to increase your value.

Surround yourself with supporters who cheer you on and challengers who keep you sharp. Both are critical at every stage of your career.

Be your best self—on the inside and outside. What people see is their first introduction to what they'll get.

Know that you can't have it all. No one can. But today women do have choices we've never had before. Assess your options honestly and choose the best ones for you.

If you fake it, you won't make it far. No matter what your insecurities or shortcomings, honesty is always the best policy.

If you want to stand out in a man's world, embrace what sets you apart as a woman. Use your XX factor to get ahead.

If you need a favor or advice from someone, just ask. Use your voice and develop a tone that makes people want to help . . . and don't forget to truly listen.

If something feels unachievable, demonstrate a little chutzpah first before you count yourself out.

If you've really hit a roadblock, know there's always more than one direction you can go. Don't be afraid to zigzag.

If your gut says go, check your other five senses before following it. Intuition is wonderful, but alone it's rarely enough.

Sweat the small stuff. At the end of the day, it always adds up to something big.

Realize that winning isn't everything, but knowing how to lose is. With the right mindset, you can take your flops and flip them.

Don't be afraid to mix work and play. With fun and friendship on the job, you'll inevitably do a better job.

Put a premium on kindness. Live with humility. Learn how to joke at your own expense. Be the kind of person you'd want to be around.

Always, always, always look on the bright side. It makes everything a little easier and a hell of a lot more enjoyable.

And remember: Change is only something to fear if you refuse to face it.

I've spent a lifetime working in television. And TV is, at its core, a platform for storytelling. But here's something I don't think people think about nearly enough: Our lives are platforms for storytelling, too—and if we make the most of them, the stories of our lives are a lot more interesting (and far more real and rewarding) than anything on the screen.

Over fifteen chapters, I've laid out my own story. I can't know exactly how your story will play out, because I can't predict every possible challenge you might face: a restructure at work, a new boss, a family crisis, another pandemic. I can't predict every opportunity that might come your way, either: the job offers you might receive, the important connections you might forge, the right places you might be at the right times that have the potential to change your life. My hope, though, is that this book gives you the tools and truths (and attitude) you need to take control of your story and write those next chapters yourself. Once you do, I'm confident you'll be able to create a career—and live a life—more rewarding than any screen or page could capture.

I'm sure as hell still creating—and living—mine! That's the truth!

# Acknowledgments

**What We're Told:** *"It takes a village . . ."*

**The Truth:** *"It takes way more than a village . . ."*

## MY TAKE

It takes multiple interconnected, caring, compassionate, and collaborative communities to help support, write, edit, design, market, launch, and simply survive writing a book, not to mention being persuaded to even attempt to do it in the first place.

My foundation in all things is my loving, giving, supportive, and patient family, who endured my epic obsession with writing this book. As always, they cheered me on. Tremendous thanks to:

My wise and incredibly nurturing husband, Dale, whose support never wavered, even though he was constantly forced to take a back seat to my computer. His perspective, insights, and critiques pushed me to reach for a higher bar.

My son, Jesse, who generously read and critiqued every word of the proposal and helped edit the second draft of the manuscript, as always, with focus, smarts, insight, and humor—and, in his inimitable style, spared me (or at least my words) no mercy. And his wife, Elizabeth, whose charisma, positive energy, and leadership helped inspire some of the ideas in these pages.

Though I spared her "reading detail" due to the 6,700 miles and fourteen-hour time difference between us, I'm grateful to my daughter, Ki Mae, for sharing her thoughts; for our years of purposeful (and fun) "chick-chats," which have enriched this book and my life; and, most important, for the joy she, Ro, Maya, and Niko bring into my life.

## NAIL IT

Next, my wide-ranging professional community, whose work, smarts, intelligence, and patience propelled me to this place where I'm typing actual acknowledgments.

Jordana Narin, a bright young talent, who was an invaluable help in brainstorming, refining, and filtering my ideas. Her challenging mind and gifted craft will, I believe, take her to unlimited heights.

Lyric Winik, a master wordsmith, who managed to take my 95,000+ words and hone them down to 80,000 without losing an iota of voice, substance, or clarity. She taught (and is still teaching) me tons. Thank you, Binky, for bringing Lyric into my book, and, more important, into my life.

Speaking of Binky, also known as Amanda Urban, she is the queen of literary agents and a no-nonsense (as she would phrase it), no-bullshit (as I would phrase it) human who encouraged me for years to write a book. Binky is the reason you're reading these words. At CAA, Bryan Lord not only encouraged me to write this book but pushed me to embrace and own my voice. Binky and Bryan also generously shared the talents of Kate Child and Christine Lancman.

At the unrivaled Simon & Schuster, my publisher, Richard Rhorer, embraced the idea and the book. From our very first meeting, I trusted his instincts. And especially my sage S&S editor, the smart, collaborative, and talented Doris Cooper. Now she's not simply my editor but my friend. And Simon Element's marketing and publicity leads, Elizabeth Breeden and Jessica Preeg, who have been supportive since the start.

A special nod to Carly Loman for creating a beautiful, clean, distinctive design that captured both the words and the message. And to Jason Holzman and Rachel Gogel for a great cover consultation.

My deep thanks to the savvy and talented Nicole Dewey; Simon Halls, my trusted confidant and gifted media whisperer; Cory Shields, the indispensable and irrepressible soul you want to have in your bunker; and the NBCU superstar and my friend Tracy St. Pierre for helping shepherd me through the media, then and now.

Craig Jacobson, the soaring eagle of legals, has been by my side professionally for more than two decades. Thank you for always being there when needed and, more important, just being there as my friend.

During this process, I benefitted greatly from the generous advice of Tina Brown, Chelsea Clinton, and Adam Grant. And, of course, a salute to my favorite tough-love mentor, Barry Diller, who challenged, stretched, and championed me 'til I lived up to my worth. Even now, Barry's words are motivators.

My community gets broader, richer, and more inclusive as I realize how many characters (and characters are always welcome) have contributed to my life and my career, and to the stories in this book. It includes, from my early days at WGBH, the talented Michael Rice and Henry Becton and my incredible team of all-female producers, *and* a director at *Good Day!* who taught me early in my career what true collaboration looks like, feels like, and succeeds like. A very special shout-out to Debbie Cohen Kosofsky, who back then was a young, wide-smiling, "just ask," up-and-coming producer . . . and now is a *Today* icon, a loyal friend, an egg-offering goddess—simply my lifelong sister.

To my mentors from the early, formative days of cable television: Kay Koplovitz, Steve Brenner, Dave Kenin, and Rod Perth. Always a wild, fun ride.

At NBCU, thank you to Jeff Zucker, a motivating and loyal leader, who entrusted me with the USA Network and believed in me from the moment I started on his watch. And to Steve Burke, who trusted me with the rest of the cable portfolio and with launching the Peacock streaming service, and who led with clarity and directness. I'm thankful for my many colleagues in the entertainment community: the writers, directors, actors, producers, showrunners, and everyone in front of and behind the camera, who create the excellent work that I've had the privilege to experience up close.

I'm also indebted to my incredible coordinators over the years, whose talent, loyalty, and hard work ensured that I brought my best every day. A very special thank-you to Dana McGowan, who has been with me throughout this journey, for juggling her normal "daytime" work while putting in extra "all-time" hours helping me with every aspect of this project. You are a true gift.

## THE FINAL WORD

The best places, including workplaces, are the ones where you find your friends. Close to last, but very far from least, are my dear, dear friends all around the country—and most of all my Westport posse, who encouraged me to write *15 Lies*, and some of whom generously read it, critiqued it, edited it, discussed it, shepherded it, and always supported it.

And to the *FlossieBird Five*... my four 1961 (and on) bunkmates, who taught me at a very young age what teamwork, trust, loyalty, commitment, fun, and true friendship really are.

Finally, to Bodhi and Risa, my ever-present—on the bed, under my desk, by the door to the shower—dog-mates, who made sure I was never lonely, regardless of the hour or how "dog tired" I was. It's true: dogs are a (wo)man's best friend . . . and that's no lie!

# Notes

### 3. Have Friends In High Places / Find Truth-Tellers In Every Location

1. Grace Winstanley, "Mentoring Statistics You Need to Know—2023," Mentorloop.com, February 15, 2023.

### 4. It's What's On The Inside That Counts / What's On Our Outsides Matters, Too

1. Eric Wargo, "How Many Seconds to a First Impression?" Association for Psychological Science, July 1, 2006.
2. Albert Mehrabian and Susan Ferris, "Inference of Attitudes from Nonverbal Communication in Two Channels," *Journal of Consulting Psychology* 31, no. 3 (1967).

### 5. You Can Have It All / You Will Have Choices

1. Population Reference Bureau analysis of data from the US Census Bureau, *Current Population Survey* (March Supplement), 1970 to 2000; and Howard N. Fullerton Jr., "Labor Force Participation: 75 Years of Change, 1950–98 and 1998–2025," *Monthly Labor Review* (December 1999).
2. Oksana Leukhina and Amy Smaldone, "Why Do Women Outnumber Men in College Enrollment?" *On the Economy* (blog), Federal Reserve of St. Louis, March 15, 2022.

### 6. Fake It 'Til You Make It / Face It 'Til You Make It

1. Paul Knopp and Laura M. Newinski, "KPMG Study Finds 75% of Female Executives Across Industries Have Experienced Imposter Syndrome in Their Careers," KPMG, October 7, 2023.
2. Katty Kay and Claire Shipman, "The Confidence Gap," *Atlantic*, May 2024.
3. Pauline Rose Clance and Suzanne Imes, "The Imposter Phenomenon in High Achieving Women: Dynamics and Therapeutic Intervention," *Psychotherapy Theory, Research and Practice* 15, no. 3 (Fall 1978).

## 7. It's A Man's World / Only If You Let It Be

1. Leonard Sax, "Sex Differences in Hearing: Implications for Best Practice in the Classroom," *Advances in Gender and Education* 2 (2010).
2. C. Dawson, "Gender Differences in Optimism, Loss Aversion, and Attitudes towards Risk," *British Journal of Psychology* 114, no. 4 (2023).
3. Michael Brush, "Here's Why Women Fund Managers Regularly Outperform Men, Based on Newer Research: It's Not about Risk Aversion, which Older Studies Have Concluded. It's More about Decision-Making Skills," CBS MarketWatch, October 23, 2020.
4. Michal Shmulovich, "What the Mossad's Female Agents Do—and Don't Do—for the Sake of Israel," *Times of Israel,* September 15, 2012.
5. Judith A. Hall, "Gender Effects in Decoding Nonverbal Cues," *Psychological Bulletin* 85, no. 4 (1978).
6. Megan Brenan, "Americans No Longer Prefer Male Boss to Female Boss," Gallup Workplace, November 16, 2017; Pat Wechsler, "Women-Led Companies Perform Three Times Better than the S&P 500," *Fortune,* March 3, 2015; Jack Zenger and Joseph Folkman, "Research: Women Are Better Leaders During a Crisis," *Harvard Business Review,* December 20, 2020; and Kimberly Fitch and Sangeeta Agrawal, "Why Women Are Better Managers than Men," *Gallup Business Journal,* October 16, 2014.
7. Rakesh Kochhar, "The Enduring Grip of the Gender Pay Gap," Pew Research Center, March 1, 2023.
8. Andrew M. Penner et al., "Within-Job Gender Pay Inequality in 15 Countries," *Nature Human Behavior* 7 (November 24, 2022).
9. Sara Silano, "Women Founders Get 2% of Venture Capital Funding in US," Morningstar, March 6, 2023.

## 8. Talk Is Cheap / Talk Is A Valuable Currency

1. Gil Greengross and Geoffrey Miller, "Humor Ability Reveals Intelligence, Predicts Mating Success, and Is Higher in Males," *Intelligence* 39, no. 4 (2011).
2. T. Bradford Bitterly et al., "Risky Business: When Humor Increases and Decreases Status," *Journal of Personality and Social Psychology* 112, no. 3 (2017).

## 10. There's Nowhere To Go But Up / Success Has Multiple Directions

1. Herminia Ibarra and Morten T. Hansen, "Women CEOs: Why So Few?" *Harvard Business Review,* December 21, 2009.

## 11. Trust Your Gut / Check Your Gut

1. Adam Hadhazy, "Think Twice: How the Gut's 'Second Brain' Influences Mood and Well-Being," *Scientific American,* February 12, 2010; and Yijing

Chen et al., "Regulation of Neurotransmitters by the Gut Microbiota and Effects on Cognition in Neurological Disorders," *Nutrients* 13, no. 6 (June 19, 2021).

2. Ruairi Robertson, "The Gut-Brain Connection: How It Works and the Role of Nutrition," Healthline, July 21, 2023.

## 13. The Winner Takes All / Winning Isn't Everything

1. Anne Fausto-Sterling et al., "Multimodal Sex-Related Differences in Infant and in Infant-Directed Maternal Behaviors during Months Three through Twelve of Development," *Developmental Psychology* 51, no. 10 (October 2015).
2. Carolyn Edwards et al., "Play Patterns and Gender," Faculty Publications, Department of Psychology, University of Nebraska–Lincoln, 2001.
3. Emily Mondschein et al., "Gender Bias in Mothers' Expectations about Infant Crawling," *Journal of Experimental Child Psychology* 77, no. 4 (2000).
4. Karolina Boxberger and Anne Kerstin Reimers, "Parental Correlates of Outdoor Play in Boys and Girls Aged 0 to 12—A Systematic Review," *International Journal of Environmental Research and Public Health* 16, no. 2 (2019).
5. Daniel Voyer and Susan D. Voyer, "Gender Differences in Scholastic Achievement: A Meta-Analysis," *Psychological Bulletin* 140, no. 4 (2014).
6. Claudia Goldin, "Gender and the Undergraduate Economics Major: Notes on the Undergraduate Economics Major at a Highly Selective Liberal Arts College," Harvard University, notes, April 12, 2015.

## 14. Don't Mix Work With Play / All Work And No Play Makes Everyone Dull

1. Alexander Sterling, "Employees Spend Almost 30% of Their Time at Work," Manage Business, November 15, 2023; Bob Nelson, "Why Work Should Be Fun," *Harvard Business Review*, May 2, 2022; and Ruth Umoh, "This Study Identified the 5 People That Make Up a 'Work Family'—Which One Are You?" CNBC.com, December 14, 2017.
2. Alok Patel and Stephanie Plowman, "The Increasing Importance of a Best Friend at Work," Gallup Workplace, August 17, 2002.
3. Karen Jehn and Priti Pradhan Shah, "Interpersonal Relationships and Task Performance: An Examination of Mediation Processes in Friendship and Acquaintance Groups," *Journal of Personality and Social Psychology* 72, no. 4 (1997).
4. "The Business Case for Addressing Loneliness in the Workforce," news room.cigna.com; and Michelle Cleary et al., "Boredom in the Workplace: Reasons, Impact, and Solutions," *Issues in Mental Health Nursing* 37, no. 2 (2013).

5. Brian Brim and Dana Williams, "Defeating Employee Loneliness and Worry with CliftonStrengths," Gallup CliftonStrengths, April 21, 2020.

6. Lindsay McGregor and Neel Doshi, "How Company Culture Shapes Employee Motivation," *Harvard Business Review,* November 25, 2015.

7. Leanne Italie, "Gallup: Just 2 in 10 US Employees Have a Work Best Friend," Associated Press, February 7, 2023; Dina Denham Smith, "What to Do When You Don't Trust Your Employee?" *Harvard Business Review,* August 17, 2023; and Jim Harter, "US Employee Engagement Drops for First Year in a Decade," Gallup Workplace, January 7, 2022.

8. Kaori Sakurada et al., "Associations of Frequency of Laughter with Risk of All-Cause Mortality and Cardiovascular Disease Incidence in a General Population: Findings from the Yamagata Study," *Journal of Epidemiology* 30, no. 4 (2020); and Solfrid Romundstad et al., "A 15-Year Follow-Up Study of Sense of Humor and Causes of Mortality: The Nord-Trøndelag Health Study," *Psychosomatic Medicine* 78, no. 3 (April 2016).